FOCUS

Interactive Grammar for Students of ESL

SECOND EDITION

Barbara Robinson

The University of Akron

CAMBRIDGE
UNIVERSITY PRESS

To Hannah, Becca, and Sabah:

The ones who help me keep the valuable and

important things of life in focus.

PUBLISHED BY THE PRESS SYNDICATE OF THE UNIVERSITY OF CAMBRIDGE
The Pitt Building, Trumpington Street, Cambridge, United Kingdom

CAMBRIDGE UNIVERSITY PRESS
The Edinburgh Building, Cambridge CB2 2RU, UK
40 West 20th Street, New York, NY 10011–4211, USA
477 Williamstown Road, Port Melbourne, VIC 3207, Australia
Ruiz de Alarcón 13, 28014 Madrid, Spain
Dock House, The Waterfront, Cape Town 8001, South Africa

http://www.cambridge.org

First published by St. Martin's Press, Inc. 1995

3rd printing 2003

Printed in the United States of America

Library of Congress Cataloging-in-Publication Data Available

ISBN 0 521 65754 7 Student's Book
ISBN 0 521 65753 9 Instructor's Manual
ISBN 0 521 65752 0 Workbook

Acknowledgments
Page 2: Scott Camazine/Photo Researchers; *Page 54* (top): Library of Congress; *Page 54*
(bottom left): The Bettman Archive; *Page 54* (bottom right): Courtesy Air France; *Page 59:*
Jean Claude Lejeune/Stock, Boston; *Page 69* (left): Photo Researchers, Inc.; *Page 69*
(right): © A.W. Ambler from National Audubon Society; *Page 71:* © Ronald H. Cohn/The
Gorilla Foundation; *Page 109:* © Gerry Cranham; *Page 111:* © Ruth Orkin 1955, 1983; *Page
155:* John Nordell/The Picture Cube; *Page 172:* Reprinted by permission of Leo Michael;
Page 181: Ellis Herwig/Stock, Boston; *Page 182* (bottom): HERMAN copyright Jim Unger.
Reprinted with permission of Universal Press Syndicate. All rights reserved; *Page 196:*
MARMADUKE reprinted by permission of UFS, Inc.; *Page 212:* reprinted by permission
of Ann Landers and Creators Syndicate; *Page 213:* PEANUTS reprinted by permission of
UFS, Inc.; *Page 222:* Eva Demjen/Stock, Boston; *Page 224* (top left): © David Barnes; *Page
224* (top right): © Teri Leigh Stratford; *Page 224* (bottom left): © George E. Jones III; *Page
224* (bottom right): © Tom McHugh; *Page 225:* MISS MANNERS reprinted by permission
of UFS, Inc.; *Page 245:* © Wally McNamee; *Page 247:* Reprinted by permission of
Associated Press; *Page 272:* © Jan Lukas; *Page 314:* © Photo by James D. Anker; *Page 318:*
Passage from *Arthur C. Clarke's Mysterious World*, by Simon Welfare and John Fairley,
published by A & W Publishers, Inc. Used by permission; *Page 320:* AP/Wide World
Photos; Page 321: Photo of child on lap, by Bruce Roberts from *Family of Man*, p. 117,
© 1955. Used with permission of Photo Researchers; *Page 326:* Reprinted by permission of
Ann Landers and Creators Syndicate; *Page 328:* © Photo by James D. Anker; *Page 329:*
© Robin Engh; *Page 330:* © Señor McGuire; *Page 334:* "Time in a Bottle," Jim Croce,
© 1971, 1972 DENJAC MUSIC COMPANY, MCA MUSIC, A Division of MCA INC. All
rights administered by DENJAC MUSIC COMPNAY, 40 West 57th Street, New York, NY
10019. All Rights Reserved. Used by Permission; *Page 341: People Weekly* © BILL
CRAMER; *Page 347: People Weekly* ©1993 TIME INC.

Preface

FOCUS is an intermediate-level grammar text for students of English as a Second Language. Students at the intermediate level are often familiar with many of the forms and structures of English. Their mastery of these structures, however, is often limited. There is, at this level, a need to develop an overall framework of the organization of English. Students need to practice familiar forms in new and creative ways. They need to develop accuracy and fluency. They need to recognize the inseparable relationship between form, meaning, and usage. Students have different strategies for learning grammar. Some students learn best inductively; others learn from explicit rules. Some students need written explanations; others learn from examples. Some find the visual explanations of diagrams and charts most useful; others learn what "sounds" right without formalizing any rules. Most students probably use a combination of learning strategies.

FOCUS meets the challenge of the intermediate student by offering an eclectic interactive approach to learning grammar. First, it is accessible to students with a wide variety of learning styles. The text encourages students to take an active role in discovering the rules, meanings, and uses of different grammatical structures. In addition, each grammar point offers a written explanation and numerous examples. Chapters also include visual explanations in the form of tables, diagrams, drawings, and photographs. Students get extensive oral practice of grammatical material in exercises that range from structured practice to free discussion. Throughout the text, students are given the opportunity to use their knowledge and creativity to communicate their own ideas while interacting with content, grammar, and each other.

Although the text is especially useful for students in academic ESL programs, the grammatical and contextual material of *FOCUS* is appropriate for all adult students at the intermediate level.

This edition of *FOCUS* features a new, clear format designed to make the material easily accessible to the students and "user friendly" for the instructor. Also included in the new edition are detailed explanations with additional examples, and extra oral and written exercises. The new *FOCUS* comes with an Instructor's Manual that contains guidelines for presenting the material in *FOCUS* as well as suggestions for additional writing assignments and communicative activities.

Organization of the Text

FOCUS deals with structures that are key at the intermediate level: the meanings and forms of the verb system, modal auxiliaries, word order, clause structure, and noun phrases. Each chapter of *FOCUS* is woven around a grammatical situation in order to examine the structures that often occur in that situation. Although each chapter is designed to build on information from preceding chapters, instructors may be able to better accommodate the needs of their students by teaching chapters in a different sequence. The Instructor's Manual offers suggestions for alternative arrangements of the material.

Organization of Each Chapter

Each chapter focuses on a number of structures that occur within a grammatical situation. Each chapter consists of the following elements:

Getting Ready to Focus: Introductory "Orientation" Contexts

First, the grammatical situation is introduced with a thought-provoking context such as a photograph, a problem to solve, a cartoon, a dialogue, or a series of questions. The introductory situations or contexts are designed to elicit discussion and to provide an orientation to the grammar structures that follow, much the same way that pre-reading exercises prepare the students for subsequent reading passages. The emphasis in the discussion should be on meaning rather than on the accuracy of new forms.

Focus

Grammatical information is given in the sections called *Focus*. These sections contain explanations, tables, examples, and reference material for a specific grammar point. The Focus sections can be used for discussion in class or for study at home. Suggestions for using the Focus sections are provided in the Instructor's Manual.

Practice

Each Focus section is accompanied by a group or groups of *Practice* exercises for oral use in class. The Practices have a variety of formats and contexts, all of which are designed to maintain the inseparable link between form, meaning, and usage in communication. The Practices encourage students to use their own knowledge and ideas to respond to situations or to exchange information with their classmates while using the grammar structures that are in Focus. The Practices can also serve as a springboard for discussions and supplementary oral and written practice.

Close-Up

The *Close-Up* section focuses on specific details that may occur within a grammatical situation. Topics encountered in this section include prepositions, multiple-word verbs, time expressions, and special functions of a structure. The reference material can be presented in class or assigned for study at home. Each Close-Up also has an oral practice for use in class.

A Wider Angle

Each section labeled *A Wider Angle* offers students the opportunity to communicate their ideas in an extended context. A Wider Angle consists of two parts: an oral communication activity and a writing practice. The first part encourages oral practice by asking students to carry out certain tasks in groups, in pairs, or as individuals. The tasks in this part may include a short prepared talk, an interview, a debate, or a group presentation. The topics and tasks are designed to naturally elicit many of the structures practiced in the chapter. Detailed instructions for implementing these communicative activities as well as suggestions for additional activities and topics are included in the Instructor's Manual.

The second part of A Wider Angle is called *Writing Practice.* As the name suggests, students are asked to write short compositions on a variety of topics. Writing Practice gives students the opportunity to communicate their ideas while using target structures in a context that extends beyond the sentence level. The Instructor's Manual contains additional suggestions for writing topics.

Developing Your Skills and Knowledge: Chapter Exercises

The exercises at the end of each chapter provide written practice at the sentence level. These exercises can be assigned for homework after students have practiced the material from the Focus sections in class. Additional written exercises are available in the *Workbook*.

Appendices

The appendices contain reference material on spelling, pronunciation, irregular verbs, prepositions, and multiple-word verbs.

The Instructor's Manual

The new edition of *FOCUS* comes with an Instructor's Manual that contains:

1. Suggestions for presenting the Focus material
2. Suggestions for using and expanding the Practices
3. Instructions for A Wider Angle
4. Notes about potential problems
5. Additional teaching points that may be appropriate
6. Suggestions for additional oral and written exercises
7. Suggestions for additional composition topics
8. Suggestions for activities beyond the classroom
9. Answer keys for Practices and Exercises
10. Chapter tests with answer key
11. Suggestions for alternative sequencing

Workbook for *FOCUS*

The supplementary *Workbook* contains:

1. Additional written exercises for each *FOCUS* chapter
2. Additional teaching points for independent study or for in-class use
3. Practice with prepositions

Acknowledgments

I would like to give heartfelt thanks to my colleagues at the English Language Institute at The University of Akron, who have been with me all the way: To Dr. Kenneth J. Pakenham for his insights, understanding, and unfailing moral support. To Martha J. McNamara and Debra Deane, who served as continual sources of enthusiasm, sympathetic sounding boards, and voices of encouragement. To Karen Andrews, whose creative ideas have been incorporated into a number of exercises throughout the text.

Many thanks to my colleagues and peers in the field who read and reviewed the second edition of *FOCUS* and offered their valuable input on its structure and content: Isabel Y. Jennings, San Antonio College; Ila Jean Kragthorpe, Moorpark College; Linda D. Kushnir, University of New Orleans; Heidimarie Hayes Rambo, Kent State University; Mary Ellen Ryder, Boise State University; Wallis Sloat, William Rainey Harper College; and Diane Yokel, University of Denver, English Language Center. A note of appreciation is also extended to the students in the ELI at The University of Akron, whose feedback helped give *FOCUS* its final form.

My gratitude goes to the staff at St. Martin's Press for bringing this project to fruition, especially to Acquisitions Editor Naomi Silverman for her patience, insight, support, and delightful sense of humor.

I would also like to thank my friends and family, whose support and interest in the project served as an energizing force. And once again, an extra special note of thanks goes to Sabah Kimyon for being there from start to finish.

Contents

CHAPTER 6   **Activities in Progress**   **108**

CHAPTER 7   **Objects and Word Order**   **133**

CHAPTER 8 **Future Situations** **154**

CHAPTER 9 **Events and Experiences Related to the Present** **180**

1 General Facts and Situations

Daily Routines

Think about your typical day. What are some of the things that you do every day?

Now read about Carol:

Carol is a sophomore at the university. Like many American students, she also has a part-time job. She works as a waitress at an Italian restaurant. Carol doesn't have a lot of free time, so she has to organize her time very carefully. Here is how she spends a typical weekday.

7:00 A.M.	gets up; takes a shower; gets dressed
7:45 A.M.	has breakfast; reads the morning newspaper
8:30 A.M.	walks to the university
8:45 A.M.	studies at the university library
10:00 A.M.	goes to French class
11:00 A.M.	goes to economics class
12:00 P.M.	eats lunch with friends in the Student Center
1:00 P.M.	goes to sociology class
2:00 P.M.	goes jogging or works out in the gym
3:00 P.M.	goes home; showers; gets ready for work
4:00 P.M.	takes the bus to Tony's Restaurant, where she works
4:40 P.M.	has dinner at the restaurant before starting work
5:00 P.M.	begins work
9:00 P.M.	goes home and studies
11:00 P.M.	watches the evening news on TV
11:30 P.M.	goes to bed

Notice that this schedule gives general information about how Carol spends her time every day.

General or Scientific Facts: Facts about Snow

Do you have any experience with snow? What do you know about snow?

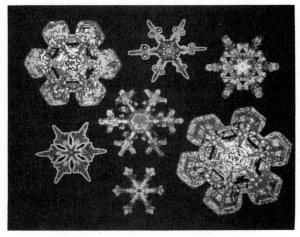

FIGURE 1–1

Now read the following information:

Snow forms in very cold weather. Water vapor in a cloud freezes and forms ice crystals. These ice crystals bump into each other and stick together. When they stick together, they become very heavy and fall to the ground as snowflakes. Almost all snowflakes are symmetrical and have six sides (see Fig. 1–1).

Notice that this information about snow is generally or always true. These are scientific facts that do not change.

In this chapter, you will practice talking about general facts, habits, and customs.

FOCUS 1 Simple Present Tense Verb Forms

The *simple present tense** of most verbs has two forms.

A.   -S/-ES form (third person singular)

Subject	Base Form + -S or -ES**	Examples
he	make + **-S**	A bartender **makes** drinks.
she	finish + **-ES**	Carol **finishes** class at 1:50.
it	serve + **-S**	The restaurant **serves** Italian food.

B.   Form without -S/-ES (first person singular and plural, second person singular and plural, third person plural)

Subject	Base Form + 0 (no -S/-ES)	Examples
I	make	I **make** friends easily.
you	finish	You usually **finish** class at 5:00 P.M.
we	like	My friends and I **like** pizza.
they	go	Carol's friends often **go** to Tony's.

The *base form* of the verb is the infinitive form without the word **TO.** For example, the infinitive form is **TO BE.** The base form of this verb is **BE.** The infinitive form is **TO GO.** The base form of this verb is **GO.**

FOCUS 2 Uses of the Simple Present Tense

The *simple present tense* can refer to habitual actions, general situations, or facts; it refers to situations that are not limited to one specific time.

---

*The rules for simple present tense in Focus 1, 3, and 4 are true for all verbs *except* the verb **BE.** The simple present tense rules for the verb **BE** are different. You can study about the simple present tense of the verb **BE** in Focus 5.

You can find spelling and pronunciation rules for the **-S/-ES form (third person singular) in Appendix A.

A. Customs and regular routines

This use of the *simple present tense* often includes a general time expression.

> *On Sundays,* my parents *usually* **go** to church.
> Pedro **calls** his family *every weekend.*
> Americans **celebrate** Labor Day *in September.*

B. General or scientific facts

> Mr. and Mrs. Wilson **live** on the tenth floor.
> My apartment **has** two bedrooms.
> Snow **forms** in very cold clouds.

PRACTICE 2–1   Using the **-S** Form

Complete each sentence with the -S form of the verb in parentheses. Think about the pronunciation and spelling of the -S/-ES ending.

1. (organize) Carol _____ her day very carefully.

2. (get up) She _____ every morning at seven o'clock.

3. (have) She usually _____ juice, coffee, and cereal for breakfast.

4. (walk) In good weather, she _____ to the university.

5. (go) In winter, however, she often _____ by bus.

6. (study) She _____ at the library first thing in the morning.

7. (keep) She _____ in good shape by running four miles every day.

8. (rush) After jogging, she _____ to work.

FOCUS 3   Negative Sentences with the Simple Present Tense

A. Forming a negative simple present tense verb

A negative verb in English uses an auxiliary ("helping verb") and the word **NOT**. The auxiliaries for the simple present tense are **DO** and **DOES**. The auxiliaries **DO** and **DOES** can be followed *only with the base form of a verb.*

Affirmative Sentences	Negative Sentence Patterns		
	HE/SHE/IT +	**DOES NOT** +	**Base Form**
Carol **eats** lunch on campus.	She	**does not**	**eat** dinner there.
The cafeteria **serves** hot food.	It	**does not**	**serve** cold sandwiches.
	I/YOU/WE/THEY +	**DO NOT** +	**Base Form**
She and her friends **eat** lunch together.	They	**do not**	**eat** dinner together.
I **like** to bring my lunch to school.	I	**do not**	**like** cafeteria food.

B. Contractions

A *contraction* is two words joined together with an apostrophe ('). English speakers often use contractions in conversation. However, they are not appropriate in formal writing. The contraction for **DO NOT** is **DON'T**; the contraction for **DOES NOT** is **DOESN'T**.

Formal		Conversational
Carol **does not have** a car.	→	Carol **doesn't have** a car.
I **do not have** much free time.	→	I **don't have** much free time.

PRACTICE 3-1   Using the Simple Present Tense

A.   Talk about the habits of people you know. Use the cues to give <u>true</u> *information about the routines of your friends and family. Your sentences can be negative or affirmative. You can choose any of the cues that you wish. Fill in empty brackets with your own cues.*

EXAMPLE   my father + (not) get up early + every day

My father gets up early every day.

(My father doesn't get up early every day.)

Subject +	Verb Phrase +	Time
Most of my friends	(not) drink coffee/tea/juice	every day
My roommate(s)	(not) eat a big breakfast/lunch/dinner	every week
My neighbor(s)	(not) get up early	in the morning/afternoon/evening
My sister/brother	(not) sleep late	on weekends
My mother/father/parents	(not) stay up late	after breakfast/lunch/dinner/class
My wife/husband	(not) smoke	before breakfast/lunch/dinner/class
My son/daughter/children	(not) get regular exercise	on Sunday mornings
[ ]	(not) watch TV	on Saturday nights
	(not) talk on the phone a lot	[ ]
	(not) take a nap	

B.   Are there any customs or habits here that you find surprising or unusual? What are some things that people here do that people in your country don't usually do? Are there any customs in your country that don't exist here? Consider, for example, the following topics: **eating habits, clothes, work habits, student life, families.** *Discuss some of these differences with your classmates.*

EXAMPLES   1. Some American professors wear jeans to class. Professors in my country don't wear jeans to class. They wear suits.

2. Americans eat a lot of fast food. They don't eat a lot of fish. In my country, we eat a lot of fish.

FOCUS 4   **YES/NO** Questions and Short Answers

A question that calls for an answer of "yes" or "no" begins with an auxiliary. You can reply to a **YES/NO** question with a short answer. In questions with the simple present tense, use the auxiliaries **DO** or **DOES** with the base form of the verb. A short answer uses a subject pronoun and an auxiliary. Look at the following examples:

Question					Short Answer			
Auxiliary	+	Subject	+	Base Form Verb		YES/NO	+	Pronoun	+	Auxiliary
Does		Carol		**drive**	to work?	→	No,	she	**doesn't.**
Does		her job		**pay**	well?	→	Yes,	it	**does.**
Does		her boss		**get**	angry very often?	→	No,	he	**doesn't.**
Do		you		**have**	a job?	→	Yes,	I	**do.**
Do		we		**use**	the book every day?	→	No,	we	**don't.**
Do		I		**speak**	too fast?	→	No,	you	**don't.**
Do		students		**need**	an ID card?	→	Yes,	they	**do.**

PRACTICE 4-1   **YES/NO** Questions and Short Answers

*Find out more about your classmates' housing situations here and in their native countries. Use the following cues to ask **YES/NO** questions. Your classmates should give short answers and, if possible, some additional information.*

EXAMPLE   you / live / near school?

Student A: Do you live near school?
Student B: Yes, I do. I live in a dormitory.
                     (No, I don't. I live about twenty miles away.)

A.   *In this country*

1.   you / rent / an apartment here?
2.   your place / have / air conditioning?
3.   you / like / it?
4.   you / have / any roommates?
5.   your family* / live / with you here?
6.   you / walk / to school?
7.   you / need / anything in your room?
8.   the kitchen / have / a dishwasher?

B.   *In your native country*

1.   most people / live / in apartments in your country?
2.   your family's home / have / a garden?
3.   your home / have / central heating?
4.   you / live / with any members of your extended family**?

C.   *What did you find out?*

---

*In American English, the word **FAMILY** is most often singular. However, the plural pronoun **THEY** is used to refer to the people in the family. Example: **Does** your family live here? Yes, **they do.**

The phrase **EXTENDED FAMILY refers to family members other than a father, a mother, and children. For example, your extended family may include grandparents, aunts, uncles, cousins, and in-laws.

A. Forms of the verb BE

The verb **BE** is irregular in the simple present tense. Its base form is **BE.** It has three simple present tense forms: **IS, AM, ARE.**

I **am** from Japan. $\left. \begin{array}{l} \text{He} \\ \text{She} \\ \text{It} \end{array} \right\}$ **is** from Japan. $\left. \begin{array}{l} \text{You} \\ \text{We} \\ \text{They} \end{array} \right\}$ **are** from Japan.

Add **NOT** after the verb **BE** to make it negative:

I **am not** from China.
She **is not** from China.
They **are not** from China.

B. Contractions

The contractions for the simple present tense of **BE** take the following forms:

I **am** single.	→	**I'm** single.
I **am not** married.	→	**I'm not** married.
He **is** a teacher.	→	**He's** a teacher.
He **is not** a student.	$\left. \begin{array}{l} \\ \\ \end{array} \right\}$	**He's not** a student. He **isn't** a student.
We **are** in class.	→	**We're** in class.
We **are not** at home.	$\left. \begin{array}{l} \\ \\ \end{array} \right\}$	**We're not** at home. We **aren't** at home.

C. Using BE as the main verb

As the main verb, **BE** usually connects a subject with another *noun, an adjective, a location, a time,* or *a phrase with a preposition.*

EXAMPLES

BE + *noun:*	Carol *is* **a student.**
BE + *adjective:*	Her friends *are* **very nice.**
BE + *location:*	Her job *isn't* **on campus.**
BE + *time:*	Her classes *are* **during the day.**
BE + *phrase:*	She *is* usually **in a good mood** at work.

NOTE: The verb **BE** can never occur with the base form of another verb.

EXAMPLES   John **is** a student. John **studies** at the university.

[MISTAKE: John ~~is study~~ at the university.]

D. YES/NO questions and short answers with BE

To form a **YES/NO** question with **BE,** put the verb at the beginning of the sentence, before the subject. Questions with **BE** do not require auxiliaries. Do not use **DO** or **DOES** in questions with **BE.**

Statement					Question				
Subject	+	**Verb BE**	+	**Rest of Sentence**	**Verb BE**	+	**Subject**	+	**Rest of Sentence**
Carol		**is**		a student.	**Is**		she		a good student?
Her classes		**are**		difficult.	**Are**		they		interesting too?

A *short answer* to a **YES/NO** question with **BE** uses a pronoun subject and the appropriate form of **BE**. Negative short answers usually use contractions. However, if the answer is "yes," it is necessary to use the full form.

EXAMPLES	Is Carol a student?	Yes, she **is.**
		[MISTAKE: Yes, ~~she's.~~]
	Is she a high school student?	No, she **isn't.**
		No, she**'s not.**
	Are you a graduate student?	No, I**'m not.***
	Are you an undergraduate student?	Yes, I **am.**
		[MISTAKE: Yes, ~~I'm.~~]

PRACTICE 5-1   **YES/NO** Questions with the Verb **BE**

*Use the following cues to ask your classmates **YES/NO** questions about their hometowns. They should respond with short answers and give additional information if possible.*

EXAMPLE   you / from a small town?

Student A: Are you from a small town?
Student B: No, I'm not. I'm from Bangkok. It's the capital.
             (Yes, I am. I'm from a small town near Bangkok.)

1.   you / from a big city?
2.   your hometown / near an ocean?
3.   your hometown / famous?
4.   streets in your hometown / very wide?
5.   the downtown area of your hometown / crowded during the day?
6.   most of the shops / open in the evenings?
7.   your hometown / very different from this city?

PRACTICE 5-2   Using **DO/DOES** or the Verb **BE**

A.   Circle all of the responses that can be used to complete the question. Draw a line through the responses that cannot be used. Explain your choices.

1.   Are you usually _____ in the morning?

a. ~~eat breakfast~~	d. thirsty	g. tired
(b.) in a good mood	e. take a shower	h. happy to get up
c. grouchy	f. drink coffee	i. want to sleep more

2.   Do you often _____?

a. call your country	e. upset about your	g. homesick
b. late to class	mistakes	h. feel homesick
c. come late to class	f. get upset about	i. tired in class
d. stay up late	your English	

---

*There is no contraction for **AM NOT**. [MISTAKE: No, I ~~amn't~~.]

B. *Complete each YES/NO question with one word. Use: **IS, AM, ARE, DOES,** or* ***DO.*** *Your classmate will answer the question with a short answer.*

EXAMPLES   Student A: **Is** Carol a student?
                     Student B: Yes, she is.
                     Student A: **Does** she work on campus?
                     Student B: No, she doesn't.

1. _____ you hungry?
2. _____ you usually get hungry in class?
3. _____ your stomach ever growl in class?

4. _____ you sometimes late to class?
5. _____ you feel embarrassed when you come late?
6. _____ your classmates sometimes come to class late?

7. _____ your teacher give you a lot of homework?
8. _____ the homework usually easy for you?
9. _____ you tired of studying English?
10. _____ your classes difficult for you?

PRACTICE 5-3   More Questions and Answers

*Use the following cues to ask your classmates **YES/NO** questions about their eating customs and habits. They should give short answers, and, if possible, some additional information. Fill in the empty brackets with your own cues.*

EXAMPLES   you / drink / tea in the morning?

               Student A: Do you drink tea in the morning?
               Student B: Yes, I do. I drink two cups.
                          (No, I don't. I drink coffee.)

               tea / expensive in your country?

               Student A: Is tea expensive in your country?
               Student B: No, it isn't. It's very cheap.
                          (Yes, it is. We import it from India.)

1. you / drink / coffee for breakfast?
2. the coffee in this country / different from coffee in your country?
3. people in your country / have a meal late in the evening?
4. breakfast / an important meal for you?
5. you / bring / your lunch to school here?
6. you / like / the food in this country?
7. the food in this country / strange?
8. fast food / popular in your country?
9. you / miss food from your country?
10. [?]

Prepositions of Location

The words **IN, ON, AT** are *prepositions*. They are often used as *prepositions of location*. This means that they can be used to indicate *where* something is. Each of these prepositions has its own meaning and its own special uses.

IN: The preposition **IN** is generally used to mean *within an area*. Use **IN** with geographic places: *continents, countries, regions, states, provinces, cities, towns*. Use **IN** also with enclosed areas: *buildings, rooms*. **IN** can also mean *inside something*.

> Chicago is **in** Illinois.
>
> My aunt lives **in** San Francisco.
>
> The telephone is **in** the kitchen.
>
> The letter from the immigration office is **in** that envelope.

ON: The preposition **ON** is often used to show that something is *on top of something*. Use **ON** also with *streets, page numbers, floors of buildings*.

> My notebook is **on** my desk.
>
> The White House is **on** Pennsylvania Avenue.
>
> Mr. Johnson lives **on** the fifth floor.
>
> Please do the exercises **on** page 45 for homework.

AT: The preposition **AT** can show general locations. **AT** emphasizes the location where an activity takes place.

> Lauren is **at** a party.
>
> Sam and Jane are **at** a concert.
>
> My roommate is **at** the post office.
>
> John is **at** the doctor's office.

Use **AT** also with specific street addresses: *number and street*.

> The driver's license bureau is **at** 1437 State Road.
>
> Mr. and Mrs. Quinn live **at** 923 East 57th Street.

Close-Up

PRACTICE **PREPOSITIONS OF LOCATION**

Answer each of the following questions with a complete sentence that includes a preposition of location: IN, ON, AT.

1. Where is Toronto?
2. Where does the leader of your country live?
3. Where does the president of the United States live?
4. Where do you usually study?
5. Where is the nearest library?
6. Where do you buy your school supplies?

7. Where do you see a lot of your friends?
8. Where is Practice 5–2 in this chapter?
9. Where do you keep pictures of your family and friends?
10. Where do you keep your keys?

FOCUS 6   Adverbs of Frequency

1. What are some of the things that you <u>almost never</u> have time to do in the morning?
2. What do you <u>usually</u> do when you get home from class?
3. What do you <u>often</u> do in your free time?
4. Is there any type of food that you <u>seldom</u> eat?

In the questions above, what kind of information do the underlined words give?

A.   Introduction to adverbs of frequency

The words **ALMOST ALWAYS, USUALLY, OFTEN, SELDOM** are examples of *adverbs of frequency*. *Adverbs of frequency* give a general idea of how often something occurs. Use them with the simple present tense to refer to routines and habits. *Adverbs of frequency* range from **ALWAYS** (100 percent of the time) to **NEVER** (0 percent of the time). Some of these adverbs have a negative meaning. The following chart gives examples of some common adverbs of frequency.

Type	Adverb of Frequency	Example		Meaning
Positive	always	Carol **always** takes a shower in the morning.	→	*every day*
	almost always	She **almost always** reads the morning paper.	→	*almost every day*
	usually	She **usually** has lunch with her friends.	→	*most days*
	often	She **often** goes jogging in the afternoon.	→	*many days*
	sometimes	Carol is **sometimes** late for work.	→	*some days*
Negative	seldom	She **seldom** eats dinner at home.	→	*not often*
	rarely	She **rarely** goes to bed before midnight.		
	hardly ever	Yes, she **hardly ever** misses class.		
	almost never	She **almost never** gets sick.		
	never/not ever	She **never** watches TV during the day.	→	*not at all*
		She doesn't **ever** watch TV during the day.		
Question	ever?	Does she **ever** have time to relax?	→	*at any time?*

B.   Negative adverbs of frequency

A negative adverb of frequency does not usually occur with a negative verb.

EXAMPLE   Carol rarely **eats** dinner at home.
[MISTAKE: Carol ~~doesn't rarely eat~~ dinner at home.]

C.   Questions with EVER

To ask about general frequency, use the adverb of frequency **EVER** in a **YES/NO** question with the simple present tense. An answer to this type of question usually includes an expression of frequency.

EXAMPLE   Do you **ever** feel homesick?   Yes, all the time.
　　　　　　　　　　　　　　　　　　　　　Yes, sometimes.
　　　　　　　　　　　　　　　　　　　　　No, never.

D. Word order with adverbs of frequency: middle position

Frequency adverbs often occur in the middle of the sentence, near the verb. We will call this **middle position.*** Many adverbs in English can occur in this position. The rules for placing an adverb in middle position depend on the type of sentence. Notice the word order in the following examples of frequency adverbs in *affirmative sentences, negative sentences, questions,* and *short forms*.

Middle Position for Frequency Adverbs		
Sentence Type	**Position**	**Examples**
affirmative sentences	after forms of **BE**	Carol *is* **usually** on time for work.
	before other simple present tense verbs	She **always** *eats* lunch at school.
negative sentences	(*Different adverbs have different positions in negative sentences. See examples for each adverb below.*)	
ALWAYS/EVER	after a negative auxiliary or form of **BE**	I *don't* **always** *have* time for breakfast.
		My roommate *doesn't* **ever** *miss* breakfast.
SOMETIMES	before a negative auxiliary or form of **BE**	Carol **sometimes** *doesn't eat* breakfast.
		She **sometimes** *isn't* in a good mood in the morning.
USUALLY/OFTEN	before <u>or</u> after a negative auxiliary or form of **BE**	The restaurant customers **often** *don't leave* big tips.
		They *don't* **often** *leave* big tips for her.
		They **usually** *aren't* very generous.
		They *aren't* **usually** very generous.
questions	after the subject	Does *Carol* **always** eat lunch on campus?
		Are *you* **ever** homesick for your country?
		What do *you* **usually** do in your free time?
short answers	before the auxiliary or form of **BE**	Do you ever go dancing? → No, I **never** *do*.
		Are you ever homesick? → Yes, I **sometimes** *am*.

PRACTICE 6-1   Adverbs of Frequency

*A.   Add an adverb of frequency to each of the following sentences to make a **true** statement about the customs of your native country. Put the adverb in **middle position**. You may make the verb negative if you wish.*

---

*You may also see some adverbs of frequency at the beginning of a sentence (*initial position*) and at the end of a sentence (*final position*).

Initial position: The adverb of frequency **SOMETIMES** also frequently occurs at the beginning of a sentence:

   Sometimes I miss food from my country.

The adverbs **USUALLY** and **OFTEN** can also occur at the beginning of a sentence for emphasis:

   Where do you eat lunch every day? → **Usually** I eat on campus, but sometimes I go home for lunch.
   Do you always eat lunch? → No, **often** I just skip it.

Final position: You may also see the adverbs **SOMETIMES** and **OFTEN** at the end of a sentence (final position) to show a contrast or special emphasis.

   Do you *always* study in the library? → Well, I study there **sometimes,** but not always. I prefer to study at home.
   You don't study in the library, do you? → Yes, I do. As a matter of fact, I study there quite **often.**

Adverbs of Frequency: **always, almost always, often, usually, sometimes, rarely, seldom, hardly ever, almost never, never**

EXAMPLES Women in my country smoke in public.

Women in my country **never** smoke in public.

Women in my country **often** smoke in public.

Women in my country **don't usually** smoke in public.

1. We take our shoes off before entering a house.
2. At universities in my country, professors wear jeans to class.
3. In my country, university professors erase the blackboards in their classes.
4. In my country, shops are closed for a lunch break.
5. In my country, shops are open on Sundays.
6. People in my country talk a lot during meals.
7. Dinner is the main meal of the day in my country.
8. University students in my country have part-time jobs.
9. In my country, we shake hands with our friends when we see them.
10. In my country, we greet our friends with a kiss on both cheeks.

B. *Now, think about this country. Are the customs you described in this exercise different in this country? How?*

EXAMPLE People in this country almost never take their shoes off before entering a house.

PRACTICE 6-2 Questions with **EVER**

Use the following cues to ask your classmates **YES/NO** questions with **EVER**. They should respond to each question with a short answer that includes a frequency adverb and an auxiliary. They may also give additional information if they wish.

EXAMPLE you / [ever] tired of speaking English?

Student A: Are you **ever** tired of speaking English?
Student B: **Yes, I sometimes am.** It's very difficult for me.
   (**No, I never am.** I like to practice my English.)

1. your family / [ever] call you?
2. you / [ever] get letters from friends in your country?
3. you / [ever] write letters to your friends?
4. your neighbors here / [ever] noisy?
5. you / [ever] talk to your neighbors here?
6. American newspapers / [ever] carry news about your country?

A WIDER ANGLE

Short Talks

Practice using the structures and vocabulary that you have learned in this chapter when you talk about the following topics.

TOPIC 1: Tell the class about the daily routine of a friend or a member of your family. For example, you can talk about the daily routine of your roommate, a grandparent, a brother or sister, an aunt or uncle, a cousin, your spouse, one of your children, one of your parents, or your best friend. When you finish, your classmates can ask you some **YES/NO** questions for additional information about that person's routines.

TOPIC 2: Tell the class about how the daily routine of a student here is different from the daily routine of a student in your native country.

Writing Practice

Write a short composition on one of the following topics:

TOPIC 1: Write a composition that describes the weather and the seasons in your country. If you wish, you can begin your composition like this:

In _____, *we have* _____ *seasons. These seasons are . . .*
     (country)   *(number)*

TOPIC 2: Write a composition about how you spend a typical weekend in this country.

DEVELOPING YOUR SKILLS AND KNOWLEDGE

Chapter Exercises

EXERCISE 1   ## Simple Present Tense—Scientific Facts

The following sentences give facts about different types of precipitation. Complete each sentence with the simple present tense of the verb indicated.

1. The word *precipitation* _____ water in the air and the
                         (refer to)
   weather it _____.
             (produce)

2. Clouds _____ water vapor. When the temperature of
          (consist of)
   the cloud _____, the water vapor
               (cool)
   _____ drops of water. Gravity _____
      (form)   *(pull)*
   these drops of water to the ground as rain.

3. Snowflakes _____ when water vapor of a cloud
               (form)
   _____ very cold and _____ ice
      (get)   *(turn into)*
   crystals. These ice crystals _____ together to form
                         (stick)
   snowflakes. The snowflakes _____ to the ground as
                     (fall)
   snow when they _____ heavy. Almost every*
                (become)
   snowflake _____ six sides, but snowflakes
             (have)
   _____ alike. Each* snowflake _____
  (not / look)   *(be)*
   different from other snowflakes.

---

*__Each__ and **every** are singular. They are used with the **-S** form of the verb:
  Each student *wants* to learn English well.
  Every language *has* its own rules.

EXERCISE 2   YES/NO Questions

*Complete the following conversational exchange between Jerome and Alicia by writing an appropriate **YES/NO** question. Remember: The short answer gives a response to the question. Information that comes after the short answer is additional new information.*

EXAMPLE   Yolanda: <u>Are you from Venezuela?</u>
Elena: No, I'm not. I'm from Spain.

JEROME: Hi! My name is Jerome.

ALICIA: Hi Jerome! My name is Alicia.

JEROME: _____?

ALICIA: No, I'm not. I'm from Brazil.

JEROME: Brazil? Wow! _____?

ALICIA: No, we don't. We speak Portuguese in my country.

JEROME: Oh, that's right. I always forget about that. Well, _____
_____?

ALICIA: Yes, I am. I am a student in the intensive English language program

JEROME: Really? I know a lot of students in that program. _____
_____?

ALICIA: Yes, I do. I know her because she is in my grammar class.

JEROME: _____?

ALICIA: No, they aren't. My entire family is in Brazil.

JEROME: _____?

ALICIA: No, I don't. I live in a dormitory.

JEROME: The dorm?! _____?

ALICIA: Yes, it is. Sometimes It's so noisy that I can't sleep!

JEROME: I can imagine. Dormitories are often noisy! _____
_____?

ALICIA: Yes, I do. In fact, I have two roommates: one from Quebec and one from Nebraska.

JEROME: _____?

ALICIA: No, they don't. But that's good. The fact that they don't speak Portuguese means that I have to speak English all the time!

JEROME: _____?

ALICIA: Yes, they are. They are very friendly and very funny! I am lucky.

EXERCISE 3   Prepositions of Location

*Fill in each blank with **IN, ON,** or **AT**.*

1.   Chan: Where's my coat?

     Keo: It's _____ the closet.

CHAN: No, it isn't.

KEO: Maybe it's _____ the bedroom.

CHAN: You're right. It's _____ the bed.

2. RITA: Excuse me. Is Dr. Simpson's office _____ this floor?

SECRETARY: No, it isn't. I'm afraid you have the wrong building. I think his office is _____ the building across the street.

3. TEACHER: For homework tonight, please do the exercises _____ your workbook _____ page 25.

4. RAMON: Where's the party tonight?

PETER: It's _____ Tony's house. He lives _____ Washington Boulevard.

RAMON: What's his address?

PETER: I think he lives _____ 3640 Washington Boulevard.

5. SING KYU: Is Pamela _____ her office?

MS. PALMER: No, she isn't. She's _____ a conference in St. Louis.

6. SECRETARY: Where do you live?

STUDENT: I live _____ a dormitory _____ Summer Street.

EXERCISE 4   Adverbs of Frequency

The Midwest is an area of the United States that includes Ohio, Indiana, Iowa, Illinois, Michigan, Wisconsin, Minnesota, and Missouri. The following sentences give information about the weather in those states. Rewrite each sentence using the adverb of frequency in parentheses. Put the adverb in the middle position and make any necessary changes in the verb.

EXAMPLE   It is foggy in the morning. (often)

It is **often** foggy in the morning.

1. Summers in the Midwest are hot and sticky. (usually)
2. The weather there begins to get cooler in October. (almost always)
3. However, it doesn't snow before November. (rarely)
4. November is a rainy month. (often)
5. It snows as late as April. (sometimes)
6. It doesn't snow in May. (almost never)
7. Flowers don't bloom before May. (seldom)

EXERCISE 5   Chapter Review

*Here are some different ways to talk about the weather. Use the subject **IT** when describing the weather.*

IT	+	Verb BE	+	Adjective
It		is		foggy / rainy.
It		is		sunny / cloudy / hazy.
It		is		windy / breezy.
It		is		wet / dry / humid / sticky / muggy.
It		is		hot / warm / pleasant.
It		is		cold / cool / chilly / freezing.

IT	+	Verb
It		snows.
It		rains.
It		hails.

A. Complete each of the following **YES/NO** questions with **DO, DOES, IS,** or **ARE**. Respond with information about the weather in your native country. Write a short answer with a frequency adverb. If possible, give some additional information.

EXAMPLE   Question: ___Does___ it ever snow in your country?
                 Answer: **Yes, it often does.** Winters in my country are very cold.

                 (**No, it never does.** My country has a tropical climate.)

1. _____ it ever rain for long periods of time in your region?

2. _____ it ever foggy in your hometown in the morning?

3. _____ they ever close schools in your country because of bad weather?

4. _____ it ever humid in your hometown?

5. _____ your region ever experience tornadoes or other violent storms?

6. _____ people ever worry about floods in your country?

7. _____ people ever discuss the weather in your country?

B. Now write three **YES/NO** questions of your own that you would like to ask one of your classmates about the weather in his or her country.

2 Exchanging Information about General Situations

```
┌─────────────────────────────────┐
│   THE BIG PICTURE               │
│                                 │
│   Information Questions         │
│   Communicating Ability         │
│   Communicating Necessity       │
│   Time Clauses                  │
└─────────────────────────────────┘
```

AT A GLANCE

Getting Information

Looking for an Apartment

Situation: Imagine that you are looking for an apartment to rent. An advertisement in the newspaper says:

> **Apartment for Rent**
> **Call 555-8658**

What do you want to know about the apartment before you decide to look at it? What questions do you want to ask when you call for information about the apartment?

Finding a Roommate

Situation: Imagine that you are looking for a roommate to share your two-bedroom apartment. You need a roommate because you cannot afford to pay the rent by yourself.

What are some different ways to find a roommate?

Look at the following list, and put a check in front of the topics you would like to ask about when choosing a roommate:

_____ study habits   _____ hobbies and leisure time activities

_____ eating habits   _____ smoking habits

_____ sleeping habits   _____ cooking abilities

Is there anything else that you would like to know about someone before inviting that person to be your roommate? What other things would you like to ask about?

_____

> **In this chapter, you will practice asking for and giving information about general facts, routines, and customs.**

_____

FOCUS 1   Information Questions

A question that asks for specific new information begins with a question word or phrase. Some examples of question phrases are: **WHAT . . . ? WHAT TIME . . . ? WHEN . . . ? HOW FAR . . . ?** Can you think of any other question words or phrases?

A.   Word order in information questions

    1.   If the main verb is a form of **BE,** put the verb in front of the subject.

Question Phrase	+	BE	+	Subject	+	Rest of Sentence
What		**is**		your name?		
Where		**are**		you		from?
How much		**is**		the rent?		

    2.   If the main verb is any other simple present tense verb, put the auxiliary **DO** or **DOES** in front of the subject. Use the *base form* of the verb after the subject.

Question Phrase	+	DO/DOES	+	Subject	+	Base Form Verb	+	Rest of Sentence
What		**do**		you		**study**		at the university?
How much		**does**		the landlord		**require**		for a deposit?
How late		**do**		you		**stay up**		at night?

B.   Negative questions

Use a contraction to ask a negative question.*

    Why **doesn't** this apartment have a desk?

    Why **aren't** you happy with your apartment?

_____

*It is also possible to ask a very formal negative question without a contraction. Put **NOT** after the subject. This type of negative question is not very common in everyday conversation.

    Why **does** this apartment **not have** a desk? Why **are** you **not** happy with your apartment?

C. Using question phrases

1. **WHERE . . . ?** asks about a *place.*

   Question: **Where** do you usually do your laundry?
   Answer: At a laundromat.

2. **WHEN . . . ?** asks about *time.*

   Question: **When** do we have to pay the rent?
   Answer: At the beginning of the month.

3. **WHAT TIME . . . ?** asks for *time on a clock.*

   Question: **What time** do you usually go to bed?
   Answer: At around 11:30.

4. **WHY . . . ?** asks for a *reason or purpose.*

   Question: **Why** do you want to find a roommate?
   Answer: Because I can't afford to pay the rent by myself.

5. **HOW OFTEN . . . ?** asks about *frequency.*

   Question: **How often** does the landlord clean the carpets?
   Answer: Once a year.

6. **HOW LONG . . . ?** asks about a *period or length of time.*

   Question: **How long** are your classes?
   Answer: They're 50 minutes each.

7. **HOW . . . ?** can ask about many different things.

   HOW . . . ? can ask about *health or general well-being.***

   Question: **How** are you?
   Answer: Pretty good. (Fine. Not too bad. Great.)

   HOW . . . ? can ask about a *method of doing things.*

   Question: **How** do you usually pay the rent?
   Answer: I usually pay by check.

   HOW . . . ? can ask about a *manner of doing something.*

   Question: **How** does your roommate drive?
   Answer: He drives very cautiously.

8. **WHAT . . . ?** has several uses.

   WHAT . . . ? can ask about *things.*

   Question: **What** do you usually eat for breakfast?
   Answer: I usually have juice, cereal, and tea.

   WHAT . . . ? can ask about an *activity.* Use the verb **DO** to ask about activities. The answer usually has a different verb.

   Question: **What** do you *do* in your free time?
   Answer: I *play* sports and *go* to movies.

---

*The question **HOW ARE YOU?** asks about a person's well-being. The question **HOW DO YOU DO?** means "It's nice to meet you." The answer to this question is also "How do you do?"

9. **WHAT KIND OF + (noun) . . . ?** asks about a *specific type or brand of something.*

> Question: **What kind of movies** do you like?
> Answer: I like detective movies.

> Question: **What kind of cereal** does Carol eat for breakfast?
> Answer: She eats oatmeal. (She eats cornflakes.)

10. **WHO . . . ?** asks about *people.*

> Question: **Who** is your favorite movie star?
> Answer: My favorite movie star is Sylvester Stallone.

D. Special questions

1. To ask about *jobs or professions,* use the question word **WHAT** with the simple present tense form of the verb **DO.** You can also use the expression **DO FOR A LIVING.**

> Question: **What** *does your father do?*
> Answer: He's a businessman.

> Question: **What** *do you do for a living?*
> Answer: I'm an elementary school teacher.

2. To ask about *methods of transportation,* use the question word **HOW** with the verb **GET (TO).**

> Question: **How** *do you get to school?*
> Answer: By bus. (By taxi. By subway. By car.)

> Question: **How** *do you get to your job?*
> Answer: I drive. (I walk. I get a ride. I take a bus.)

3. To ask about *how much time is necessary to do something,* use the question phrase **HOW LONG** with the verb **TAKE.** Notice that the subject is **IT.** Notice also that the action verb uses the infinitive form of the verb (**TO + base form**).

> Question: **How long** *does* it *take you to get to school?*
> Answer: *It takes* me 15 minutes by car.

> Question: **How long** *does* it *take you to eat* breakfast?
> Answer: *It usually takes* me half an hour.

4. To ask for *an opinion or impression of something,* use the question word **HOW.** Notice the different ways to ask this type of question.

> Question: **How** *do you like American food?*
> Answer: I think it's pretty good.

> Question: **How** *is the food in the dormitory?*
> Answer: It's terrible.

PRACTICE 1-1   Information Questions

Mr. Morena is a travel agent. The following schedule shows his daily routine:

6:30 A.M.   gets up; gets ready for work
7:00 A.M.   leaves house; drives downtown to work
8:00 A.M.   arrives downtown; stops to have coffee and a muffin at a coffee shop

8:30 A.M.	begins work at the travel agency
12:30 P.M.	goes out to a vegetarian restaurant for lunch
1:30 P.M.	returns to work
5:30 P.M.	gets off work; goes to a nearby health club to work out
6:30 P.M.	drives home
7:30 P.M.	arrives home; fixes and eats dinner
8:30 P.M.–12:00	[?]

Use the following cues to ask questions about Mr. Morena's routine. Your classmate should respond with information from the schedule. If the information is not on the schedule, use your imagination to give information about Mr. Morena. Fill in empty brackets with your own cues.

EXAMPLE: What time / get up every day?

            Student A: What time does Mr. Morena get up every day?

            Student B: He gets up at six-thirty.

1. what / do for a living?
2. where / the travel agency?
3. how / get to work?
4. what time / leave his home?
5. how long / it / take him to get to work?
6. where / eat / breakfast?
7. what kind of food / eat for lunch?
8. why / (not) go directly home after work?
9. [What time . . . ?]
10. [What . . . ?]
11. [Where . . . ?]
12. [?]

FOCUS 2   Questions with **WHO** and **WHAT** as the Subject

The question words **WHO** and **WHAT** can ask for information about the subject of the sentence. **WHO . . . ?** asks about *somebody*. **WHAT . . . ?** asks about *something*.

In the following examples, notice that the question word (**WHO/WHAT**) *is* the subject of the question. Also notice how the word order in these questions is different from the question word order that is explained in Focus 1.

Subject	+	Verb	+	Rest of Sentence
Somebody		needs		a roommate.
Who		**needs**		a roommate?
Rick		needs		a roommate.
Something		is		expensive.
What		**is**		expensive?
The apartment		is		expensive.

Rules to remember:
1. When the question word **WHO** or **WHAT** is the subject of the question, do not use the auxiliary **DO** or **DOES**.
2. Use regular statement word order.

3. When **WHO** or **WHAT** is the subject, always use the singular form of the verb. Although the question always has a singular verb, the answer may be singular or plural.
4. A short answer to this type of question can use an auxiliary or form of **BE**.

EXAMPLES

Question	Short Answer
Who **needs** a roommate?	Rick **does.**
Who **lives** in the dorm?	Maria and Carmen **do.**
Who **is** noisy?	The students in the dorm **are.**
What **is** expensive?	The rent for Rick's apartment **is.**
What **is** broken?	The TV and washing machine **are.**
What **bothers** Rick?	The noise from the refrigerator **does.**

PRACTICE 2–1 Questions with **WHO** as the Subject

In an apartment or house, the *tenant* is the person who pays the rent to live there. The *landlord* is the person who owns the rental property. When a tenant decides to rent an apartment, he or she often signs a *lease*, or contract. This contract outlines the responsibilities of both the tenant and the landlord.

*Interview a classmate who has experience renting an apartment, room, or house here or in his or her native country. Ask questions with **WHO** to find out who has the following responsibilities. Your classmate should respond with a short answer. Fill in empty brackets with your own questions.*

EXAMPLES   make up the lease
Student A: **Who** makes up the lease?
Student B: The landlord **does.**

sign the lease
Student A: **Who** signs the lease?
Student B: The landlord and the tenant **do.**

1. pay for the electricity?
2. clean around the outside of the building?
3. be responsible for getting rid of bugs and insects?
4. provide the furniture?
5. provide the refrigerator and stove?
6. be in charge of the security of the building?
7. [?]

PRACTICE 2–2 More Questions with **WHO** as the Subject

A.   *Interview a classmate who lives with other people here or in his or her native country. Ask questions with **WHO** to find out who usually does the different household chores, such as shopping, cooking, washing dishes, paying bills, putting children to bed, fixing things, taking care of the yard, and so on. Your classmate will answer with a short answer.*

EXAMPLES   Student A: **Who** usually cooks dinner in your house?
Student B: My roommate **does.**

Student A: **Who** usually washes the dishes?

Student B: I **do.**

B. *What did you find out from your classmate?*

Questions with **WHO(M)** and **WHAT** as the Object

The question words **WHO(M)** and **WHAT** can also ask for information about someone or something other than the subject. They can ask about objects. If the question word is *not* the subject, use regular question word order. Be sure to keep all necessary prepositions in the question.

1. Rick wants to talk about **SOMETHING.**
   ↓
   What does he want to talk **about?**
   About his rent.

2. Rick wants to live with **SOMEONE.**
   ↓
   Who(m) does he want to live **with?**
   With Joe and Ali.

When the question word is *not* the subject, you can use **WHO** or **WHOM. WHO** is often used in conversational English. Prepositions stay with the verb in this type of conversational question.

Conversational: **Who** does Rick want to live **with?**

Questions with **WHOM** are formal. In formal questions, prepositions often come before the question word. If the preposition comes before the question word, use only **WHOM. WHO** is not possible in this situation.

Formal: **With whom** does Rick want to live?

PRACTICE 3-1 Questions with **WHO** as the Object

Use each of the following cues to form a YES/NO question for one of your classmates. Your classmate will respond with a short answer. If your classmate answers "yes," ask a second question using WHO(M). This time, your classmate will answer with a complete sentence.

EXAMPLE live with somebody?

Student A: **Do** you live with somebody?

Student B: Yes, I do.

Student A: **Who** do you live with?

Student B: I live with my uncle and his family.

1. [usually] come to school with somebody?
2. [usually] sit next to somebody in class?
3. [ever] eat lunch with anybody?
4. [ever] write letters to anybody?
5. [often] get letters from somebody?
6. [sometimes] visit somebody on weekends?
7. [often] think about somebody from your country?
8. [ever] call anybody on the telephone?
9. [ever] confide in anybody when you have a problem?

Questions with **WHO** and **WHAT**

*Rick is unhappy because his apartment is very old and has a lot of problems. To find out more about these problems, use the following cues to form questions with **WHO** or **WHAT**. Your classmate should use his or her imagination to answer each question.*

EXAMPLE   Rick has problems with **something** in his apartment.

Student A: **What** does he have problems with?
Student B: He has problems with cockroaches.
             (He has problems with the plumbing.)

1. **Something** often breaks.
2. Rick often complains about **something.**
3. **Someone** usually comes over to fix this problem.
4. Rick also has problems with **something else.**
5. He often talks to **someone** about this.
6. **Someone** is very noisy.
7. Rick pays a lot of money for **something.**
8. **Something** almost never works.
9. **Someone** is responsible for fixing it.

CLOSE-UP   **Expressions of Time and Frequency**

A.   Other expressions of frequency

The following expressions give *specific information* about *how often* an action or situation occurs within a particular time period:

How Often	Time Period
once / one time	
twice / two times	a day / a week / a month / a semester / a year
several / many / four times	
Carol goes to the bank **once a week.**	
She gets a paycheck **twice a month.**	
Carol goes jogging **four or five times a week.**	
every	
every other	day / week / month / semester / year
every three/four/ten →	days / weeks / months / years
Rick complains about his rent **every month.**	
Carol gets a paycheck **every other week.**	
Leap year occurs **every four years.**	

B.   Expressions of time

When the following expressions are used with a simple present tense verb, they give information about *when* or *what time* an action or situation generally occurs.

IN: Use the preposition **IN** with *seasons, months,* and *general time periods of the day.*

> **in** (the) spring / (the) summer / (the) fall or autumn / (the) winter
> **in** May / January / November
> **in** the morning / the afternoon / the evening

> > Students often have a vacation **in the summer.**
> > Rick's family usually goes skiing **in December.**
> > Carol goes to the library **in the morning.**

ON: Use the preposition **ON** with *specific days, including the weekend.*

> **on** Monday(s)   **on** Halloween
> **on** Sunday morning(s)   **on** weekends
> **on** October 31   **on** the weekend

> > Americans celebrate Halloween **on October 31.**
> > I don't usually go to the library **on Friday nights.**
> > Carol doesn't get up early **on weekends.**

AT: Use **AT** with *time on a clock.* Use **AT** also with **NIGHT.**

> > Carol usually gets up **at seven o'clock.**
> > She has lunch **at noon.**
> > She watches the news **at 11:00 P.M.**
> > She is always asleep **at midnight.**
> > She doesn't like to stay up late **at night.**

FROM–TO: The preposition **FROM** occurs with the prepositions **TO** or **UNTIL** to indicate a *time period.*

> > Carol works at the restaurant **from 5:00 P.M. to 9:00 P.M.**
> > Students are on vacation **from June until September.**

Close-Up

PRACTICE   **RETURNING THE QUESTION**

In informal conversations, when someone asks you a question, you can "return" the question with the expressions **WHAT ABOUT . . . ?** or **HOW ABOUT . . . ?**

EXAMPLE   Dave: Do you live near school?

Beth: No, I don't. I live about 30 minutes from here. **What about you?**

Dave: I live about two blocks from campus.

Beth: How's your apartment?

Dave: It's OK, I guess. **How about your apartment? (How about yours?)**

Beth: It's much too small. I want to move as soon as possible.

*Use the following cues to ask your classmate questions. Your classmate should answer each question with a complete sentence, and then return the question with **HOW ABOUT** . . . ? or **WHAT ABOUT** . . . ? Fill in the empty brackets with your own cues.*

EXAMPLE   how often / you / hold national elections in your country?

           Student A: How often do you hold national elections in your country?

           Student B: We hold elections every seven years. **How about in your country?**

           Student A: We hold elections every four years.

1.   how often / you / go shopping for groceries?
2.   how long / it / [usually] take you to clean your house?
3.   when / you / have time to relax?
4.   how often / you / eat out?
5.   who / you / [usually] eat out with?
6.   how often / you / [?]
7.   when / you / [?]
8.   what time / you / [?]

FOCUS 4   Ability, Permission, and Opportunity: Modal Auxiliary **CAN**

What are some things that you can do fairly well? (Think, for example, about sports, hobbies, musical instruments, and so on.) What are some things that you cannot do as well as you would like to be able to?

A.   Introduction to modal auxiliaries

English has a group of special auxiliaries called *modal auxiliaries.* Examples of modal auxiliaries are **CAN, COULD, MAY, MIGHT, WILL, WOULD, SHALL, SHOULD,** and **MUST.** A modal auxiliary adds extra meaning to the verb. Notice, for example, the difference between these two sentences:

    I **drive** to school every day. (*This is my habit.*)
    I **can drive.** (*I have the ability to drive.*)

Some modal auxiliaries have more than one meaning. In this Focus section, you will learn some of the uses of **CAN.** You will practice other modals and their uses in other chapters.

B.   General rules for modal auxiliaries

All of the modal auxiliaries follow these grammar rules:

1.   A modal auxiliary has only one form for all subjects.
2.   A modal auxiliary is always the first auxiliary of the verb.
3.   A modal auxiliary does not occur with the auxiliaries **DO/DOES.**
4.   A modal auxiliary is followed by a verb or another auxiliary in the *base form.*
5.   A verb can have only one modal auxiliary.

C.   Using the auxiliary CAN

The auxiliary **CAN** often adds the meaning of present *ability, opportunity,* or *permission* to the verb.

Which of these meanings does **CAN/CAN'T** add to the verb in each of the following sentences?

1. I **can't water ski.** I've never learned how.
2. We **can't water ski** here. That sign says "No Skiing."
3. You **can't water ski** around here because there aren't any lakes.
4. **Can** you **swim?**
5. **Can** I **swim** in this pond, or is it against the law?
6. **Can** you **swim** around here anywhere, or are most of the lakes far away?

D. Forming sentences with CAN

1. Use **CAN** with the base form of a verb. To make the verb negative, use **CANNOT** or the contraction **CAN'T**.

Subject	+	Auxiliary	+	Base Form Verb
		"ability"		
		"opportunity"		
		"permission"		
I		cannot		**ski.**
We		can't		**leave** yet.
You		can		**use** my calculator.
It		can		**help** you with your calculations.
She		can't		**stay** here very long.
He		can't		**drive.**
They		cannot		**understand** me very well.

2. To form a question, put **CAN** before the subject. Use **CAN** or **CAN'T** in short answers.

a. YES/NO questions and short answers
Can you **swim?**   Yes, I **can.**
Can your sister **drive?**   No, she **can't.**

b. Information questions
How many languages **can** you **speak?**   Three.
Where **can** I **get** a cup of coffee?   In the cafeteria.

PRACTICE 4-1   Using **CAN** and **CAN'T**

*Give an example of something these people or things **can** do and of something they can't do.*

EXAMPLES   My mother . . .

My mother **can speak** English, but she **can't write** it.
My mother **can swim,** but she **can't swim** very fast.

1. A computer . . .
2. Doctors today . . .
3. On a plane, passengers . . .
4. An international student who is here on a student visa . . .
5. A tenant . . .
6. I . . .

Some *modal expressions* have the same meaning as modal auxiliaries. These expressions do not use a special auxiliary. Look at the following examples:

Computers **can make** quick calculations.

Computers **are able to make** quick calculations.

You **can't smoke** in this building.

You **aren't allowed to smoke** in this building.

I **can't drive**.

I **don't know how to drive**.

A.   BE ABLE TO + (base form verb)

BE ABLE TO is an expression that often indicates *ability*, usually some type of physical ability. **BE ABLE TO** can also refer to opportunity. This expression is always followed by a *base form verb*. To talk about present ability, use the simple present tense of the verb **BE**. In the present tense, **CAN** is used more often than **BE ABLE TO**.

Subject	+	BE	+	ABLE TO + Base Form Verb
I		**am** (not)		**able to swim** quickly.
He		**is** (not)		**able to see** very well.
You		**are** (not)		**able to run** five miles.

To form a question, put the form of **BE** before the subject. Use a form of **BE** in short answers.

1. YES/NO questions

   Are you **able to understand** American TV shows? Yes, I **am**.

   Is your family **able to visit** you here often? No, they **aren't**.

2. Information questions

   What **is** a computer **able to do?**

   How **are** doctors **able to save** someone with a bad heart?

B.   BE ALLOWED TO + (base form verb)

The expression **BE ALLOWED TO** can be used to talk about *permission*. This expression is always followed by a *base form verb*. To talk about present permission, use the simple present tense form of the verb **BE**.

EXAMPLES   We **aren't allowed to speak** our native language in class.

Am I allowed to use the library? Yes, you **are**.

An international student **is allowed to work** on campus part-time.

C.   KNOW HOW TO + (base form verb)

An expression that refers to *learned ability* is the phrase **KNOW HOW TO (do something)**. The verb **KNOW** is not an auxiliary. It is a regular verb. In the simple present tense, it uses the auxiliary **DO** or **DOES** for questions, negative sentences, and short answers. This expression is always followed by a base form verb.

EXAMPLES   **Do** you **know how to play** tennis? Yes, I **do.**

John **doesn't know how to cook** very well.

I **know how to play** that song on the guitar.

Talking about Ability and Permission

A.   Use the following cues to ask your classmates YES/NO questions using the auxiliary CAN. Your classmate will respond with a short answer and additional information if possible.

EXAMPLE   you / sing very well?

Student A: **Can** you **sing** very well?

Student B: Yes, I **can.** I love to sing folk songs.

(No, I **can't.** I have a terrible voice.)

1.   your best friend / drive a motorcycle?
2.   your father (mother) / see well without glasses?
3.   you / play a musical instrument?
4.   people from your country / travel to Canada without a visa?
5.   your best friend / play a sport?
6.   the teacher / speak your native language?
7.   someone who is sixteen years old / drive in your native country?
8.   you / jog five miles?
9.   you / do any magic card tricks?
10.   the teacher / erase the top of the blackboard?

B.   Now, report what you found out from your classmates. Do NOT use CAN. Use a form of BE ABLE TO, BE ALLOWED TO, or KNOW HOW TO.

EXAMPLES   1. Mali **knows how to sing** very well. She loves to sing folk songs.

2. Rita **isn't able to sing** very well. She says she has a terrible voice.

FOCUS 6   Necessity and Obligation: **MUST/HAVE TO**

What are some things that are necessary for human life?
What are some things that are necessary for <u>you</u> to be happy?

A.   Talking about necessity

1.   The modal auxiliary **MUST** can indicate that something is *necessary.* If it is necessary for you to do something, you have no choice. You must do it whether you want to or not. It can also indicate that there is an obligation for you to do something whether you want to or not.

If you hear a fire alarm, you **must leave** the building immediately.

2.   The expression **HAVE TO** can also indicate necessity and obligation. **HAVE TO** is not an auxiliary. It is a regular verb. In conversational English, people use **HAVE TO** more often than **MUST** to express necessity.

If you hear a fire alarm, you **have to leave** the building immediately.

B.   Forming sentences with MUST and HAVE TO

MUST and **HAVE TO** are always followed by a base form verb.

Subject	+	MUST/HAVE TO "necessity"	+	Base Form Verb	+	Rest of Sentence
I		have to		eat		in order to live.
I		must		eat		in order to live.
They		have to		work		to earn a living.
They		must		work		to earn a living.
He		has to		get		a visa to visit Canada.
He		must		get		a visa to visit Canada.

C. Negative sentences with MUST and HAVE TO

In negative sentences, **MUST** and **HAVE TO** have different meanings.

> 1. Negative sentences with **HAVE TO**

To show that something is *not necessary,* use the simple present tense of the expression **(NOT) HAVE TO.**

> Joe **doesn't have to pay** for the utilities in his apartment.
>
> *(His landlord does not require him to do this.)*
>
> Many desert plants **don't have to have** a lot of water to live.
>
> *(It is not necessary for them to have a lot of water. They can survive without it.)*

> 2. Negative sentences with **MUST***

Use **MUST NOT + (base form verb)** to show that it is necessary or important *not* to do something. In other words, this expression means **"DON'T DO IT!"**

> Students **must not come** to class late.
>
> *(It is important that students **not** come to class late!)*
>
> You **must not get** discouraged about your progress in English.
>
> *(Don't get discouraged!)*

D. Questions with MUST and HAVE TO

The most common way of asking about necessity is with the expression **HAVE TO.**

> **Do** you **have to pay** for your electricity? No, I **don't.**
>
> **Does** your sister **have to get up** early for class? Yes, she **does.**
>
> What time **do** you **have to be** at school every day? At 9:00 A.M.

Occasionally you might hear questions with **MUST.** This type of question, however, is not very common.

> **Must** you **leave** so soon? Yes, I really **must.**

PRACTICE 6–1 Talking about Necessity and Obligation

A. Use the following information to form sentences about things that are necessary and not necessary. Use an appropriate form of HAVE TO or MUST.

EXAMPLE   Joe **has to pay** for electricity, but he **doesn't have to pay** for gas.

(Joe **must pay** for electricity, but he **doesn't have to pay** for gas.)

---

*You can find more information about **MUST NOT** in Chapter 10.

subject	NECESSARY	NOT NECESSARY
1. Joe	pay for electricity	pay for gas
2. Chang	pay income tax	pay property taxes
3. Bruce and his roommate	pay the phone bill	pay the water bill
4. Carol	work during the week	work on weekends
5. landlords	provide locks on doors	provide a TV
6. actors	know how to act well	be good-looking
7. I	. . . on weekdays	. . . on weekends

B. *Match the phrase in the first column with the appropriate situation in the second column.*

_____ You don't have to shout.

a. It is not necessary for you to shout. I can hear you very well.

_____ You must not shout.

b. Please don't shout. The baby is sleeping.

_____ You don't have to wait for me.

c. Don't wait for me. You'll be late to your next class.

_____ You must not wait for me.

d. It is not necessary for you to wait for me, but you can if you want to.

C. *Use **HAVE TO** or **MUST** to answer the following questions.*

1. What are the requirements for serving in the military in your country?
2. What do soldiers in basic training have to do?
3. Do soldiers in your country have any special privileges that ordinary citizens do not have? In other words, is there anything that a soldier does not have to do while he is in the military?
4. What are some things that a soldier must not do?
5. What do you know about the requirements for military service in this country?

GETTING READY TO FOCUS

Different Customs

What happens in your country when a high school student comes to class late? What about a university student?

Coming to Class Late

Read the following situation:

A student at an English Language Institute overslept and got to class almost 15 minutes late. When he arrived, his class, of course, had already started. The instructor was explaining something to the students.

When he got to the class, he stood outside the door and knocked, even though the door was open. The instructor looked surprised.

Instructor: Yes?

Student: Good morning, my teacher. Can I come in?

Instructor: Yes, of course.

Student: I'm sorry I'm late. You see, I forgot to set my alarm and . . .

Instructor: It's okay. Please just have a seat. We're in the middle of a lesson.

(After class:)

Student: I'm sorry I was late, teacher. I forgot to set my alarm.

Instructor: I understand. But there's something you should probably know. In this country, if a student is late, he tries to enter the class as quietly as possible so that he doesn't interrupt the lesson. He usually takes the first seat he can find, and he almost never says a word. If he wants to apologize or explain, he waits until after class.

Student: Really? I didn't know that. In my country, it is very different. When a student gets to class late, he cannot enter until the teacher gives him permission. So, when he gets to the class, he knocks on the door and waits for the teacher to let him come in. I am very sorry, my teacher.

Instructor: No problem. It's just a different custom, that's all. Speaking of different customs, it is not the custom here for students to say "my teacher." Students call their teachers by name.

Student: Really? That seems very strange to me, but I will try to remember that. Thank you, Dr. Reed.

Instructor: Sure. See you tomorrow!

How are the customs in this student's country different from the customs at universities here?

FOCUS 7   General Time Clauses

A.   Introduction to clauses

The term *clause* refers to a group of words that has a subject and a verb. An *independent* or *main clause* is a complete sentence by itself. A *dependent* or *subordinate clause*, however, is *not* a complete sentence by itself. Even though a *dependent clause* contains a subject and a verb, it must be connected to a main clause. Most dependent clauses are connected to the main clause with a *connecting word*.

1.   Independent clause:

The teacher doesn't like to stop in the middle of a lesson.

In some countries, late students knock on the classroom door.

2.   Dependent clause:

Students here don't usually knock on the door **when they are late.**

As soon as they get to class, they try to find a seat.

In this chapter, you will practice using one type of dependent clause—*time clauses*. You will study other types of dependent clauses in other chapters.

B. Forming time clauses

1. A *time clause* shows *when* or *in what situation* another action or situation takes place. Use the simple present tense to talk about general situations.

Late students try to find a seat **as soon as they get to class.**

↑

(When do late students try to find a seat?)

I feel very embarrassed **when I am late to class.**

↑

(When do you feel embarrassed?)

2. A *time clause* can come *before* or *after* the main clause. The clause that contains the important or new information usually comes at the end of the sentence. If the new information is in the main clause, the time clause comes first. When a time clause goes *before* the main clause, there must be a comma after the time clause. If the new information is in the time clause, the time clause comes after the main clause. When the time clause comes after the main clause, no comma is needed.

Question: What does a student in your country do when he is late to class?

Answer: **When a student is late, he usually knocks on the**

⌣ time clause ⌣ main clause—new information

classroom door.

Question: When does a student knock on the classroom door?

Answer: **He knocks on the door when he is late.**

⌣ main clause ⌣ time clause—new information

3. A *time clause* is not a complete sentence by itself. It is connected to a main clause with a *time word* or *time phrase*. Some examples of time words and phrases are **BEFORE, AFTER, WHEN, AS SOON AS,** and **WHENEVER.**

Main Clause	Time Clause
Subject + Verb + Rest of Clause	**Time Word + Subject + Verb + Rest of Clause**
American students never knock	**before** they enter a classroom.
They apologize to the teacher	**after** the class is over.
Students don't say anything	**when** they come into class late. *(at that time)*
They usually try to find a seat	**as soon as** they get to class. *(immediately after)*
I feel very embarrassed	**whenever** I am late for class. *(every time)*

PRACTICE 7-1 General Time Clauses

A. *Using the time word in parentheses, answer each of the following questions with a sentence that includes **a time clause**. (Notice that the new information will be in the time clause. This means that the time clause should follow the main clause in these sentences.)*

EXAMPLE   When do people say "Bless you"? (when)

They say "Bless you!" **when somebody sneezes.**

1. When do people say "So long"? (when)
2. When do people say "Have a good time"? (when)
3. When do people say "Have a nice day"? (before)
4. When do people say "Good luck"? (before)

5. When do people say "I appreciate it"? (after)
6. When do you feel nervous? (whenever)
7. When do you feel homesick? (whenever)
8. When do people in your country have a big party? (when)

B.   *Using the following cues, form questions to find out what your classmates generally do in different situations. Begin each question with **What do you usually do . . . ?"** Your classmate should respond to each question with a complete sentence. Follow the example.*

EXAMPLE   . . . when / someone / sneeze?

Student A: <u>What do you usually do</u> **when someone sneezes?**
Student B: I say, "Bless you."

1. . . . when / you / have a headache?
2. . . . when / you / get nervous?
3. . . . just before / a test / begin?
4. . . . after / you / finish your homework?
5. . . . as soon as / you / get home from class?
6. . . . when / you / not understand the teacher?

C.   *What did you find out about your classmates?*

A WIDER ANGLE

Interviews

Find out more about customs and lifestyles in a classmate's native country. Choose one of the following topics, and interview your classmate to learn as much as possible about that topic.

TOPIC 1:   Find out how they celebrate the New Year in your classmate's country. For example, you can ask about food, parties, clothes, special activities, or customs for this holiday.

TOPIC 2:   Find out how different members of your classmate's family usually spend their free time. You can ask about activities in different seasons and weather conditions, on weekends and on weekdays, or during long vacations.

Writing Practice

Write a short composition on one of the following topics.

TOPIC 1:   Write about an important or favorite holiday in your country. How do people celebrate this holiday?

TOPIC 2:   Interview someone from this country to find out what he or she does during a typical day. Write about your friend's daily routine. How is it different from yours?

TOPIC 3:   Write about someone who has a very unusual daily routine. You can write about a real person, or you can use your imagination and write about a person that you make up. Examples of people with unusual routines are *a person who works the night shift, a mother with a newborn baby,* or *someone who is most active at night.*

TOPIC 4:   Describe a typical wedding in your country.

Chapter Exercises

EXERCISE 1   **Information Questions**

Carol's mother is talking on the telephone to Lucia Spadaro, an old family friend. They are trying to catch up on what has been going on in each other's lives. Lucia wants to hear all about Carol. Part of their conversation follows. Complete the conversation by writing an appropriate question.

LUCIA: Well, tell me about Carol. _____?

CAROL'S MOM: Oh, she's just fine.

LUCIA: That's good. _____?

CAROL'S MOM: Yes, she is. She's a sophomore at the university.

LUCIA: A sophomore already? My! How time flies!_____

_____?

CAROL'S MOM: She lives in her own apartment.

LUCIA: _____?

CAROL'S MOM: No, she doesn't. She can't afford to buy a car yet.

LUCIA: No car!? _____?

CAROL'S MOM: She usually walks. Her place is pretty close to campus.

LUCIA: _____?

CAROL'S MOM: It's on Atwater near the library.

LUCIA: Oh, yes. I know that apartment complex. Those are nice

apartments! _____?

CAROL'S MOM: Yes, she does. She has a part-time job as a waitress.

LUCIA: Really? _____?

CAROL'S MOM: At Tony's Restaurant.

LUCIA: My goodness! Carol is a busy young woman!

CAROL'S MOM: Yes, she certainly is.

EXERCISE 2   **Questions with WHO and WHAT**

A.   *Answer the following questions with a short answer.*

EXAMPLE   Question: Who fixes your breakfast?
                  Answer: My husband does.
                              (Nobody does.)
                              (I do.)

1.   Who teaches this class?
2.   Who speaks Japanese in this class?
3.   Who is the leader of your country?
4.   Who does your laundry?
5.   What is difficult for you in English grammar?

*B.   Ask about the identity of **something** or **somebody** in each of the following situations by writing a question with **WHO** or **WHAT**. Use the cues in parentheses to answer the question with a short answer or phrase. Fill in empty brackets with your own cues.*

EXAMPLES   **Somebody** works at Tony's restaurant. (Carol)
Who works at Tony's restaurant?
Carol does.

Carol has lunch with **somebody** every day. (her friends)
Who(m) does Carol have lunch with?
With her friends.

1. **Something** gives Maria headaches. (loud music)
2. **Something** gets rid of headaches. (aspirin)
3. These books belong to **somebody.** (that student over there)
4. The movie *Gone With the Wind* is about **something.** (the American Civil War)
5. **Somebody** often calls me. [   ]
6. I often think about **somebody.** [   ]
7. I often think about **something.** [   ]
8. **Somebody** is sometimes late to class. [   ]
9. **Somebody** plays soccer. [   ]
10. **Something** happens to water when the temperature reaches 32°F. [   ]

EXERCISE 3   General Time Expressions

Answer each of the following questions with a complete sentence.

1. What time does your first class begin?
2. How long does your first class last?
3. What time do you usually get home after school?
4. How often does your teacher give tests?
5. When do you usually study?
6. How often do you get help with your homework?
7. When do high school students in your country have a long vacation?

EXERCISE 4   Ability, Opportunity, and Necessity

Different Housing Situations

International students at colleges and universities around the country have different housing situations. For example, some students live *at home with their relatives;* others live *in a dormitory;* others share *a house with students from this country;* others live *in apartments by themselves.* Each of these different housing situations has advantages and disadvantages.

A.   Write about the advantages and disadvantages of these different housing situations by completing the sentences below. Add any additional information or explanations that you wish.

1. a. Students who live in a house with their relatives can . . .
   b. In addition, they don't have to . . .
   c. However, students who live with their relatives can't . . .
   d. They have to . . .

2. a. If you live in a dormitory, you can . . .
   b. Dormitories are also nice because you don't have to . . .
   c. However, if you live in a dormitory, you have to . . .
   d. You can't . . .

3. a. Students who share a house with native English speakers can . . .
   b. However, students who live with native English speakers have to . . .
   c. And sometimes they can't . . .

4. a. If you live in an apartment by yourself, you can . . .
   b. You don't have to . . .
   c. However, if you live in an apartment by yourself, you can't . . .
   d. You have to . . .

B. *What kind of housing situation do you prefer? Write a short paragraph about the type of living situation that is best for you. You can choose one of the situations from Part A, or you can write about a different type of housing situation. Be sure to give at least three reasons for your choice.*

EXERCISE 5 **General Time Clauses**

Give general information about schools and education by completing the following sentences.

1. In my country, when a university student is late, _____
   _____.

2. When a professor in my country enters the classroom, _____
   _____.

3. Before a student can enroll in a university in my country, _____
   _____.

4. Before an international student can enroll in a university in this country, _____.

5. In some countries, a student usually stands up when _____
   _____.

6. I get nervous in class whenever _____
   _____.

7. Every day after my classes are over, _____
   _____.

8. I always study before I _____
   _____.

3 *Past Events*

┌─────────────────────────┐
│ **THE BIG PICTURE** │
└─────────────────────────┘

The Simple Past Tense

Time Clauses

AT A GLANCE

Past Events

Toshio's Itinerary

*Rising Sun Travel Agency
Kioi-cho, Chyoda-ku
Tokyo, Japan
(03) 264-1124*

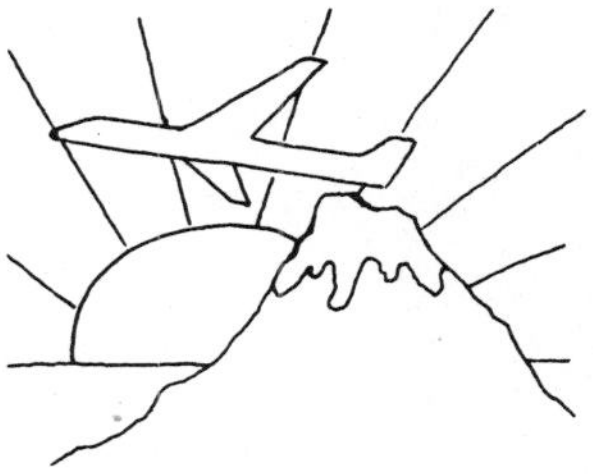

For: Kimura / Toshio

08 Jan. 95--Sunday

Depart: Tokyo, Narita Airport   3:45 P.M.   JAL   **Flight:** 04   Economy class

Arrive: San Francisco   8:50 A.M.   Nonstop

FIGURE 3–1

Look at Toshio's ticket (Fig. 3–1) and answer the following questions.

1. Where did Toshio buy his ticket to the United States?
2. What day did he leave Tokyo?
3. What time did his plane leave?
4. What was the number of his flight?

On Sunday morning, Toshio got up early because he had to finish packing his suitcases for his trip to California. At noon, he and his parents caught a special bus to the airport. The bus took about an hour and a half to get to the airport. Toshio didn't talk much during the ride because he was nervous and excited. This was his first trip outside of Japan!

When Toshio got to the airport, he checked in at the Japan Airlines ticket counter. He checked his luggage there and got his boarding pass and seat assignment. After he said good-bye to his folks, he went through a security check and passport control. It was only two-thirty, so he killed some time* by looking in some of the duty-free shops.

Finally, around 3:15 P.M., an attendant announced the departure of his flight, and Toshio was able to board the plane. He had an aisle seat in the first class section. His flight was comfortable, and the flight attendants were very friendly. They served him Japanese food and tea for dinner. After dinner, he watched an American movie. Fortunately, he was able to listen to it in Japanese! When the movie was over, Toshio went to sleep. He woke up several hours later when he heard the flight attendant announcing their arrival in San Francisco. It was time to start thinking in English!

In this chapter, you will practice talking about past events that occurred at a specific time.

---

*Someone's "folks" means "parents." The phrase "kill some time" is used to mean "pass the time."

Uses of the Simple Past Tense

The **simple past tense** can refer to actions, events, or situations that took place at a specific time in the past. This verb tense shows that the action or situation is finished.

A. Completed actions

Toshio **took** Japan Airlines to the United States on January 8, 1995. He **arrived** in San Francisco around 9:00 A.M.

B. Situations that existed during a specific past time period

Toshio **felt** very nervous during the bus ride to the airport.

C. Past habits or actions repeated in the past

When he was in high school, Toshio *often* **thought** about visiting the United States.

Simple Past Tense Verb Forms*

The simple past tense has only one form for all subjects.

A. Regular simple past tense verbs

Regular simple past tense verbs have the ending **-ED.** You can study the spelling and pronunciation rules for the regular **-ED** ending in Appendix A.

I **waited** at the airport yesterday.

You **arrived** on time yesterday.

Toshio **watched** a movie on the plane.

The flight attendants **served** him dinner on the plane.

B. Irregular simple past tense verbs

Many common verbs have irregular simple past tense forms. You can study these irregular simple past tense forms in Appendix B.

I **came** to this country last year.

You **got** here on time yesterday.

Toshio **had** dinner on the plane.

The flight attendants **ate** dinner on the plane, too.

C. Negative simple past tense verbs

To form the negative of a simple past tense verb, use the auxiliary **DID** with **NOT.** The contraction for **DID NOT** is **DIDN'T.** The auxiliary **DID/DIDN'T** can occur *only* with the *base form* of a verb.

Affirmative Verb	Negative Verb			
	Subject +	Auxiliary +	Base Form Verb +	Rest of Sentence
Toshio's sisters **went** to a party.	They	**did not**	**go**	to the airport.
Toshio **talked** to them before leaving.	He	**didn't**	**talk**	much on the bus.
I **slept** a lot during my flight.	I	**didn't**	**sleep**	the night before.

*The rules for simple past tense verbs in Focus 2 and 3 refer to all verbs *except* the verb **BE.** The simple past tense rules for the verb **BE** are different. You can study the simple past tense of the verb **BE** in Focus 4.

Regular Simple Past Tense Verbs

Complete each sentence with the simple past tense of the verb in parentheses.

1. (fasten) Toshio _____ his seatbelt as soon as he sat down.

2. (look) He _____ at the safety information in the seat pocket.

3. (relax) After the plane took off, Toshio _____ in his seat.

4. (serve) They _____ both Japanese and American food on the plane.

5. (want) Toshio _____ Japanese food.

Irregular Past Tense Verbs

See how many irregular verbs you already know. Complete each sentence with the simple past tense form of the verb in parentheses.

1. (get) Toshio _____ up early on Sunday.

2. (have) He _____ a lot of things to do.

3. (put) He _____ some photographs of his family in his wallet.

4. (catch) Toshio and his parents _____ the bus at a hotel nearby.

5. (take) They _____ the bus to the airport.

6. (go) At the airport, he _____ through passport control.

7. (buy) He _____ a cup of coffee in the waiting area.

8. (read) While he was waiting for his plane, he _____ a magazine.

9. (find) When he boarded the plane, he _____ his seat quickly.

10. (feel) He _____ nervous and excited!

Affirmative and Negative Sentences

*A. The following statements do not give accurate information about Toshio's trip. Change each to a **true** statement by making the verb negative. Then give additional information.*

EXAMPLE   False: Toshio took a taxi to the airport.

True: Toshio **didn't take** a taxi to the airport. He **took** a bus.

1. Toshio finished packing on Saturday night.
2. He slept late on Sunday morning.
3. It took Toshio and his parents four hours to get to the airport.

4. Toshio talked a lot during the bus ride.
5. On the plane, he ate American food.
6. Toshio had a seat by the window.

B. Now think about your trip to this country. Tell your classmates how your trip here was different from Toshio's trip.

EXAMPLES   I didn't take a bus to the airport. My father drove me.

I didn't have an aisle seat. I sat by the window.

FOCUS 3   Questions and Answers in the Simple Past Tense

To form questions in the simple past tense, use the auxiliary **DID** with the *base form* of a verb. Put **DID** *before the subject.* To give a short answer to a question in the simple past tense, use **DID** or **DIDN'T** with a *subject pronoun.*

Auxiliary	+	Subject	+	Base Form Verb	+	Rest of Sentence		Answer
Did		Toshio		**take**		a taxi to the airport?		No, he **didn't.**
Did		his parents		**go**		with him?		Yes, they **did.**
Did		you		**have**		a nice flight?		Yes, I **did.**
How **did**		they		**get**		to the airport?		They **went** by bus.
When **did**		his plane		**leave**		for San Francisco?		It **left** at 3:45 P.M.
Where **did**		you		**sit**		on the plane?		I **sat** near the front.

PRACTICE 3–1   Questions and Answers

Interview a classmate to find out more about his or her flight to this country. Use the following cues to form questions. Your classmate should answer each information question with a complete sentence. For each YES/NO question, your classmate should give a short answer and some additional information, if possible. Fill in empty brackets with your own cues.

EXAMPLES   when / you / leave your country to come here?

Student A: When **did** you **leave** your country to come here?
Student B: I **left** my country on January 8 of last year.

you / fly on Japan Airlines?

Student A: **Did** you **fly** on Japan Airlines?
Student B: No, I **didn't.** I **flew** on Northwestern Airlines.

1. when / you / leave your country to come here?
2. what airline / you / take?
3. you / have a nice flight?
4. how long / it / take you to get here?
5. you / visit any other countries on your way?
6. how many times / your plane / stop?
7. you / travel alone?
8. you / bring a lot of baggage with you?
9. what / you / do on the plane?
10. what / you / eat on the plane?

11. you / see a movie on the plane?

12. [?]

FOCUS 4 Simple Past Tense Forms of the Verb **BE**

A. Simple past tense forms of the verb BE

The verb **BE** is irregular in the *simple past tense.* Unlike other past tense verbs, the verb **BE** has two forms.

I
It
He   } **was** cold on the plane.
She

We
You   } **were** cold on the plane.
They

B. Negative sentences

To make the verb negative, add **NOT** after **WAS** or **WERE**. The contraction for **WAS NOT** is **WASN'T**; the contraction for **WERE NOT** is **WEREN'T**.

The plane **was not** on time. We **were not** on time. (*full form*)

The plane **wasn't** on time. We **weren't** on time. (*contraction*)

C. Questions and short answers

To form a question, put **WAS** or **WERE** before the subject. In short answers, use a subject pronoun with **WAS, WERE,** or their negative forms.

BE +	Subject +	Rest of Sentence	Answer
Was	your flight	comfortable?	Yes, it **was.**
Were	you	nervous?	No, I **wasn't.**
Were	your parents	nervous?	No, they **weren't.**
When **was**	your flight?		It **was** at 3:00 P.M.
How **were**	the flight attendants?		They **were** very nice.

PRACTICE 4-1 Questions and Answers

*Use **DID, WAS,** or **WERE** to complete the following **YES/NO** questions. Your classmate should respond to each question with a short answer and additional information, if possible.*

EXAMPLE   _____ you nervous the day you left your country?

Student A: **Were** you nervous the day you left your country?

Student B: No, I **wasn't.** But I was very excited and happy.

1. _____ you excited about coming here?

2. _____ the weather nice the day you left?

3. _____ you get up early that day?

4. _____ you have a lot of things to do that day?

5. _____ your suitcases heavy?

6. _____ any of your friends at the airport when you boarded the plane?

7. _____ your plane on time?

8. _____ your family sad to see you leave?

9. _____ anybody cry when you left?

10. _____ you cry?

FOCUS 5   Questions about the Subject: **WHO** and **WHAT**

When **WHO** or **WHAT** is the subject of the question, use the simple past tense of the verb with regular statement word order. Do <u>not</u> use the auxiliary **DID**. Use an auxiliary or form of **BE** to give a short answer about the subject. Remember, when **WHO** or **WHAT** is the subject, always use the singular form of the verb.

Somebody checked Toshio's hand luggage.

Who checked it? The security guards **did.**

Something set off the metal detector.

What set off the metal detector? Toshio's belt buckle **did.**

Somebody was at the airport to say good-bye.

Who was at the airport to say good-bye? His parents **were.**

PRACTICE 5–1   Questions with **WHO**

Find out more about your classmate's trip here. Use the following cues to ask questions with WHO. Your classmate should respond to each question with a short answer.

EXAMPLE   travel with you?

   Student A: **Who traveled** with you?
   Student B: Nobody **did.** I came alone.

1. get your visa for you?
2. buy your airline ticket?
3. help you pack your bags?
4. give you a present before you left?
5. call you before you left?
6. drive you to the airport?
7. be at the airport to say good-bye?
8. be sad to see you leave?

FOCUS 6   Questions about an Object: **WHO(M)** and **WHAT**

When the question words **WHO** or **WHAT** are *not* the subject of the question, use regular question word order. Put the auxiliary **DID/DIDN'T** before the subject of the question. Use the *base form* of the main verb.

Toshio rode on the bus with **somebody.**

Conversational:	**Who** did he ride with?
Formal:	**Whom** did he ride with?
	With whom did he ride?

PRACTICE 6-1   More Questions with **WHO**

Continue to get information about your classmate's trip. Use the following cues to ask YES/NO questions. If your classmate answers YES to a question, ask a second question with WHO. Your classmate should then respond with a complete sentence.

EXAMPLE   call anybody before you left?

Student A: **Did you call** anybody before you left?
Student B: Yes, I did.
Student A: **Who did you call?**
Student B: I called my girlfriend.

1.   hug anybody when you left?
2.   wave to anybody when you left?
3.   be next to anyone on the plane?
4.   think about anyone on the plane?
5.   talk to anyone during the flight?
6.   bring pictures of anyone?

CLOSE-UP   **Past Time Expressions**

A.   Asking about past time

The question expressions **WHEN . . . ?** and **HOW LONG AGO . . . ?** ask for a *specific time in the past.* Any past time expression can answer the question **WHEN . . . ?** The answer to the question **HOW LONG AGO . . . ?** often includes a time expression with **AGO.**

Specific Time Question	Specific Time Answer
When did you get to this country?	I got here **last year.**
When did you arrive in this city?	I arrived here **a few weeks ago.**
When did you graduate from high school?	I graduated **on June 20, 1994.**
How long ago did you get your passport?	I got it **several months ago.**
How long ago did you get your degree?	I got my degree **a year ago.**

Note: The question expression **HOW LONG . . . ?** asks *"How much time . . . ?"*

| **EXAMPLES** | How long did it take you to get here? | It took 14 hours. |
| | **How long** was your flight? | It was 14 hours. |

B. Time adverbs FIRST/LAST

The time adverb **FIRST** means *"the first time."* The time adverb **LAST** means *"the most recent time."* Like frequency adverbs, these time adverbs go in *middle position,* near the verb.

> When did you **first** take a plane? I **first** took a plane in 1992.
>
> How long ago did you **last** take a plane? I **last** took a plane two months ago.

C. Past time expressions

The following expressions refer to a *specific past time.* Use them with the simple past tense to answer the questions **WHEN . . . ?** and **HOW LONG AGO . . . ?**

---

1. **YESTERDAY:** refers to the day before today

   yesterday, yesterday morning, yesterday afternoon, yesterday evening

   I slept late **yesterday morning.**

   Did you have a good time at the picnic **yesterday?**

---

2. **LAST:** * refers to the time period just before the present one

   last week, last month, last semester, last year, last Monday, last night

   Mr. Park bought a new car **last month.**

   Where did you go **last Friday night?**

*Do not use prepositions or the article **THE** with past time expressions containing **LAST**.
   [Mistake: I bought a new car ~~in~~ last month. I bought a car ~~the~~ last month.]

---

3. **BEFORE LAST:** refers to the time period just before the last one

   (the) day before last, *(the) week before last, (the) month before last*

   Simone arrived here **the week before last.**

   I called you **the night before last,** but you weren't home.

*You can also say **THE DAY BEFORE YESTERDAY**.

---

4. **AGO:** refers to a point in time that is a specific time period before now

   a week ago, two years ago, a few minutes ago, a long time ago

   I ran into an old friend **a little while ago.**

   The Amish settled in the United States **a long time ago.**

   Keesha got married **three years ago.**

---

5. **EARLIER:** refers to a point sometime before now. It may refer to a point in time during a specific time period.

   earlier, earlier today, earlier this week, earlier this month

   Where were you **earlier this morning?**

   Dwayne applied to the university **earlier this month.**

---

6. **THE OTHER:** refers to a recent past time. It is used when the speaker does not remember the exact day or when the exact day is not important.

the other day, the other morning, the other afternoon, the other night

I saw a great movie **the other night.**

Were you at home **the other evening** when the big storm hit?

7. **IN THE PAST:** refers to general situations in the past, usually in contrast to the present

In the past, extended families frequently lived together.

In the past, people led simpler lives.

Close-Up

PRACTICE **QUESTIONS AND ANSWERS**

*A. Use the following cues to ask a classmate a question about past events. Begin each question with the question expression **HOW LONG AGO . . .?** or **WHEN . . .?** Your classmate should answer with a complete sentence.*

EXAMPLE   you / [first] fly in an airplane?

Student A: **When** did you first fly in an airplane?
Student B: I first flew in a plane **five years ago.**

1. you / [last] eat traditional food from your country?
2. you / [last] cook traditional food from your country?
3. you / [first] eat at a fast-food restaurant here?
4. you / [last] eat at a fast-food restaurant here?
5. you / [last] see your family?
6. your family or relatives / [last] write a letter to you?
7. you / [last] make a call to your country?
8. you / [first] think about coming here?
9. you / [last] go to a movie?
10. you / [first] start studying English?

B. Find out about one of your classmates' vacations. Use the following cues to form questions. Your classmate should answer with as much information as possible. Fill in empty brackets with your own cues.

EXAMPLE   your country / have many nice places for vacation?

Student A: Does your country have many nice places for vacation?
Student B: Yes, it does. It has some beautiful beaches.

1. your country / have many nice places for vacation?
2. your family / [ever] take vacations together these days?
3. how often / you / go on vacation?
4. when / you / [last] go somewhere for vacation?
5. where / you / go?
6. who / you / go there with?
7. how long / it / take you to get there?
8. how long / you / stay there?
9. [?]

Number the following events in the order in which they happened. What happened first? Second? Third? Fourth? In other words, what is the **sequence of events?**

_____ Toshio went to the waiting area to wait for his flight.
_____ Toshio got to the airport.
_____ Toshio got his boarding pass.
_____ Toshio checked in at the ticket counter.

A.   Using time clauses

Time clauses in the simple past tense give information about the order or sequence of past events. The connecting time word in the clause shows which event happened first.

In the following examples, decide which action occurred first: the action in the main clause or the action in the time clause.

Main Clause +	Time Clause
Toshio checked in at the counter	**as soon as** he got to the airport.
He wrote his name on his luggage	**before** he checked it at the counter.
He got his boarding pass	**when** he checked in at the counter.
He went to the waiting area	**after** he got his boarding pass.
His parents waited with him	**until** he went through passport control.
Toshio sat down	**once** he got to the waiting area.

A time clause can come before or after the main clause. If the main clause contains new or important information, the time clause comes first. When the time clause comes before the main clause, it must be followed by a comma. If the important or new information is in the time clause, the time clause comes after the main clause. No comma is needed.

What did Toshio do as soon as he got to the airport?
As soon as Toshio got to the airport, he checked in at the counter.

What did he do after he got his boarding pass?
After he got his boarding pass, he went to the waiting area.

When did he say good-bye to his parents?
He said good-bye to them **before he went to the waiting area.**

B.   Using time words

The connecting time word of the time clause indicates the order things happened.

1.   BEFORE, AFTER
First Toshio got his boarding pass. Then he said good-bye to his parents.

    a.   He got his boarding pass **before** he said good-bye to his parents.

    b.   **After** he got his boarding pass, he said good-bye to his parents.

2. **WHEN, AS SOON AS, ONCE**

These time words are similar to **AFTER.** They emphasize that one completed action immediately followed another completed action.

First he found his seat on the plane. Then he sat down.

a. **When** he found his seat, he sat down.

b. **As soon as** he found his seat, he sat down.

c. **Once** he found his seat, he sat down.

The time word **WHEN** can also indicate that two actions happened at the same time or at almost the same time.

a. **When** I dropped the dish, it broke.

b. Mario hurt his ankle **when** he fell.

A time clause with **WHEN** can also refer to a past time period.

a. I always studied in the library **when** I was a student.

b. Consuelo met a lot of interesting people **when** she lived overseas.

3. **UNTIL**

This time word focuses on the ending point of an action that continued for a period of time. The situation or action of the main clause continued over time. The time clause shows when the situation or action finished.

His parents waited with him for a while. Then he went to his gate, and they left.

a. They waited **until** he went to his gate.

b. They didn't leave **until** he went to his gate.

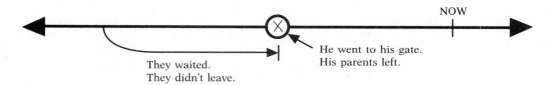

It is impossible to say: They left until he went to his gate. The verb **LEAVE** does not continue over a period of time. Instead it is possible to say: They left **when** he went to his gate.

PRACTICE 7-1   Past Time Clauses

A.   Using the time word that is given, combine each of the following pairs of sentences into one sentence. Change nouns to pronouns where appropriate. Think about the sequence of events. Which action occurred first?

EXAMPLE   (as soon as)   a. Toshio found his seat.

b. Toshio sat down.

As soon as Toshio found his seat, he sat down.

(Toshio sat down **as soon as** he found his seat.)

1. **(when)**

a. Toshio sat down in his seat.

b. Toshio fastened his seatbelt.

2. **(once)**

    a. The plane reached a high altitude.

    b. The captain turned off the seatbelt sign.

3. **(before)**

    a. The flight attendants served cocktails and drinks.

    b. The flight attendants served dinner.

4. **(after)**

    a. Toshio watched a movie.

    b. Toshio finished dinner.

5. **(until)**

    a. He stayed awake.

    b. The movie was over.

6. **(when)**

    a. The movie was over.

    b. He went to sleep.

B. *Each set of pictures below shows a sequence of events that happened **yesterday**. Using the time words that are given, make sentences with time clauses in the simple past to show the sequence of events.*

EXAMPLE

    a. **(after)** Toshio watched a movie after he ate dinner on the plane.

    b. **(when)** When the movie was over, he went to sleep.

1. a. **(until)**
   b. **(when)**

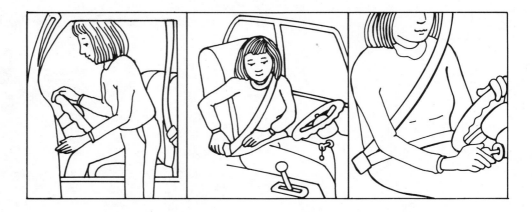

2. a. **(as soon as)**
   b. **(before)**
   c. **(until)***

GETTING READY TO FOCUS

Past Situations

The Changing World

New technology continues to change the way we live. Think about traveling, for example. Today we can travel quickly and easily by jet. In the past, however, it was different.

How did people travel long distances many years ago?

---

*Hint: You will need to use a negative verb in this sentence.

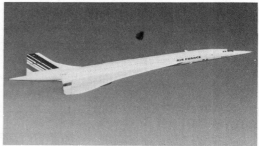

Even air travel has changed a great deal. How is air travel today different from air travel 50 years ago?

FOCUS 8   Past Situations That No Longer Exist: **USED TO**

According to the following statements, what do we know about the general situation in the past? What do we know about the general situation now?

> People **used to fly** on propeller planes, but now they fly on passenger jets.

> Women **didn't use to be** flight attendants, but nowadays women often perform this job.

The special verb expression **USED TO / DIDN'T USE TO** compares a past situation to the present situation. This verb expression usually indicates that a past situation does not exist anymore. **USED TO** is unusual because it can occur in only one verb tense—the simple past. In addition, unlike other past tense verbs, this expression usually occurs without a specific past time.

The *base form* of a verb always follows **USED TO / DIDN'T USE TO**.

A. Understanding USED TO / DIDN'T USE TO

Subject	+	USED TO (before: yes) (now: no)	+	Base Form Verb	+	Rest of Sentence
Only men		used to		be		flight attendants.

Subject	+	DIDN'T USE TO (before: no) (now: yes)	+	Base Form Verb	+	Rest of Sentence
Women		didn't use to		have		this job.

B. Forming sentences with USED TO/DIDN'T USE TO

AFFIRMATIVE STATEMENTS

People **used to travel** long distances by ship.

NEGATIVE STATEMENTS

People **didn't use to travel** by jet.

QUESTIONS AND ANSWERS

Did people **use to travel** by horse? Yes, they **did.**

Did people **use to take** jets? No, they **didn't.**

How **did** people **use to travel?** By wagon.

Do you get nervous on planes? No, but I **used to.**

C. Contrasting the past and the present

We can emphasize the contrast between the past situation and the present situation by adding a clause that begins with **BUT, BUT NOW . . . ,** or **BUT NOT ANYMORE:**

I used to jog, **but I stopped last year.**

I used to jog, **but now I don't.**

I used to jog, **but I don't anymore.**

I didn't use to chew gum, **but now I do.**

I used to be scared to fly, **but I'm not anymore.**

PRACTICE 8-1   **USED TO**

A.   Use the information in the following statements to answer the questions. Your answer may be "yes," "no," or "I don't know."

1.   Michael used to work for a travel agency.

   a. Does Michael have experience working at a travel agency?
   b. Does Michael work at a travel agency now?
   c. When did he work at a travel agency?

2.   Carol didn't use to like spinach.

   a. Does Carol like spinach now?
   b. Did she like spinach when she was younger?
   c. When did she start to like spinach?

B.   Respond to the following questions with complete sentences.

1.   Is there any kind of food that you didn't use to like? What? When did you begin to like this food?

2. Think back to your childhood days. What did you use to do in your free time? What did you use to be afraid of?

3. Clothing fashions change all the time. Think about fashions in your country when your grandparents were your age. What did people use to wear in your country? What do they wear now?

4. What do teenagers do for fun these days? What did teenagers use to do for fun?

FOCUS 9   Ability, Opportunity, and Permission in the Past

A.   COULD

The modal auxiliary **COULD** can talk about ability, opportunity, and permission in the past. To make the verb negative, add **NOT** after the auxiliary. The contraction for **COULD NOT** is **COULDN'T. COULD** and **COULDN'T** can be followed only by a *base form verb*. Like other past tense verbs, **COULD** and **COULDN'T** refer to a specific past time or context.

> During the early years of air travel, only men **could work** as flight attendants.
>
> In the past, women **couldn't work** as flight attendants.
>
> During Toshio's flight, passengers **could choose** Japanese or American food.
>
> They **could not** order Italian food!
>
> Toshio **could see** the movie screen very well from his seat on the plane.
>
> He **couldn't understand** the movie in English.

B.   BE ABLE TO + (base form verb)

1.   It is also possible to use the expression **WAS/WERE ABLE TO + (verb)** to talk about past abilities and opportunities.

During Toshio's flight, . . .

Subject +	BE (past) +	ABLE TO + Base Form Verb ("ability") +	Rest of Sentence
. . . passengers	were	able to choose	Japanese or American food.
. . . they	were not	able to order	Italian food.
. . . some passengers	weren't	able to see	the screen well.
. . . Toshio	was	able to see	the screen very well.
. . . he	was not	able to understand	the movie in English.
. . . Toshio	wasn't	able to sleep	for a long time.

2.   The expression **USED TO BE ABLE TO + (base form verb)** compares past abilities and opportunities in the past with those in the present.

Subject +	"before" +	"ability" +	Action +	"ability now"
I	used to	be able to	**run** five miles,	but now **I can't.**
We	didn't use to	be able to	**travel** easily,	but now we **can.**

C.   Questions and answers

Could you **speak** English before you came here?	Yes, I **could.**
	No, I **couldn't.**
Were you **able to understand** the flight attendants?	Yes, I **was.**
	No, I **wasn't.**
Did people **use to be able to watch** movies on planes?	No, they **didn't.**

PRACTICE 9-1 Using **COULD** and **BE ABLE TO**

*A.   Find out about the past abilities of your classmates. Use the cues to make
YES/NO questions with COULD. Your classmate will respond with a short answer
and, if possible, additional information.*

EXAMPLE   speak a foreign language // when / you / in elementary school?

> Student A: **Could** you **speak** a foreign language when you were in
> elementary school?

> Student B: No, I **couldn't.** I didn't start learning English until I was
> in high school.

1.   read // when / you / four years old?
2.   ride a bike // when / you / in elementary school?
3.   stay up all night // when / you / in high school?
4.   speak any English // when / you / in elementary school?
5.   understand the flight attendants // when / you / fly here?

*B.   What did you find out about your classmates? Make sentences about your
classmates using a form of BE ABLE TO, BE ALLOWED TO, or KNOW HOW TO.*

EXAMPLE   Boris **wasn't able to speak** English in elementary school. He
started learning English in high school.

C.   Think back to your childhood.
1.   What are some things that you used to be able to do?
2.   What are some things that you didn't use to be able to do?

FOCUS 10 Past Necessity and Obligation

A.   HAD TO + (base form verb)

Use the expressions **HAD TO** or **DIDN'T HAVE TO** with a *base form verb* to talk
about *things that were or were not necessary in the past.* The expression **HAD TO**
refers only to actions that actually took place. It is not possible to use the modal
auxiliary **MUST** to talk about necessity in the past.

Subject	+	**HAD TO** ("necessity")	+ Base Form Verb	+ Rest of Sentence
Before air travel, people		**had to**	travel	overseas by ship.
When they came here, the Amish		**didn't have to**	change	their lifestyle.

B.   USED TO HAVE TO + (base form verb)

Use the expression **USED TO HAVE TO** and **DIDN'T USE TO HAVE TO** with a
base form verb to compare past and present necessity.

Subject	+	Before	+	"necessity"	+	Action	+	"necessity" now
People		used to		have to		**travel** by ship,		but now they **don't.**
I		didn't use to		have to		**cook** for myself,		but now I **do.**

C. Questions and answers

Did you **have to get** a visa to come here?   Yes, I **did.**
Did you **have to open** all of your bags at customs?   No, I **didn't.**
How many bags **did** you **have to open**?   I only **had to** open one.
Did people **use to have to travel** overseas by ship?   Yes, they **did.**

PRACTICE 10-1   Ability and Necessity in the Past

A.   Yesterday, only three students showed up for a meeting to plan the class party. Following is a list of some of the students who couldn't attend the meeting. Why weren't they able to come? What did they have to do? Use the cues to explain why they weren't there yesterday. Fill in empty brackets with your own cues.

EXAMPLE   Melissa / go to the dentist

Melissa **couldn't go** to the meeting because she **had to go** to the dentist.

1. Miriam / stay after class to talk to a professor
2. Karl / take his car to the garage
3. Ali / wait for an overseas phone call from his family
4. Sarah / drive her aunt to the airport
5. Tanya and her husband / [   ]
6. I / [   ]

B.   Complete the following sentences with true information.
1. Before I could come to this country, I had to. . . .
2. In my country, I didn't use to have to . . . , but now I do.
3. In order to communicate over long distances, people used to have to. . . .

C.   There are many wonderful things about modern society as well as many problems. Imagine how people lived one hundred years ago. List some of the disadvantages and advantages of living back then. Use the expressions COULD/COULDN'T, HAD TO/DIDN'T HAVE TO, BE ABLE TO as appropriate.

EXAMPLES   (disadvantage)   People **couldn't communicate** over long distances quickly.

(advantage)   People **didn't have to worry** so much about crime.

A WIDER ANGLE   Interviews

Interview a classmate to get as much information as possible about one of the following topics:

TOPIC 1:   The last party your classmate had or attended.

TOPIC 2: Your classmate's visit to a place in this country.

TOPIC 3: Some of the things your classmate did to prepare for coming to this country.

Writing Practice: My Trip to This Country

Write a composition about your trip to this country. You can write, for example, about the things you did during the trip, about how you felt, about any problems you had, and about any interesting situations or people you encountered. If you wish, you can begin your composition like this:

I left my country on _____ . That day, I woke up at _____ .

DEVELOPING YOUR SKILLS AND KNOWLEDGE

Chapter Exercises

EXERCISE 1 ## Simple Past and Present Tense Verbs

*During his flight, Toshio read an interesting article about the Amish people of the United States. In the following passage, you will learn more about the Amish people. Fill in each blank with the **simple past tense** or **simple present tense** form of the verb cue.*

During the sixteenth century, some people in Europe

_____ to feel dissatisfied with the Roman Catholic Church.
    (begin)

In Switzerland, a man named Ulrich Zwingli _____ the
                                        (criticize)

Roman Church for participating in politics. He _____ a
                                                    (form)
religious group called the Anabaptists. The powerful Roman Catholic

Church _____ Zwingli's ideas and _____
              (not / like)   (not / allow)
this new group to worship freely. In fact, the Church

_____ many of Zwingli's followers. As a result, many
        (persecute)
Anabaptists _____. Others _____ in the
                  (die)   (hide)
caves and mountains of Germany and Switzerland.

The Amish _____ a religious group descended from the
                  (be)
Anabaptists. In the late 1700s, many Amish people _____
                                                          (come)
to America, where people could worship more freely. The first Amish

families _____ in Pennsylvania. Later, many Amish
              (settle)
families _____ west because there was plenty of good land
              (migrate)
in Ohio and Indiana.

Today, more than 80 percent of the Amish in the United States

_____ in Ohio, Indiana, and Pennsylvania. The Amish of
        (live)
today still _____ many of the same traditions that their
                  (follow)
ancestors in Switzerland _____ years ago. Many Amish
                                (follow)
still _____ any modern conveniences or electricity.
        (not / use)
Although they _____ English in school, they
                    ([usually] learn)
_____ a special type of German in their homes. Keep in
        (speak)
mind, however, that the Amish _____ foreigners. They
                                        (not / be)
_____ here more than two hundred years ago.*
        (come)

EXERCISE 2   Questions and Answers

*A.   Write one word or contraction to complete each of the following questions and
short answers. Use **IS, AM, ARE, WAS, WERE, DO, DOES, DID,** or the negative
form.*

1.   _____ the Amish come to the United States a long time ago?

     Yes, they _____ .

*Sources: Good, Merle and Phyllis. 20 Most Asked Questions about the Amish and Mennonites
(Lancaster, Pennsylvania: Good Books, 1979).
Hostetler, John A. Amish Life (Scottdale, Pennsylvania: Herald Press, 1980).

2. _____ they originally from Europe? Yes, they _____ .

3. _____ they free to follow their religion in Europe? No, they

_____ .

4. _____ they first settle in Pennsylvania? Yes, they _____ .

5. _____ most Amish families today speak English at home? No,

they _____ .

6. _____ the Amish Americans? Yes, they _____ .

7. _____ they forget their religion and traditions when they came

here? No, they _____ .

B.   *Imagine that you have just met some Amish people. Write down three questions that you would like to ask them about their culture and lifestyle. Do not ask about things that you already know.*

C.   *Now imagine that you have just met someone who visited your country last year. Write down three questions that you would like to ask that person about the trip.*

EXERCISE 3   Past Time Expressions

A.   *Respond to each of the following questions with a complete sentence.*

1. When did you last have food from your country?
2. How long ago did you first learn how to cook?
3. When did you last cook a dish from your country?
4. How long did it take you to make it?
5. How often do you usually fix food from your country?
6. How long ago did you last go to a party?
7. How long did you stay at that party?

B.   *Complete the following conversation between Joe and Sue by writing an appropriate question for each response.*

JOE: _____?

SUE: Pizza? Let me see. I think I first had it when I was in high school.

JOE: _____?

SUE: I loved it! I have eaten it many times since that first time.

JOE: _____?

SUE: A couple of weeks ago.

JOE: _____?

SUE: At Tony's Pizza Place.

JOE: _____?

SUE: It was pretty good.

JOE: _____?

SUE: I eat there about once a month.

EXERCISE 4   Time Clauses

Last month, Carmen and Roberto, a young couple from Honduras, took a trip to Florida. The following sentences describe some of the things that happened after they landed at the airport in Miami. Combine each pair of sentences into one sentence with a time clause. Use one of the following time words: WHEN, BEFORE, AFTER, AS SOON AS, ONCE, UNTIL.

EXAMPLE   They got off the plane.
They went to the baggage claim area.
As soon as they got off the plane, they went to the baggage claim area.

1. a. They got their luggage.
    b. They got in line for customs.

2. a. It was their turn to go through customs.
    b. They showed their passports to the customs officer.

3. a. He looked at their passports.
    b. He asked them to open one of their suitcases.

4. a. He tried to close the suitcase.
    b. The zipper broke.

5. a. The other people in line had to wait.
    b. He finished fixing the suitcase.

EXERCISE 5   USED TO

Elizabeth is a student from Argentina. Her life here is different in many ways from life in her country. The following chart gives information about Elizabeth in the past and Elizabeth now.

Before	Now
She was a secretary.	She's a student.
She had long hair.	She has short hair.
She wore glasses.	She wears contact lenses.
She lived alone.	She lives with a roommate.
A maid did her housecleaning.	She does her own housecleaning.
She smoked.	She doesn't smoke.
She didn't chew gum.	She chews gum.
She never went jogging.	She goes jogging regularly.

1.   *Using the information on the chart, write five sentences about Elizabeth. Use* **USED TO** *and* **BUT**.

EXAMPLE   She **used to wear** glasses, **but** she doesn't anymore. Now she wears contact lenses.

2.   *Now write five sentences about Elizabeth using* **DIDN'T USE TO** *and* **BUT**.

EXAMPLE   She **didn't use to wear** contact lenses, **but** now she does.

3.   Write *five sentences about yourself using* **USED TO** *or* **DIDN'T USE TO** *and* **BUT**.

EXAMPLE   I never **used to cook, but** now I cook for myself every day.
I **used to be** shy, **but** I'm not anymore.

EXERCISE 6   **Ability and Necessity**

Complete each sentence by using the appropriate form of one of the following expressions with the verb cue indicated. Each blank must contain one of these expressions, or its negative form.

CAN	MUST
COULD	HAVE / HAS TO
IS / ARE / WAS / WERE ABLE TO	HAD TO

Make the verb negative if necessary.

In the past, planes did not have smoking and nonsmoking sections.

Smoking was not restricted to certain rows. Smokers _____
(smoke)

in any seat. People who didn't like cigarette smoke _____
(do)

anything about it. They _____ in the middle of smokers
(sit)

whether they liked it or not! These days, however, there are very strict

regulations about smoking. People _____ on any flight
(smoke)

within the United States. This protects the passengers and crew so that

they _____ cigarette smoke.
(breathe)

4 *Reacting in Conversations*

```
┌──────────────────────────────────────────────────┐
│  ┌──────────────────────────┐                      │
│  │   THE BIG PICTURE         │                      │
│  └──────────────────────────┘                      │
│  Using Auxiliaries                                 │
│  Too / Either / So / Neither                       │
│  Tag Questions                                     │
│                                                    │
└──────────────────────────────────────────────────┘
```

AT A GLANCE

Keeping a Conversation Going

Reactions

Imagine that you are walking with a friend. How can you respond to the following comments?

What does your friend expect you to do or say when he or she tells you these things? How will your friend feel if you do not respond at all?

Echoes

What is an **echo?** Where can you hear an echo? If you shout, "Hello, everybody!" in the mountains, which of the following echoes might you hear?

1. "Hellooooo"
2. "... body ... body ... body"
3. "... loooooo"
4. "Hi, there"
5. "Good-bye"

> In this chapter, you will practice some different ways to respond in conversation. One way to react in English is with a type of "echo." You will practice using short form auxiliaries as "echoes" in conversation.

FOCUS 1   Introduction to "Echo" Auxiliaries

Look at the following short forms. What phrase does each short form stand for?

Jim:	Do you have a pet?
Olga:	No, I **don't. Do** you?
Jim:	No, I **don't** either. But I'd like to get a dog someday.
Olga:	You **would?** How come?*
Jim:	Well, dogs are very friendly and devoted to their owners.
Olga:	So **are** cats.
Jim:	No, they **aren't.** Cats can be affectionate, but they are so independent!

In English, it is common to use a subject with a short form auxiliary or the verb **BE** to represent an entire phrase. You have already practiced short form auxiliaries in answers to **YES / NO** questions. (Do you have a pet? No, I **don't.**) As you will see in this chapter, there are many other ways to use auxiliary short forms, especially in conversations. These short form auxiliaries "echo" or represent the verb phrase of the full sentence.

There are two points to remember about using "echo" auxiliaries.

   1.   Choose the auxiliary that corresponds to the verb tense and form of the full verb.

EXAMPLES	Statement:	I **have** a pet snake. (*simple present verb*)
	Response:	You **do!?** (*simple present auxiliary*)
	Statement:	I **used to** have a puppy. (*simple past verb*)
	Response:	So **did** I. (*simple past auxiliary*)
	Statement:	My dog **could do** some tricks. (*modal auxiliary* **COULD**)
	Response:	Really? Mine **couldn't.** (*modal auxiliary* **COULD**)
	Statement:	A snake **isn't** very affectionate. (*the verb* **BE**)
	Response:	Neither **are** fish. (*the verb* **BE**)

   2.   If the auxiliary is negative, you can use a contraction in a short form. However, if the auxiliary is affirmative, do not use a contraction.

EXAMPLES	Statement:	Guess what?**
	Response:	What?
	Statement:	My snake isn't in its tank!
	Response:	It **isn't!?**
	Statement:	No. My snake is gone!
	Response:	It **is!?** I'm out of here!† See you later!

****HOW COME** means *"Why?"* It is used in informal conversation.

**GUESS WHAT? is an informal conversational expression that means *"I have something to tell you."* The usual response is *"What?"*

†The expression *"I'm out of here!"* means *"I'm leaving right now."* It is used only in informal conversation.

"Echo" Reactions with **TOO / EITHER** and **SO / NEITHER**

"Echo" auxiliaries can show that one situation is different from or similar to another situation.

A. Situations that are similar

The expressions **TOO, EITHER, SO,** and **NEITHER** indicate that two situations are similar in some way. These expressions often occur with short forms.

1. Affirmative sentences: **TOO** and **SO**

Use **TOO** or **SO** with an affirmative auxiliary or form of **BE** to "echo" an affirmative statement. **TOO** and **SO** have the same meaning. They both show that two affirmative situations are similar. However, each expression requires a different word order pattern. **SO** comes at the beginning of the reaction; **TOO** comes at the end. It is not possible to change the word order pattern.

Speaker #1: Affirmative Comment	Speaker #2: Affirmative Reaction		
	Subject + Auxiliary + TOO	or	SO + Auxiliary + Subject
I **have** a pet bird.	I **do** too.		So **do** I.
My bird **can say** a few words.	Mine **can** too.		So **can** mine.
My bird **was** a gift.	Mine **was** too.		So **was** mine.
I **got** it for my birthday.	I **did** too.		So **did** I.
We **have** several pets at home.	We **do** too.		So **do** we.

2. Negative sentences: **EITHER** and **NEITHER**

Use **EITHER** or **NEITHER** to "echo" a negative statement. They both show that two negative situations are similar. However, each expression requires a different word order pattern. **EITHER** comes at the end of the reaction and occurs with a *negative* auxiliary or form of **BE**. **NEITHER** comes at the beginning of the reaction. **NEITHER** means "not either." Because **NEITHER** already has a negative meaning, it does not occur with a negative auxiliary.

Speaker #1: Negative Comment	Speaker #2: Negative Reaction		
	Subject + Auxiliary + NOT + EITHER	or	NEITHER + Auxiliary + Subject
My pet bird **can't sing.**	Mine **can't** either.		Neither **can** mine.
I **don't have** a big cage.	I **don't** either.		Neither **do** I.
My bird **isn't** very big.	Mine **isn't** either.		Neither **is** mine.
My bird **never goes** outside.	Mine **doesn't** either.		Neither **does** mine.

B. Situations that are different

You can use a subject with a short form auxiliary or form of **BE** to show that two situations are different. If two situations are different, *do not use* **TOO, EITHER, SO,** or **NEITHER**.

Speaker #1: Comment	Speaker #2: Opposite Reaction
	Subject + Auxiliary
I **like** cats better than dogs.	Really? I **don't.**
My favorite pet **is** a cat.	Really? Mine **isn't.** I prefer dogs.
I **didn't have** any pets growing up.	Really? I **did.** I had a pet bird.

Reacting with **TOO** and **EITHER**

*A.   For each of the following statements, use an auxiliary with **TOO** or **EITHER** to give an example of something that is similar.*

EXAMPLES   Comment: Dogs make good pets. (cats)
Reaction: Cats **do too.**

Comment: I don't like snakes. (I)
Reaction: I **don't either.**

1.   India has a lot of different snakes. (Thailand)
2.   Tigers hunt for food. (wolves)
3.   Owls can see well in the dark. (lions)
4.   Human babies can't take care of themselves. (monkey babies)
5.   Camels don't need a lot of water to survive. (snakes)
6.   Some snakes are poisonous. (some spiders)
7.   Garter snakes aren't dangerous to humans. (black snakes)

*B.   What is your reaction to each of the following comments? Use an auxiliary short form with **TOO** and **EITHER** to indicate a similar situation. Use an auxiliary alone to indicate a different situation. Give additional information if you wish.*

EXAMPLES   Comment: I want a pet.
Reaction: I **do too.** I would like to get a dog.
(Really? I **don't.** Pets are too much work.)

Comment: I didn't have any pets as a child.
Reaction: I **didn't either.**
(Oh, I **did.** I got a cat when I was six years old.)

1.   I think it is interesting to learn about animals.
2.   I can't keep pets in my home here.
3.   I couldn't have a pet when I was a child.
4.   I am not very interested in animals and wildlife.
5.   I am afraid of snakes.
6.   I like to watch television shows about nature and animals.

Reacting with **SO** and **NEITHER**

*For each of the following statements, use an auxiliary with **SO** or **NEITHER** to give an example of something that is similar. Fill in empty brackets with your own cues.*

EXAMPLES   Comment: Dogs make good pets. (cats)
Reaction: **So do** cats.

Comment: I don't like snakes. (I)
Reaction: **Neither do** I.

1.   A dolphin is a mammal. (a whale)
2.   Dolphins are very intelligent. (gorillas)
3.   Some snakes aren't dangerous. (some sharks)
4.   Dinosaurs used to roam the world. (different mammals)
5.   The buffalo was once in danger of extinction. (the bald eagle)
6.   Poachers kill a lot of animals. (pollution)
7.   Humans can use tools. (chimpanzees)

8.   Birds don't have fur. [   ]
9.   Giraffes don't eat meat. [   ]
10. Turtles lay eggs. [   ]
11. Snakes are cold-blooded animals. [   ]
12. Snakes scare me. [   ]

PRACTICE 2-3   Comments and Reactions

*Use the following cues to make **true** statements about your situation and opinions. You can make affirmative or negative statements. Your classmate should use short form auxiliaries to react to your comments.*

EXAMPLES   I / (not) have / a dog

a. Student A: I **don't have** a dog.
   Student B: I **don't either. (Neither do** I.) (I **do.)**

b. Student A: I **have** a dog.
   Student B: I **do too. (So do** I.) (I **don't.)**

1.   I / (not) afraid of dogs
2.   I / (not) comfortable when I see pets inside a house
3.   I / (not) have a pet when I was young
4.   I / (not) like cats
5.   People in my country / (not) own dogs for protection
6.   My hometown / (not) have a zoo

CLOSE-UP   **Combining Sentences: TOO, EITHER, SO, NEITHER**

Look at the following two photographs. Do you notice any similarities between the elephant and the other animal, a hyrax?

The elephant's only known living "relative" is a small mouse-sized animal called a hyrax. *Although these animals seem to be very different, they are similar in some ways. These similarities are enough to indicate to scientists that they are related to each other.*

As you can see in the following examples, "echo" auxiliary short forms can be used in combining sentences.

A. Combining things that are the same: AND . . . TOO/EITHER; AND . . . SO/NEITHER

If the information about the subjects in both sentences is the same, use the connecting word **AND** to combine the sentences. Use short form auxiliaries with **TOO** and **SO** to combine affirmative statements. Use short form auxiliaries with **EITHER** and **NEITHER** to combine negative statements.

   1. A hyrax has flat toenails. An elephant has flat toenails too.

      A hyrax has flat toenails, **and an elephant does too.**

      A hyrax has flat toenails, **and so does an elephant.**

   2. Elephants don't have other relatives. Hyraxes don't have other relatives.

      Elephants don't have any other relatives, **and hyraxes don't either.**

      Elephants don't have any other relatives, **and neither do hyraxes.**

B. Combining things that are different: BUT . . .

If the information about the subjects is different, use the connecting word **BUT** with a short form auxiliary.

   1. An elephant is very large. A hyrax isn't large.

      An elephant **is** very large, **but a hyrax isn't.**

   2. A hyrax doesn't have a trunk. An elephant has a trunk.

      A hyrax **doesn't have** a trunk, **but an elephant does.**

Close-Up

PRACTICE   **SENTENCE COMBINING**

A. Interview a classmate using one of the following sets of cues to form questions. Your classmate should respond to each question with a short answer.

EXAMPLE   you / like cats?

             Student A: Do you like cats?

             Student B: No, I don't.

                       (Yes, I do.)

INTERVIEW 1:

    1.   you / like to swim in the ocean?

    2.   you / afraid of sharks?

    3.   your hometown / have an aquarium?

    4.   you / tell [=*ability*] / the difference between a shark and a dolphin?

    5.   you / go to the beach for vacation last year?

INTERVIEW 2:

    1.   you / like to go hunting?

    2.   your government / allow hunting?

    3.   your area / have a lot of interesting birds?

    4.   you / think / it / important to save animals from extinction?

    5.   your country / have any wildlife reservations?

B.   Now form sentences comparing your situation and opinions to your classmate's.
Use the connecting words AND or BUT with short form auxiliaries.

EXAMPLES   Ming doesn't like cats, **and** neither **do** I.
                Ming doesn't like cats, **and** I **don't** either.
                Ming doesn't like cats, **but** I **do.**

FOCUS 3   "Echo" Questions and Exclamations

What is the purpose of the "echo" auxiliaries in the following conversation?

Paula: Did you read this story about animal communication?
Sarah: No, I didn't. **Did you?**
Paula: Yes, I did. It was fascinating. Dr. Francine Patterson of Stanford
          University taught a gorilla to communicate with sign language.
Sarah: **She did?!**
Paula: Believe it or not, she did. In fact, Koko the gorilla can use more than
          500 signs to communicate facts and feelings.
Sarah: **She can?!**
Paula: Yes. Isn't that amazing?

A. "Echo" questions

You can return a **YES/NO** question with a short "echo" question using the following pattern: *auxiliary + subject?*

Yes/No Question:	Did you read about Koko?
Response with "Echo":	No, I didn't. **Did you?** (*Did you read about Koko?*)
Reply to response:	No, I didn't either.
Yes/No Question:	Are you interested in animal communication?
Response with "Echo":	Oh yes, very! **Are you?** (*Are you interested in animal communication?*)
Reply to response:	Yes, I am too.

B. "Echo" exclamations

You can show surprise by reacting to a statement with a short "echo" exclamation. Use the following pattern: *subject + auxiliary?!*

Statement:	Koko the gorilla can communicate her feelings with sign language.
Response with "Echo":	**She can?!** That's amazing!
Statement:	And listen to this! A chimpanzee named Lana uses a computer keyboard to communicate.
Response with "Echo":	**She does?!** I'd love to see that.

PRACTICE 3-1   "Echo" Questions and Exclamations

*A.   Use the following cues to make **YES/NO** questions. Your classmate should respond with a short answer and then ask you for the same information with an "echo" question. You should then respond to your classmate's question.*

EXAMPLE	you / have a dog?
	Student A: Do you have a dog?
	Student B: No, I don't. **Do you?**
	Student A: No, I don't either.

1. you / [ever] watch educational television?
2. you / ride [= *ability*] / a horse?
3. people in your country / [often] keep pets in the house?
4. you / worried about the future of wildlife in your country?
5. you / see the last *National Geographic* special on TV?

B.   The following are statements about Koko the gorilla. You should respond to each one with an "echo" exclamation to show surprise.

EXAMPLE	Statement:	Dr. Patterson taught Koko how to use American Sign Language.
	Echo Response:	**She did?!**

1. Koko the gorilla is famous in the United States.
2. Koko used sign language to ask for a kitten as a birthday present.
3. Koko was very gentle with her kitten.
4. When the kitten bit or scratched her, Koko didn't get angry.

5. Koko often uses sign language to communicate her feelings.
6. She can even remember and "talk" about past events.

Sources: Coon, Dennis. *Introduction to Psychology—Exploration and Application* (St. Paul, Minnesota: West Publishing Company, 1980).
Patterson, Dr. Francine. *Koko's Kitten* (New York: Scholastic, Inc., 1985).

FOCUS 4 More Reactions in Conversation

The following expressions give other ways to react in conversation.

A. Expressing an opinion: I THINK SO / I DON'T THINK SO

Pedro: Do handicapped people ever use monkeys to help them in their daily lives?

Chan: **I think so.** It seems I saw something about that on TV.

Pedro: Do they ever use trained cats?

Chan: **I don't think so.** At least, I've never heard of it.

B. Agreeing with another opinion: I THINK SO TOO / I DON'T THINK SO EITHER

Jill: I think that it is important for us to protect animals from extinction.

Kathy: **I think so too.**

Jill: I don't think that people should kill elephants for their ivory.

Kathy: **I don't think so either.**

C. Expressing a hope or desire: I HOPE SO / I HOPE NOT

Barb: Is your wife expecting a fur coat for her birthday?

Scott: **I hope not.** I am against the entire idea of fur coats.

Barb: I wonder if she will be happy with an artificial fur jacket.

Scott: **I hope so,** because that's what I got her.

D. Expressing regret: I'M AFRAID SO / I'M AFRAID NOT

Student: Do poachers still kill alligators for their leather?

Dr. Franks: **I'm afraid so.** Alligators may be extinct one day.

Student: Do all governments enforce strict laws against hunting endangered animals?

Dr. Franks: **I'm afraid not.** Many governments do not have the resources to protect wild animals.

All of these reactions can also be used with a subject and an "echo" auxiliary.

Pedro: Do people still hunt whales?

Mary: *I'm afraid* **they do.**

Pedro: Is whale hunting by big companies legal in the United States?

Mary: *I don't think* **it is.** But I don't know for sure.

Reactions with **HOPE**, **THINK**, and **BE AFRAID**

A. *Complete the following responses with a subject and short form auxiliary.*

EXAMPLE   Question: Is the water cold?
Response: I'm afraid ____it is____.

1. QUESTION: Does this city have any good restaurants?

   RESPONSE: I think _____ .

2. QUESTION: Do you have time to go eat something with me after class?

   RESPONSE: Sorry. I'm afraid _____ .
   STATEMENT: Maybe we can do it another time.

   RESPONSE: I hope _____ . I would enjoy that.

3. STATEMENT: Our guests are very late. I wonder if they are lost.

   RESPONSE: I hope _____ .
   QUESTION: Did you give them a map to the house?

   RESPONSE: No, I'm afraid _____ . I forgot to do that.
   QUESTION: Do they have our phone number?

   RESPONSE: I think _____ .

B. *Complete each of the following responses with **one** word or contraction.*

EXAMPLE   Question: Is the water cold?
Response: I'm afraid ____so____ .

1. QUESTION: Are there any sharks in this area?

   RESPONSE: I sure hope _____ .

2. QUESTION: Is this beach safe for swimming?

   RESPONSE: I think it _____ .

3. QUESTION: I'm not a good swimmer. Does the water get deep quickly as you walk out?

   RESPONSE: I'm afraid _____ . You'd better be careful.

4. QUESTION: Did you remember to bring the sunscreen?

   RESPONSE: I think _____ . Look in my bag.

5. STATEMENT: Those waves are pretty high. I don't think we should go in the water.

   RESPONSE: I don't think so _____ .

6. STATEMENT: I think we should just sit on the beach.

   RESPONSE: I think so _____ .

FOCUS 5   Tag Questions

Another type of question that is very common in conversational English is a *tag question.*

A. Using tag questions

There are three basic uses for tag questions:

1. **To give an opinion and ask for a reaction**

   Koko is amazing, **isn't she?**

2. **To react with surprise or disbelief**

   Koko can't really communicate, **can she?**

3. **To ask for confirmation**

   Koko lives with Dr. Patterson, **doesn't she?**

In this chapter, you will practice using tag questions to *ask for confirmation*. Speakers often use tag questions to make sure that their information is correct. Tag questions can be answered with a short answer.

This is what I think;	am I correct?	Confirmation
Koko is a gorilla,	isn't she?	You're right. She is.
Koko isn't a chimpanzee,	is she?	No, she isn't.

B. Forming tag questions

A *tag question* has two parts: a statement, and a question added at the end. The statement part expresses the speaker's idea; the question part asks for confirmation. The question part consists of an auxiliary and a subject pronoun. The subject pronoun refers to the subject of the statement. The auxiliary refers to the verb of the statement part, but puts it in opposite form. In other words, if the verb in the statement part is *affirmative,* the auxiliary in the question part is a *negative* contraction; if the statement verb is *negative,* the auxiliary in the question part is *affirmative.*

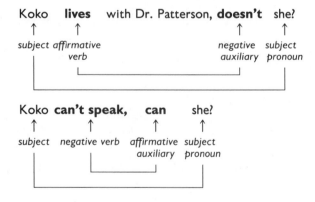

C. Answering tag questions

You can use short answers to respond to tag questions. Keep in mind that a response of "yes" occurs with an affirmative auxiliary; a response of "no" occurs with a negative auxiliary.*

Tag question:	John doesn't have a car, does he?
Response:	No, he doesn't. *(confirmation)*
	You're right. He doesn't. *(confirmation)*
	Yes, he does. (idea *not* confirmed)
Tag question:	John walks to school, doesn't he?

---

*In English, it is **not** possible to respond "Yes, he doesn't" or "No, he does."

Response: Yes, he does.   *(confirmation)*
No, he doesn't.   (idea *not* confirmed)

D.   More examples of tag questions

Tag Question Asking for Confirmation	Confirmation
I **am** late, **aren't*** I?	Yes, you **are.**
We **have** a test soon, **don't** we?	Yes, we **do.**
You **had to leave** early yesterday, **didn't** you?	Yes, I **did.**
It **snows** here in Iowa in winter, **doesn't** it?	Yes, it **does.**
Courtney **was** at the party, **wasn't** she?	Yes, she **was.**
That**'s** your brother over there, **isn't** it?	Yes, it **is.**
I**'m** not on time, **am** I?	No, you **aren't.**
We **don't have** any homework tonight, **do** we?	No, we **don't.**
You **didn't come** late, **did** you?	No, I **didn't.**
It **doesn't snow** in Hawaii, **does** it?	No, it **doesn't.**
Aaron **wasn't** there, **was** he?	No, he **wasn't.**
Those **aren't** your books on the desk, **are** they?	No, they **aren't.**

Notice that the question part of the tag question *must* have a **subject pronoun**. The pronoun for **THIS / THAT** is **IT**. The pronoun for **THESE / THOSE** is **THEY**.

> **That** is your brother over there, isn't **it?**
> **This** can't work without electricity, can **it?**
> **These** are yours, aren't **they?**
> **Those** don't belong to me, do **they?**

Notice also that when the question part is negative, it usually has a contraction.

> You live near school, **don't** you?
> I'm in the right room, **aren't*** I?

PRACTICE 5–1   Forming Tag Questions

Complete each of the following tag questions. Your classmate should answer with the expected short answer.

EXAMPLES   Student A: Koko is a gorilla, **isn't she?**
Student B: Yes, she is.

Student A: Koko isn't a chimpanzee, **is she?**
Student B: No, she isn't.

1.   Botany is the study of plants, _____ ?

2.   Zoologists study animals, _____ ?

3.   Most plants have to have water, _____ ?

4.   Ornithology isn't the study of fish, _____ ?

5.   Ornithologists study birds, _____ ?

6.   Not all birds can fly, _____ ?

---

*There is no contraction for **AM NOT**. In tag questions, use **AREN'T** instead of **AM NOT**.

7. Sharks today are a lot like sharks millions of years ago,

   _____ ?

8. We can improve our understanding of language learning from Koko,

   _____ ?

9. Koko can't speak, _____ ?

10. Koko was very young when Dr. Patterson got her,

    _____ ?

PRACTICE 5-2   Asking for Confirmation

A.   Complete each of the following sentences. Then find out if your information is correct by asking a classmate a tag question. Try to ask someone who probably knows the correct answer. Your classmate should respond with a short answer.

EXAMPLES   The capital of California is _____ .

Student A: The capital of California is **San Francisco, isn't it?**
Student B: No, it isn't. The capital of California is Sacramento.

(Student A: The capital of California is **Sacramento, isn't it?**)
(Student B: You're right. It is.)

1. The capital of Spain is _____ .

2. India exports _____ .

3. France doesn't grow _____ .

4. Henry Ford produced _____ .

5. The current vice president of the United States is

   _____ .

6. _____ was the president of the United States before

   _____ .

7. The last summer Olympics were in _____ .

B.   Do you have ideas or information about any of the following topics? Find out if your idea is correct by asking your classmate a tag question. Try to ask someone who probably knows the information you are trying to confirm. Your classmate should answer with a short answer. You should then react to your classmate's response.

EXAMPLES   the meaning of a word in your classmate's native language

Student A: "Sayonara" means "good-bye" in Japanese, doesn't it?
Student B: Yes, it does.
Student A: **That's what I thought. (I thought so.)**

Student A: "Gesundheit" means "hello" in German, doesn't it?
Student B: No, it doesn't. It means "health."
Student A: **It does? I didn't know that.**

1. the number of children (or brothers and sisters) that your classmate has

2. the place where your classmate usually eats lunch

3. the location of the nearest public library

4. the languages your classmate can speak
5. something that your classmate did or didn't do last weekend
6. the capital of your classmate's country
7. something that your classmate likes to do in his or her free time
8. the meaning of a word in your classmate's native language

A WIDER ANGLE

Conversations

A classmate should begin each of the following four conversations. You should react in any way that seems appropriate. Then your classmate should respond. Continue the conversations as long as you can. Use your imagination!

Conversation 1
STUDENT A: Guess what!

Conversation 2
STUDENT A: You will never believe what happened yesterday!

Conversation 3
STUDENT A: A good friend of mine has to leave the country immediately.

Conversation 4
STUDENT A: I just won an incredible prize!

Writing Practice

Choose one of the following topics to write about.

TOPIC 1:   A *tall tale* is a story that is filled with exaggeration. In fact, a tall tale has so many exaggerations that it cannot possibly be true.

Use your imagination to write a conversation in which you tell a friend a tall tale or surprising story. The story can come from your imagination, or else you can retell a famous tall tale from your country. Be sure to include your friend's reactions to your story. Below is an example of how your conversation might start.

You: You won't believe what happened to me yesterday!
Friend: What?
You: I caught a giant fish at Griffey Lake!
Friend: You did?! How big was it?
You: It was too big to fit in the boat.
Friend: It was? You're kidding!
You: No, I'm not. I'll tell you how I got it home. There was this octopus, see. . . .

TOPIC 2:   Write a short composition about the advantages and disadvantages of owning a pet.

TOPIC 3:   Are you a "cat person" or a "dog person"? Which animal do you prefer as a pet? Write a short composition discussing how dogs and cats differ as pets.

Chapter Exercises

EXERCISE 1 Too / Not Either

*Complete each response with an auxiliary and **TOO** or **NOT EITHER**.*

EXAMPLES

Statement: I don't like to eat fast food.
Response: **I don't either.**

Statement: I prefer to cook at home.
Response: **I do too.**

1. STATEMENT: I sometimes have trouble talking on the phone in English.

 RESPONSE: I _____ .

2. STATEMENT: My American friends speak so fast!

 RESPONSE: Mine _____ .

3. STATEMENT: I can't understand their jokes.

 RESPONSE: I _____ .

4. STATEMENT: My best friend tries to speak slowly for me.

 RESPONSE: Mine _____ .

5. STATEMENT: I couldn't understand very much when I first arrived here.

 RESPONSE: I _____ .

6. STATEMENT: We didn't have native English teachers in my country.

 RESPONSE: We _____ .

EXERCISE 2 So / Neither

*Write a short form reaction to each of the following statements. Use the subject in parentheses with an auxiliary and **SO** or **NEITHER**. Fill in empty brackets with your own cues.*

EXAMPLES

Foreign students can't vote. (permanent residents)
Neither can permanent residents.

Automobile prices rose last year. (food prices)
So did food prices.

1. Plants need nitrogen in order to live. (human beings)
2. Cactus plants can survive without much water. (camels)
3. Benjamin Franklin was a famous inventor. (Thomas Edison)

4. The United States presidential elections occur every four years. (the Olympic games)
5. Saudi Arabia never gets snow. [   ]
6. England doesn't have a president. [   ]

EXERCISE 3 **Using Auxiliaries**

Complete each sentence by writing one word or contraction in the blank.

EXAMPLE Saudi Arabia exports oil, but Japan **doesn't.**

1. France fought in World War II, and so _____ England.

2. Colombia grows coffee, and Venezuela _____ too.

3. Some areas of Ethiopia don't get a lot of rain, and neither _____ parts of the Sudan.

4. Florida gets a lot of sunshine, but the state of Washington _____ .

5. India used to be a British colony, but Saudi Arabia _____ .

6. Many people in Malaysia are Muslim, and many people in Indonesia _____ too.

EXERCISE 4 **Sentence Combining**

*A.   Combine each pair of sentences into one sentence. Use the connecting words **AND** or **BUT** with short form auxiliaries. Use **TOO** or **NOT EITHER** where appropriate.*

EXAMPLES Whales are an endangered species.
Pandas are an endangered species.
Whales are an endangered species, **and** pandas **are too.**

Pigs are intelligent animals.
Chickens are not intelligent animals.
Pigs **are** intelligent animals, **but** chickens **aren't.**

1. A shrimp is a type of shellfish.
A lobster is a type of shellfish.
2. Polar bears live in the Arctic.
Seals live in the Arctic.
3. Pandas don't kill for food.
Gorillas don't kill for food.
4. A panda doesn't hunt for food.
A wolf hunts for food.

*B.   Continue combining pairs of sentences. Use the connecting words **AND** or **BUT** with short form auxiliaries. Use **SO** or **NEITHER** where appropriate.*

1. Sally used to have a pet raccoon.
Jay used to have a pet raccoon.
2. Some mammals don't hibernate in winter.
Birds don't hibernate in winter.

3. Full-grown elephants don't have any natural enemies except humans.
   Full-grown blue whales don't have any natural enemies except humans.

4. Dolphins have to come up for air.
   Seals have to come up for air.

EXERCISE 5 Reacting with SO

Complete each conversation by writing one of the following responses in the blank. Do not use a phrase more than once.

I think so.   I hope so.
I think so too.   I hope not.
I don't think so.   I'm afraid so.
I don't think so either.   I'm afraid not.

1. QUESTION: Do you think our psychology professor will make us write a term paper?

   RESPONSE: _____ . I hate to write papers!

2. QUESTION: Do you think our psychology professor will make us write a term paper?

   RESPONSE: _____ . My roommate took her course last year, and she had to write a term paper. I think it's a course requirement. But we can ask the professor to be sure.

3. QUESTION: I hate to write papers more than anything in the world! Do we have to write a term paper in psychology class?

   RESPONSE: _____ . The teacher announced the assignment on the first day of class, when you were absent.

4. STATEMENT: We have five exams in psychology class. I don't think we should have to write a term paper on top of all that!

   RESPONSE: _____ . Five exams and all that reading are enough!

5. QUESTION: Is there a final exam in this psychology course?

   RESPONSE: _____ . The course syllabus doesn't mention anything about it.

EXERCISE 6 Tag Questions

*Complete each **tag question**. Then give a short answer to confirm the speaker's information.*

EXAMPLES Your adviser helped you with your schedule, **didn't he?**
Yes, he did.

That isn't your adviser over there, **is it?**
No, it isn't.

1. I'm in the right classroom, _____ ?

   _____

2. I can't take this course until I finish the prerequisites, _____ ?

   _____

3. Your major is chemistry, _____ ?

   _____

4. Freshmen have to take English composition, _____ ?

   _____

5. Your roommate had to get permission to drop his math class, _____ ?

   _____

6. Late registration is tomorrow, _____ ?

   _____

7. New students can't get their ID cards right away, _____ ?

   _____

8. You took 15 credits last semester, _____ ?

   _____

9. You transferred from another college, _____ ?

   _____

10. You weren't able to transfer all your credits, _____ ?

    _____

5 *Using Nouns*

THE BIG PICTURE

Count / Non-Count Nouns

Articles and Determiners

Possessives

AT A GLANCE

People, Places, and Things

Fill-in-the-Blank

Complete the following sentence with one word:

I'm thinking about the _____ that you mentioned yesterday.

You can probably think of many different words to complete the sentence. And all of your words have something in common: they belong to a group of words in English called *nouns*. A noun is a word that refers to a person, place, thing, or idea. Most languages use nouns, but different languages classify and use them differently.

Choosing a Place to Live

Think about people in your country who are your age. Do they usually live in the same place all their lives, or do they move from city to city or even to other countries? What are some reasons that people move to new places? Imagine that you can move to any city that you want. Excluding family, what things will you consider when you choose a place to live?

Places Rated in North America

North American society is quite mobile. People frequently move from one city or state or province to another. In the 1993 edition of the *Places Rated Almanac*, the authors evaluate various aspects of 343 different metropolitan areas in the United States and Canada. When evaluating these cities, the authors looked at ten different factors that seem to be important to Americans and Canadians:

living costs	job outlook	housing	transportation	education
health care	recreation	crime	the arts	climate

After taking all these factors into consideration, the authors' study concluded that in 1993, the best place to live in America was Cincinnati, Ohio, and the best place to live in Canada was Toronto.

Although they were rated as great places to live, both cities have some drawbacks along with their advantages. Cincinnati is strong in the areas of education, culture, recreation, health care, and job outlook. However, Cincinnati has a high cost of living and housing is expensive. Toronto scored very high in the areas of transportation, education, job outlook, health care, and the arts; but, like Cincinnati, it was rated low in the areas of living costs and housing.

Now look back at the last paragraph of the reading passage. Underline all the nouns that you can find.

In this chapter, you will practice using nouns to talk about people, places, and things. You will see how the English language classifies and uses nouns. You will also practice using determiners and quantity expressions that often occur with nouns. Keep in mind as you go through the chapter that English may use nouns differently from the way your language uses them. Do not be surprised if the grammar of English nouns sometimes seems illogical to you!

FOCUS 1 Introduction to Nouns

English grammar classifies nouns as *proper nouns* or *common nouns*. A *proper noun* is the name of a particular person, place, or thing. Proper nouns always begin with a capital letter. Examples of proper nouns are *Toronto, Children's Hospital, Aunt Jeanne, Main Street, Abraham Lincoln,* and *Christmas*. Nouns that refer to a thing in general are called *common nouns*. Examples of common nouns are *book, beauty, river, city, holiday,* and *grandmother*. This chapter will focus on common nouns.

In English, most common nouns fall into one of two major categories: *count nouns* and *non-count nouns*.

A. Count nouns

A *count noun* is a noun that can be *singular* (only one thing) or *plural* (more than one thing). Most, but not all, count nouns can be counted with numbers.

Examples of count nouns: **museum, factory, park**

> The Metropolitan Museum of Art is a world-famous art **museum.**
> New York City has 52 major art **museums** and **galleries.**

B. Non-count nouns

A *non-count noun* is a noun that has only one form. It cannot be counted with a number.

Examples of non-count nouns: **unemployment, pollution, water**

> Pollution is a problem in many large cities in the United States.

Does your language divide nouns into count and non-count nouns?

FOCUS 2 Count Nouns

Look at each of the nouns in the following sentences. Is the noun referring to one thing (singular) or to more than one thing (plural)? How do you know?

1. Affordable **apartments** are hard to find in San Francisco.
2. Where did you get this **book** about art? It's lovely!
3. My **clothes** are dirty. I need to wash them.
4. One important **means** of public transportation is the **subway.**
5. This TV **series** has some famous **actors.** It's excellent!
6. This park has quite a few **deer.** No one is allowed to hunt them.

___

A. Agreement with nouns

1. Singular nouns: A singular noun subject needs a singular verb. A singular noun can be replaced by a singular pronoun. A singular noun cannot usually stand alone. An article (**A, THE**) or other singular determiner (**THIS, THAT, MY, YOUR, EACH, EVERY,** etc.) must come before a singular noun.

> **The** subway **stops** near my home. **It's** very convenient.
> **This is a** nice jacket. I bought **it** downtown.

2.   Plural nouns: A plural noun subject needs a plural verb. A plural noun can be replaced by a plural pronoun. A plural noun can occur with or without a determiner.

> *Tornadoes* **are** common in many central states, but **they** do not normally occur in the northwestern United States. **These** violent *storms* frequently **come** in the spring.

B.   Regular plural noun forms

To form the plural of most nouns, add **-S** or **-ES** to the singular form. You can find spelling rules for regular plural noun forms in Appendix A.

> book → book**s**   watch → watch**es**   cit**y** → cit**ies**

C.   Irregular plural noun forms

1.   Some nouns have irregular plural forms. Some nouns change **F** to **V** and add **-ES** to form the plural:

> one knife—many kni**ves**   one half—several hal**ves**
> one wife—many wi**ves**   one loaf—several loa**ves**
> one life—many li**ves**   one leaf—several lea**ves**

> **Note:** Some nouns that end with **F** have the regular plural form.

> belief→belief**s**   chief→chief**s**   roof→roof**s**

2.   Some nouns change the spelling of the singular noun to form the plural. These nouns do not use **-S** or **-ES:**

> one man—two men   one tooth—two teeth
> one woman—two women   one goose—two geese
> one child—two children   one mouse—two mice
> one foot—two feet

3.   Some nouns use the same form for both singular and plural:

> one sheep—two sheep   one series—several series
> one deer—two deer   one means—several means
> one fish—two fish

D.   Nouns that are always plural

Some nouns occur only as plural nouns. They always take a plural verb and plural pronouns. Unlike most other plural nouns, these nouns, do *not* occur with numbers. The plural noun **PEOPLE**, however, can occur with numbers.

> **clothes:** I bought a lot of **clothes** at the sale yesterday. Here <u>they are</u>!
> **groceries:** Groceries <u>are</u> expensive these days!
> **police:** The **police** <u>are</u> allowed to carry guns in the United States.
> **people:** The **people** in this class <u>are</u> friendly.
> There <u>are</u> <u>two</u> **people** from Japan in this class.

E.   Nouns consisting of two equal parts

Some nouns in English refer to tools, instruments, or articles of clothing that consist of two equal parts joined together. Even though these nouns refer to one item, they are always *plural nouns*. They occur with plural verbs and can be replaced only by plural pronouns.

> **pajamas:** I need <u>some</u> new **pajamas.**
> **glasses:** John's new **glasses** <u>are</u> very strong.
> **scissors:** Be careful! Those **scissors** <u>are</u> sharp.

binoculars: <u>These</u> **binoculars** <u>are</u> great for birdwatching!
pants: <u>These</u> **pants** <u>are</u> comfortable.
jeans: <u>These</u> **jeans** <u>are</u> new.
trousers: Those **trousers** <u>are</u> too big for you.
slacks: I bought <u>these</u> nice **slacks** on sale.
shorts: <u>These</u> **shorts** <u>don't</u> fit me. Maybe you could wear <u>them</u>.

Unlike most other plural nouns, this type of noun does not usually occur with a number.

[MISTAKE: I have ~~three~~ **pants**.]

To count this type of noun, use the counting word **PAIR**.

Jack has on **a nice pair of** *pants*.
I bought **three pairs of** *jeans* yesterday.

PRACTICE 2-1   Singular and Plural Nouns

Complete the following comparisons with the singular or plural form of the noun.

EXAMPLE   one monkey / several **monkeys**

1. a big city / many big _____

2. a _____ of communication / several different means of communication

3. a Swiss watch / a couple of Swiss _____

4. one child / five _____

5. one bad _____ / a few bad teeth

6. a baked potato / four baked _____

7. a new TV _____ / two or three new TV series

8. a tropical fish / many tropical _____

9. a strange belief / many strange _____

10. a sharp knife / two sharp _____

11. a pair of jeans / several _____

FOCUS 3   Non-Count Nouns

Which of the following nouns can be counted with a number? Which cannot?

Cincinnati has:

| _____ museums | _____ rain | _____ universities |
| _____ unemployment | _____ dance companies | _____ cold weather in winter |

The nouns *unemployment, rain,* and *cold weather* are **non-count** nouns.
A non-count noun has only one form. It does not have a singular or plural form. A non-count noun takes a singular verb and is replaced by the singular pronoun **IT**. A non-count noun cannot have a number immediately in front of it.

Unemployment **is** one reason Americans move from one city to another. **It** forces people to look for jobs in other places.

A. Examples of some common non-count nouns

Some Types of Food

Liquids: water, oil, milk, wine, beer, juice, coffee, tea
Spices: salt, pepper, cinnamon, sugar, mint
Types of meat: meat, pork, beef, lamb, fish, chicken
Types of grain: corn, wheat, barley, rice, cereal
Milk products: cheese, ice cream, yogurt, butter
Some vegetables: * lettuce, celery, broccoli, cauliflower, cabbage, corn
Other items: fruit, soup, candy, chocolate, pasta, spaghetti, flour, bread

*Many vegetables are count nouns: tomatoes, potatoes, onions, carrots, radishes, vegetables.

Substances, Minerals, and Types of Energy

Types of metal: gold, silver, iron, tin, aluminum, nickel, steel
Sources of energy: energy, light,[†] coal, petroleum, oil, gas, electricity, gasoline
Types of material: wool, cotton, linen, silk, nylon
Other substances: air, oxygen, hydrogen, detergent, soap, sand, clay, wood, plastic, rubber

Abstract Nouns

knowledge, intelligence, health, life, truth, honesty, beauty, courage, wealth, poverty, unemployment, happiness, luck, fun

Note: The nouns **SUGGESTION, IDEA, DREAM,** and **THOUGHT** are count nouns.

Academic Subjects

mathematics, physics, economics, biology, sociology, psychology, history, chemistry, French, Spanish, engineering, pharmacy, medicine

Weather*

rain, snow, hail, sleet, fog, sunshine, humidity, weather, thunder, lightning

*Note: Most natural disasters are count nouns: storms, hurricanes, tornadoes, earthquakes, floods, typhoons

Other Non-Count Nouns

advice, communication, information, news, mail, postage, work,[†] homework, housework, grammar, vocabulary, slang, poetry, literature, music, jazz, entertainment, nightlife, recreation, traffic, transportation, violence, crime,[†] money, jewelry, furniture, machinery, equipment, industry,[†] agriculture, farming, pollution, research, luggage, baggage, garbage, junk, stuff

[†]Some nouns can be count and non-count with different meanings. (More examples of these nouns are given in Workbook Exercise 5.7.):

Non-count	Count
Crime is a problem in many cities.	The prisoner committed eight **crimes.**
Industry sometimes causes pollution.	Texas has several important **industries.**
Plants need **light** in order to grow.	Please turn off the **lights.**

B.   Using THERE + BE + (noun)

Why are the verbs in each pair of sentences different?

> **There is** a lot of rain in Seattle, Washington.
>
> **There are** a lot of hurricanes in Florida, **aren't there?** Yes, **there are.**
>
> **There was** a lot of rain last night, **wasn't there?** No, **there wasn't.**
>
> **There were** many floods in the United States several years ago.

Use **THERE** with the verb **BE** to mention that something exists. In this construction, **THERE** indicates the existence or presence of something; it does not refer to a place. **THERE** is a subject pronoun. This type of sentence needs a specific time or place in the sentence or context. The verb **BE** agrees with the noun that follows it: singular with non-count nouns, singular or plural with count nouns.

> **There was** a lot of *rain* yesterday.
>
> **There were** a lot of *floods* last year.
>
> **Was there** a storm here last night? Yes, **there was.**
>
> **Are there** a lot of *earthquakes* in your region? No, **there aren't.**

PRACTICE 3–1   Using Count and Non-Count Nouns

The expression **A LOT OF** refers to a large quantity. **A LOT OF** can occur with plural count nouns and with non-count nouns.

*A.   Use the following noun cues to make **true** statements telling where a large quantity of these things can be found. Change the noun to the plural form if necessary. Be sure to include the place where each thing exists. Your sentence should begin:* There (is / are) a lot of . . .

EXAMPLES   high mountain
　　　　　　　　There are a lot of high mountains in Nepal.

　　　　　　　　hot weather
　　　　　　　　There is a lot of hot weather in Texas.

1.　farm	6.　automobile factory
2.　farming	7.　traffic
3.　agriculture	8.　modern highway
4.　rice field	9.　new road construction
5.　heavy industry	10.　shopping center

B.   Think about this city. What is there a lot of here?

　　1.　There is a lot of . . .
　　2.　There are a lot of . . .

FOCUS 4   General Quantities

Although non-count nouns cannot occur with numbers, there are some general quantity expressions that can be used with count and non-count nouns. These expressions give a general idea about *how much* or *how many*; they do not refer to a specific number. Count and non-count nouns often use different quantity expressions with similar meanings.

A. General expressions of quantity

Quantity	Plural Count Nouns	Non-Count Nouns
Large quantities	a lot of lots of many quite a few a great many	a lot of lots of much quite a bit of a great deal of
Small quantities	a few several a couple (of)	a little
Limited quantities	not many very few only a few few	not much very little only a little little
"Zero" quantity	not any no	not any no

B. Special notes

1. **MUCH:** The quantity word **MUCH** is almost never used in *affirmative statements*. In conversation, use **A LOT OF** in affirmative sentences; in formal writing, use **A GREAT DEAL OF. MUCH** normally occurs in *questions* and *negative sentences*.

> Cleveland has **a lot of** snow. Cleveland gets **a great deal of** snow.
> Seattle doesn't get **much** snow.
> Does Toronto get **much** snow in winter?

2. **QUITE A BIT OF / QUITE A FEW:** These quantity words almost never occur in *negative* sentences. They do not occur frequently in questions.

> We get **quite a bit of** rain in our region.
> Does your region get **much** rain? Yes, we get **quite a bit.**
> We don't have **much** rain during the summer.
> We have **quite a few** violent storms during the monsoon season.

3. **LOTS OF: LOTS OF** is an informal conversational form of **A LOT OF.**

> I want to live somewhere with **lots of** snow.

C. More examples

You can see more examples of general quantity expressions in the following sentences:

(count)	There **are quite a few** dance companies in Pittsburgh.
(non-count)	There **is quite a bit of** crime in large urban areas.
(count)	There **are a great many** fine restaurants in Boston.
(non-count)	There **is a great deal of** traffic in Boston.
(count)	There **are a few** nice museums in Indianapolis.
(count)	There **are a couple** of nice museums in Toledo.
(non-count)	There **is a little** air pollution in Pittsburgh.
(count)	There **aren't many** tourists in small towns.

(non-count)	There **isn't much** cold weather in San Francisco.
(count)	There **are (very) few** tourists in small towns.
(non-count)	There **is (very) little** cold weather in San Francisco.
(count)	There **aren't any** diamond mines in Ohio.
(count)	There **are no** diamond mines in Ohio.
(non-count)	There **isn't any** snow in Honolulu.
(non-count)	There **is no** snow in Honolulu.

PRACTICE 4-1   Large Quantities

Make true *sentences using the noun cues with one of the following quantity expressions. Make the noun plural if necessary. Begin each sentence with* **THERE IS / ARE. . . .** *Fill in empty brackets with your own cues.*

a great many, a great deal of, quite a few, quite a bit of

EXAMPLE   snow / Alaska
               There's a great deal of snow in Alaska.

1. crime / large cities
2. educational opportunity / Cincinnati
3. university / Boston
4. volcano / Hawaii
5. oil / Saudi Arabia
6. desert / [   ]
7. economic problem / [   ]
8. tourism / [   ]
9. tourist / [   ]
10. sunny weather / [   ]
11. pollution / [   ]
12. [   ] / in my hometown
13. [   ] / Africa
14. [   ] / India
15. [   ] / Australia
16. [   ] / in this country

PRACTICE 4-2   Limited Quantities

A.   Use each of the following cues to form a **YES/NO** *question with* **MUCH** *or* **MANY**. *Make the noun plural if necessary. Answer the question with one of these quantity expressions:*

only a few, only a little, very few, very little

EXAMPLES   Seattle / snow
               Question: Does Seattle have **much** snow?
                           (Is there **much** snow in Seattle?)

               Answer: No, it doesn't. It gets **very little** snow.
                           (No, there isn't. It has **only a little** snow.)

               Ohio / big earthquake
               Question: Does Ohio have **many** earthquakes?
               Answer: No, it doesn't. There are **very few** big earthquakes in Ohio.

1. smog / Pittsburgh
2. highway / here / sixty years ago
3. town / Antarctica
4. news about your country / American TV
5. air pollution / the Rocky Mountains
6. health club / the United States / fifty years ago
7. doctor / rural areas of the United States

B. *What are some of the things that you like about this city or town?*

1. I like the fact that there is a great deal of . . .
2. There is also very little . . .
3. In addition, there are quite a few . . .
4. There are very few . . .
5. It is also nice that there is (are) . . .

C. *What are some things that you do not like about this city or town?*

1. Unfortunately, it has quite a bit of . . .
2. I don't like the fact that there isn't much . . .
3. There are a great many . . .
4. There are very few . . .
5. In addition, there is (are) . . .

CLOSE-UP   Limited Quantities

What is the difference between the underlined sentences in the following conversations?

A. (It's Monday. Rudy has one dollar. He isn't planning to spend it today.)

Jim: Hey, Rudy! Do you have any money you could lend me? I forgot my wallet.

Rudy: <u>I think I have **a little money.**</u> Yes. Right here. <u>I have **a few quarters.**</u> Is a dollar okay?

Jim: Great. Thanks.

B. (It's Friday. Rudy has one dollar. He needs it to buy some gas for his car.)

Bob: Listen, Rudy. Do you have an extra dollar on you? I'll pay you back first thing Monday.

Rudy: Sorry, Bob. <u>I have **very little money**</u> on me today. And I need the **few quarters** <u>I have to buy some gas.</u>

The difference between **A LITTLE / A FEW** and **LITTLE / FEW** is a difference in the attitude of the speaker. The difference is not in the quantity.

Use **A FEW** and **A LITTLE** to communicate that something exists.

Plural count noun: a few (= several)

A few people signed up for the trip, so we're going.

Non-count noun: a little (= some)
I have **a little** money I can lend you.

Use **FEW** and **LITTLE** to communicate that something is insufficient or less than expected.

Plural count noun: (very) few (= not many)
Few people signed up for the trip. We're not going.

Non-count noun: (very) little (= not much)
I have **little** money today. I can't lend you any.

Close-Up

PRACTICE   **CONTRAST OF SMALL AND LIMITED QUANTITIES**

A.   *Look at the highlighted expression in each of the following sentences. Choose the phrase that means almost the same thing.*

EXAMPLE   I **have a little** money. (= I have some money.)

　　　　　　　　(a.) have some   b. don't have much   c. don't have many

1.   I can't talk to you right now. I **have very little** time. My next class starts soon.

   a. have some   b. don't have much   c. don't have many

2.   If you need to talk to me, I **have a little** free time after lunch. Come by then.

   a. have some   b. don't have much   c. don't have many

3.   The transportation system here isn't adequate. There are **few** buses that go near my home after 6:00 P.M.

   a. some   b. not much   c. not many

4.   I'm sure you can get to that shopping center by bus. **A few** buses stop there at different times during the day.

   a. several   b. not much   c. not many

B.   *Replace the highlighted expression in each of the following sentences with one of these expressions: LITTLE, A LITTLE; FEW, A FEW. Make any necessary changes in the verb.*

EXAMPLES   I have **some** money.
　　　　　　　　I have a little money.

　　　　　　　　I **don't have much** money.
　　　　　　　　I have little money.

1.   The desert **doesn't get much** rain.
2.   The grass looks green today because we got **some** rain last night.
3.   We had **some** problems with our electricity because of the storm earlier.
4.   I'd like to get **some** information about the geography of your country.
5.   **Not many** Americans know a lot about other countries.
6.   I **don't get much** mail because I **don't write many** letters.

FOCUS 5 Counting and Measuring

In order to count non-count nouns, use other count nouns as counting words. For example, we can measure coffee by counting *pounds, cans,* or *cups:*

two cups of coffee, **one pound of** coffee, **several cans of** coffee

A. Ways to count non-count nouns

Non-Count	Examples of Counting Words
jewelry	two necklaces, a ring, several bracelets, a few pieces of jewelry
furniture	two chairs, a table, one bed, several pieces of furniture
equipment	a few machines, cranes, trucks, tools, a large piece of equipment
news	an article, a story, several news items
mail	two letters, packages, parcels; a few pieces of mail
luggage, baggage	four suitcases, one bag, two pieces of luggage
clothing	shirts, dresses, several articles of clothing
homework	assignments, exercises, two pages of reading
vocabulary	fifty words
money	fifty cents, two dollars, two dimes

B. Items at the supermarket

1. To count food items and liquids, use a measurement or container.

   Examples of measurements: two **pounds of** beef, a **quart of** milk, several **gallons of** ice cream

   Examples of containers: one **jar of** coffee, three **bottles of** soda, a few **cartons of** milk, a **box of** rice

2. Some items have special counting words:

   two **heads of** lettuce (cabbage, cauliflower)
   a **bunch of** grapes (carrots, celery, bananas)
   ten **ears of** corn
   one **loaf** / two **loaves of** bread
   four **bars** of soap (chocolate)
   several **sticks of** butter (margarine)

3. Money can be used to measure some things:

   ten dollars' worth of gas; **three dollars' worth of** grapes

C. Asking questions about specific quantities: HOW MUCH, HOW MANY

Use the question phrases **HOW MUCH + (non-count noun)** and **HOW MANY + (plural count noun)** to ask for a specific quantity of something.

How much time do you spend studying every day?	I spend three hours.
How many books do you have for this class?	We have two books.

PRACTICE 5-1   Specific Quantities

A.   Use the following cues to form questions with HOW MUCH or HOW MANY. Your classmate should answer each question with a complete sentence.

exercise / get?

              Student A: **How much exercise** do you get?

              Student B: I get about an hour of exercise a day.

1.   homework / have last night?
2.   luggage / bring to this country?
3.   jewelry / wear every day?
4.   mail / get last week?
5.   furniture / have in your room?
6.   egg / eat for breakfast?
7.   sugar / put in your tea (or coffee)?
8.   language / speak?
9.   water / drink every day?
10.   state / the United States?
11.   money / have with you today?
12.   key / carry with you every day?
13.   fruit / eat every day?
14.   rice / buy every week?

B.   *Name some of the things that are in your refrigerator and kitchen cupboards at home. Be sure to give specific quantities.*

EXAMPLES   I have **three sticks of margarine** in my refrigerator.

                 There is **a carton of milk** in my refrigerator.

GETTING READY TO FOCUS

Articles in English

Does your language have articles similar to **A, THE,** or **SOME?** Choosing an appropriate article in English can be confusing, especially if your language does not have articles, or if your language has different rules for articles.

The nouns in the following examples have different articles, and some of them don't have any articles. Can you explain their different meanings?

Jill likes **tea.**	Marc collects **rare stamps.**
She got **some tea** from a specialty store.	He has **some rare stamps** from England.
The tea that she got there was very expensive.	His uncle gave him **the English stamps.**

This section of the chapter will focus on some basic guidelines for using English articles. These guidelines can help you to choose appropriate articles when you write or speak.

FOCUS 6   Referring to General Categories of Things

A.   "Zero" article

The most common way to talk about things in general is to use a plural or non-count noun with *no* article.

plural (no article):   I'm allergic to cats. Cats make me sneeze. (*all cats; no specific cats*)

non-count (no article):   I don't drink coffee. Coffee gives me a stomachache. (*coffee in general*)

B.   A / AN*

A singular noun with the article **A** or **AN** can also refer to a general category. A singular noun most often has a general meaning in definitions or general rules.

A / AN + *singular noun:* A child needs love. (*a general rule about children*)

A saw is a tool for cutting wood. (*a definition*)

PRACTICE 6-1   General Reference to Things

A.   Use any appropriate noun from the following list to complete each sentence. Make the noun plural if necessary.

foreign car	snow	thunder	folk song
fruit	scary movie	hard test	uncooked meat
jeans	rainy day	jazz	pizza
book	snake	classical music	
French perfume	dog	rock music	

1. _____ is / are expensive in my country.

2. _____ is / are not expensive in my country.

3. I love _____.

4. I don't like _____.

5. I'm afraid of _____.

6. I don't like to listen to _____.

B.   British English and American English sometimes use different words for the same item. Match each British expression to its equivalent expression in American English. Then make a definition using the verb BE. Use the article A / AN where appropriate.

EXAMPLES   Nail varnish is nail polish.

A flat is **an** apartment.

British English		American English	
1.	lorry	a.	wrench
2.	lift	b.	French fries
3.	chips	c.	highway
4.	nail varnish	d.	potato chips
5.	flat	e.	truck
6.	pub	f.	apartment
7.	spanner	g.	elevator
8.	windscreen	h.	nail polish
9.	motorway	i.	bar
10.	crisps	j.	windshield

---

*Use the article **A** before singular nouns that begin with a consonant sound: *a house, a store, a park.*
Use the article **AN** before singular nouns that begin with a vowel sound: *an hour, an umbrella, an island.*

Referring to Specific Items

A. Some rules for using THE

The definite article **THE** can occur with singular, plural, and non-count nouns. Use the article **THE** with a noun when both the speaker and the listener know the specific thing(s) it is referring to. The speaker and the listener may know the item(s) for any of the following reasons.

1. There is only one: **The sun** is bright today.
   Please close **the door.**

2. The context specifies which one(s):   Do **the problems** on page 5.
   The party last night was fun.

3. It has been mentioned before: Albert: I bought a book and a calculator today.
   Mimi: Was **the calculator** expensive?

B. Contrasting general and specific nouns

Following are some examples that show the difference between a specific noun and a noun that refers to a general category.

General (no article)	Specific (THE + noun)
I drink **tea.**	I didn't drink **the tea** on the counter because it was too strong for me.
Tea relaxes me.	**The tea** in that store is very expensive.
I don't like **dogs.**	I don't like **the dog** that bit my child.
	I don't like **the dogs** that live next door.

Note: Do not use the article **THE** to refer to general categories of nouns.

[MISTAKE: There isn't a dog in the world that I like. I simply don't like ~~the~~ dogs.]

C. Special nouns

There are some nouns that almost always take the definite article **THE** even when the listener doesn't know the specific identity of the noun. Notice that these nouns are names of places and things that are familiar to us.*

I went to **the store.**   I went to **the post office.**
I went to **the mall.**   I went to **the bank.**
I went to **the dentist.**   I went to **the park.**
I went to **the doctor.**   I went to **the zoo.**
I went to **the hospital.**   I went to **the beach.**
I went to **the movies.**   I turned on **the radio.**
                                  I often talk on **the phone.**

PRACTICE 7-1   Referring to Specific Items

Fill in each blank with the appropriate form of the noun in parentheses. It may be necessary to use a plural form or to add an article.

EXAMPLES   (child) <u>Children</u> need love.
      (child) <u>A child</u> needs love.
      (child) <u>The children</u> who live next door are very noisy.

---

*Some nouns do not use an article: **go to jail, go to school, watch TV, go to bed.**

1. (life) It sometimes seems that _____ is not fair.
2. (life) _____ of a singer is not always as much fun as it may seem.
3. (movie) I enjoyed _____ we saw together last week.
4. (detective movie) I go to _____ all the time.
5. (noise) _____ from your radio is bothering me. Could you turn it down a little?
6. (noise) Did you know that _____ can cause stress?
7. (city / town) _____ is bigger than

   _____.

8. (city / town) _____ are bigger than

   _____.

9. (town) _____ where I grew up is famous for its hot springs.

FOCUS 8   Referring to Unidentified Things

Use the *indefinite* articles **A, AN,** and **SOME** or *no article* to refer to items that have not been mentioned or identified before. Use the indefinite article if either the listener or the speaker does not know the particular item. Indefinite articles are often used to mention a noun for the first time.

A.   Indefinite singular nouns: Use A or AN

I saw **a good movie** last night. [*The movie is mentioned for the first time; the listener does not know which movie.*]

Do you have **a pen** I can borrow? [*The speaker does not have a particular pen in mind.*]

B.   Indefinite plural and non-count nouns: Use SOME or no article

I bought **some new shoes** yesterday. I bought **new shoes** yesterday. [*The listener does not know which shoes.*]

We got **some mail** this morning. We got **mail** this morning. [*The listener does not know which mail.*]

PRACTICE 8-1   Contrasting Definite and Indefinite Articles

A.   *Read each sentence. Then use the cues to ask for additional information about the highlighted noun. Answer the question using your imagination.*

EXAMPLE   Michelle took **a train** to Baltimore last month.
                 (where / she / catch / train?)

                      Question: Where did she catch the train?
                      Answer: She caught it in Washington, D.C.

1.   Michelle visited **an aquarium** and several art museums on her trip to Baltimore.
      (what / she / see / aquarium?)

2. There were **some stingrays** and many different kinds of tropical fish there.
(stingrays / big?)

3. Michelle watched **a museum attendant** feed some of the stingrays.
(what / attendant / feed / stingrays?)

4. There was also **a very playful dolphin** at the aquarium.
(what / dolphin / do?)

B. *Read the following conversation out loud. Add the articles* **A, AN, SOME,** *and* **THE** *where necessary. Some of the blanks do not need any articles.*

NICOS: What did you do this past weekend?

ELENI: I visited Sea World.

NICOS: What's that?

ELENI: It's _____ big marine park near Cleveland.

NICOS: What do they have there?

ELENI: They have _____ dolphins, _____ aquarium, and lots of shows.

NICOS: What kind of shows?

ELENI: There is _____ show with _____ killer whale.

_____ whale performs _____ wonderful tricks.

_____ announcer usually gives _____ audience

_____ scientific information about _____ whales.

NICOS: What else is there?

ELENI: There is _____ animal show with _____ sea lions and

_____ otter. _____ sea lions are very funny, and

_____ otter is cute.

NICOS: I have never heard of _____ sea lions or _____ otters.

ELENI: Both of them are _____ mammals that can swim and get

_____ food from the sea.

FOCUS 9 Possession

English has a special form of nouns and pronouns to show that something belongs to someone. The following is a review of **possessive forms.**

A. Possessive nouns
Use the following possessive words before the noun to show possession:

singular noun + 'S	This is my **friend's** dictionary.
regular* plural noun + '	The **students'** grades were all very high.
irregular* plural noun + 'S	The **men's** locker room has a sauna.

---

*Regular plural nouns end in −**S**; use an apostrophe (') to make them possessive. Irregular nouns do not end with −**S**; use (**'S**) to make them possessive.

B.   Possessive determiners: MY, YOUR, HIS, HER, ITS, THEIR, OUR

Possessive determiners occur with all types of nouns.

These books belong to me.	They're **my** books.
Could you drive to the party?	**Your** car is big enough to take all of us.
These keys belong to Mary.	She always loses **her** keys.
The new student is Korean.	**His** name is Mr. Park.
The students have an idea.	**Their** idea sounds interesting.
I am not familiar with this machine.	What is **its** function?
This room is for us.	It's **our** room.

C.   Possessive pronouns: MINE, YOURS, HIS, HERS, THEIRS, OURS

Use **possessive pronouns** instead of a possessive word and a noun. Because they are pronouns, these words do not occur with a noun; they stand alone. They can refer to all types of nouns.

These are my books.	They're **mine.**
Let's take your car.	**Yours** is big enough for everyone.
This coat is Mr. Park's.	This coat is **his.**
These are Mary's keys.	They're **hers.**
This was the students' idea.	The idea was **theirs.**
This is our room.	This room is **ours.**

Note: There is *no* possessive pronoun for ITS. ITS always occurs with a noun.

D.   Asking about possession: WHOSE

Use the question word **WHOSE** or **WHOSE + (noun)** to find out who something belongs to. **WHOSE** can occur with all types of nouns.

This isn't my pen. **Whose** is it?	I think it's the teacher's.
Whose pen fell on the floor?	Mine did.
Whose pen did you borrow?	My roommate's.

PRACTICE 9–1   Possession

*Read the following sentences and then ask questions with **WHOSE** to find out whom the items belong to. Your classmate should answer each question with his or her own ideas.*

EXAMPLE   Student A: I didn't use my own book in class today.
               Student B: **Whose book** did you use?
               Student A: My roommate's.

1.   John didn't use his own calculator during the test this morning.
2.   Maria drove to school today, but she didn't drive her own car.
3.   Professor Smith read some poems in class today, but they weren't her own poems.
4.   The Thompsons never use their own lawn mower when they cut their grass.
5.   Somebody's car is in front of the house.

Small Group Presentations

TOPIC 1:   **The Ideal Vacation:** Divide into groups. Each group will plan a week's vacation for the class. The vacation will be next month. Discuss where you would like to go. Talk about the possible advantages and disadvantages of some different places, but do not worry about the cost of the trip! Once your group decides on a place, tell the rest of the class about it. Explain why your group chose this place. Here are some suggestions for places to go: Washington, D.C., Florida, Hawaii, Colorado, Texas, New York City, Toronto, Montreal, San Francisco, or any other place of your choice.

TOPIC 2:   **Places Rated in Your Native Country:** At the beginning of this chapter, you read about the top rated cities in the United States and Canada. Now, think about your native country (or a country where you have spent a lot of time). In your opinion, what is the best city or town to live in there? Why do you think so? (You can do this either as an individual presentation or as a group presentation with classmates who come from or are familiar with the same country.)

Writing Practice

Write a short composition on one of the following topics. Pay attention to some of the things you have practiced about nouns in this chapter: **subject/verb agreement, pronoun agreement, articles and determiners, quantity words.**

TOPIC 1:   In a short composition, discuss the strengths and weaknesses of one particular city or town as a place to live or study. Consider, for example, cultural, educational, and recreational opportunities, climate, environment, transportation, housing, cost of living, job outlook, and anything else that is important to you. Choose a place that you are familiar with, such as your hometown, a famous city in your country, or the community where you are living right now.

TOPIC 2:   In a short composition, write about a place in your country that is a good place for a vacation. Be sure to give your reasons for recommending this place. If you like, you can begin your composition like this:

If you want to take a vacation in my country, the best place to go is . . .

Chapter Exercises

Singular and Plural

Choose the words that best complete each sentence.

1.   My pants _____ too small. I can't wear
        (is / are)

_____ anymore.
     (it / them)

2. The children _____ outside when it began to rain, so
   (was / were)
   _____ came inside.
   (he / they)
3. A police officer _____ many different responsibilities.
   (has / have)
4. In some countries, the police _____ carry guns.
   (doesn't / don't)
5. Did you see the TV miniseries about the American Civil War?

   _____ started last night.
   (It / They)
6. I hurt my tooth. I think _____ broken.
   (it's / they're)
7. Clothes from Korea and China _____ often quite
   (is / are)
   inexpensive.

8. The fish in that aquarium _____ from many different
   (is / are)
   parts of the world.

9. This pair of scissors _____ very sharp.
   (isn't / aren't)
10. The scissors over there on the table _____ much
    (is / are)
    better.

EXERCISE 2 Count and Non-Count Nouns

*Use the cues to form sentences with **THERE + BE + A LOT OF**. . . . Make the noun plural if necessary, and choose an appropriate verb tense. Add any necessary prepositions. Fill in empty brackets with your own cues.*

EXAMPLES
tornado / Texas
There **are a lot of** tornadoes in Texas.

heavy rain / last week
There **was a lot of** heavy rain last week.

1. old clothes / my closet
2. advice for students / that magazine
3. poverty / many parts of the world
4. news about the economy / *The Wall Street Journal**
5. fresh tomato / grocery store / summer
6. snow / Chicago / last winter
7. nice beach / [   ]
8. humidity / [   ]

The Wall Street Journal is a highly respected American newspaper that specializes in news about business and the economy.

EXERCISE 3   Subject–Verb and Pronoun Agreement

Choose the words that best complete each sentence.

1. The information in that article _____ true.
   (isn't / aren't)
   _____ totally wrong.
   (It's / They're)

2. Groceries _____ expensive these days.
   (is / are)

3. Food _____ expensive these days.
   (is / are)

4. I love your shorts! Where did you buy _____?
   (it / them)

5. The teacher gave us a lot of _____.
   (homework / homeworks)
   _____ very difficult.
   (It was / They were)

6. Farming _____ an important source of income for this
   (is / are)
   area.

7. A lot of _____ _____ financial trouble.
   (farm / farms)   (has / have)

8. California has _____.
   (a good weather / good weather)

9. This unit has a lot of vocabulary. I can't learn _____.
   (it all / them all)

10. I bought a lot of _____ yesterday. When I got home, I
    (bread / breads)
    discovered that _____ old and stale, so I took
    (it was / they were)
    _____ back.
    (it / them)

EXERCISE 4   Much or Many

*Complete these sentences by using **MUCH** or **MANY** with each noun cue indicated.*
Make the noun plural if necessary.

EXAMPLE   The theater is crowded. There isn't / (aren't) **many** seats left.

1. Sam is getting bald. He doesn't have _____ left.
   (hair)

2. This town has _____, but it doesn't get
   (foreign restaurant)
   _____.
   (foreign film)

3. Fortunately, the teacher didn't give us _____ over the
   (homework)
   weekend.

4. The United States imports _____ from Japan.
   (car)

5. There (isn't / aren't) _____ in your field.
   (job)

6. Do you have _____?
   (clothes)

7. Does Scotland sell _____?
   (wool)

8. Do people in Scotland raise _____?
   (sheep)

EXERCISE 5 **General Quantities**

A.   Write true *sentences using the cues. In each sentence, use one of the following quantity expressions. You may use an expression more than once if necessary.*

a great deal of	a great many	a	very few	not many
quite a bit of	quite a few	several	very little	not much
a lot of	many			not any

EXAMPLE   dance company / Pittsburgh

Pittsburgh has a great many dance companies.
(There are many dance companies in Pittsburgh.)

1.   snow / my country
2.   oil / Saudi Arabia
3.   student from my country / this class
4.   oil / Japan
5.   traffic / small towns
6.   desert* / my country
7.   nice disco / this city
8.   nightlife** / this city
9.   good movie / TV / last night
10.   American TV show / TV / my country

B.   *Choose a city, state, province, or country that you know something about. Complete the following sentences.*

I'm going to write about _____.

1.   *Strengths:*

_____ has a great deal of _____.
         (name of place)
It also has quite a few _____.

It doesn't have much _____.

2.   *Weaknesses:*

It has very little _____.

In addition, it has too much _____.

It has many _____.

EXERCISE 6   **FEW / LITTLE and A FEW / A LITTLE**

*Fill in each blank with **VERY FEW, A FEW, VERY LITTLE,** or **A LITTLE.***

1.   I couldn't work in my garden last week because we had

_____ good weather.

---

* = count noun

** = non-count noun

2. We had _____ good weather last week, so I was able to cut the grass.

3. The test was more difficult than I expected. I had

_____ trouble with _____ questions.

4. David thought the test was easy. He had _____

trouble answering the questions. There were _____ answers that he didn't know.

5. The city government closed the swimming lake when they

discovered _____ pollution. A month later, they

reopened it when they were sure that _____ pollution remained.

6. I might be late for the party because I still have

_____ work to do.

EXERCISE 7 Questions and Answers

Answer each question with a complete sentence.

1. Approximately how much mail do you get every month?
2. How many letters do you write a month?
3. How much money do you spend on phone calls to your country every month?
4. How much luggage did you bring with you to this country?
5. How much bread do you eat every day?

EXERCISE 8 General Reference

Fill in each blank with the correct form of the noun indicated. Keep in mind that all of these nouns refer to general categories.

1. For some people, the most important thing in _____
(life)

is _____.
(money)

2. Some people measure _____ in _____.
(success)   (dollar)

3. Other people say that _____ can't buy
(money)

_____.
(happiness)

4. _____ (is / are) more important than
(good health)

_____.
(material thing)

5. _____ without _____ would be very
(life)   (child)
empty.

6. I am very interested in _____ and
(nature)

_____.
(wild animal)

7. Everyone has a different definition of _____.
(beauty)

EXERCISE 9   Definitions and General Rules

Fill in the blank with the appropriate form of the noun. Add the article A/AN if necessary.

1. _____ takes a lot of work.
     (baby)
2. _____ take a lot of work.
     (baby)
3. _____ is _____ for opening
     (bottle opener)   (utensil)
   _____.
     (bottle)
4. _____ is a type of meat.
     (lamb)
5. _____ is _____.
     (lamb)   (baby sheep)
6. _____ are _____.
     (lamb)   (baby sheep)

EXERCISE 10   General or Specific Reference

Fill in each blank with the correct form of the noun indicated. Use THE if it is necessary.

1. I don't enjoy watching _____ on TV.
                              (violence)
2. I couldn't believe _____ that was in the movie last
                          (violence)
   night.
3. It takes a long time for _____ to reach my country.
                                (letter)
4. I received a letter from the Internal Revenue Service yesterday.

   _____ said that I owed _____ some
     (letter)   (government)
   money.
5. _____ is beautiful. It always makes things look clean.
     (snow)
6. _____ last night made driving very difficult.
     (snow)

EXERCISE 11   Using Articles

Fill in each blank with the appropriate article: A, AN, SOME, or THE. If no article is necessary, write an "X" in the space.

EXAMPLE   I like ___X___ funny movies. I went to ___a___ funny movie
               yesterday.

1. SUE: What did you do last night?

   DAN: I went to _____ double-feature movie.

   SUE: How were _____ movies?

DAN: _____ first movie was terrible. It was _____ science-fiction movie. I don't like _____ science-fiction movies very much. But _____ second film was _____ detective story. It was great!

SUE: That's funny. I don't like _____ detective stories, but I love to go to _____ science-fiction movies. I like to read _____ science fiction too. In fact, I'm reading _____ interesting short story by Ray Bradbury. It's about _____ mysterious child.

2. BOB: I went to _____ fantastic party last weekend. _____ food there was great! _____ music was great! And _____ people there were a lot of fun.

MARY: Did you go alone?

BOB: No. I went with _____ friends.

MARY: Did you drive?

BOB: No. I got _____ ride with them. I met _____ nice people from Mexico there. They played _____ Mexican music, and they taught us _____ Mexican dance. I had _____ good time. While I was there, I ran into _____ old friend of mine from high school. I enjoyed talking to her. It's fun to see _____ old friends.

6 Activities in Progress

THE BIG PICTURE

The Present Progressive Tense
The Past Progressive Tense
Time Clauses
Stative Verbs

AT A GLANCE

Capturing the Moment

Motion Photography

FIGURE 6–1

What is the man in the picture doing (Fig. 6–1)? Is he moving? How can you tell?

Photographers can take a special kind of picture to indicate that an activity is in progress. They can also use photographs to "freeze" and focus on an activity at one particular point.

> **Like photographers, English speakers can choose a verb form that focuses on an activity while it is in progress. To focus on a particular point in the middle of an activity, English uses the progressive form. In this chapter, you will practice talking about activities in progress right now and in the past.**

FOCUS I Forming the Present Progressive Tense

A. Forming present progressive verbs

All progressive verbs have a form of the auxiliary **BE** followed by an **-ING verb.** To talk about activities in progress now, use the present form of the auxiliary **BE (AM,**

IS, ARE) with an **-ING verb.** You can find the spelling rules for **-ING** verbs in Appendix A. To make the verb negative, add **NOT** to the auxiliary or use a negative contraction.

Subject	+	BE (not) + -ING Verb	+	Rest of Sentence
The man		**is riding**		his bicycle.
He		**isn't winning**		at the moment.
Many people		**are watching**		the race.
They		**aren't riding**		in the race themselves.
I		**am trying**		to take some photos.

B.   Questions, answers, and short forms

To form a question, move the auxiliary **BE** before the subject. Use a form of the auxiliary **BE** for short forms.

Is the man **winning** the race?	No, he **isn't.**
Are the people **cheering** for him?	Yes, they **are.**
What **are** you **doing?**	I'**m taking** pictures.
Why **is** he **wearing** a helmet?	To protect his head.
Where **are** the crowds **standing?**	They'**re standing** by the road.
Who **is winning?**	An Italian man **is.**
Who **is cheering?**	The spectators **are.**
Who **are** you **taking** pictures of?	Of the racers.
You'**re using** special film, **aren't** you?	Yes, I **am.**
That guy **isn't winning, is** he?	No, he **isn't.**
Are you **enjoying** the race?	Yes, I **am. Are** you?
The German rider **is dropping out** of the race.	He **is?**
We **are cheering** for that rider.	So **am** I.

PRACTICE 1-1   Questions and Answers

Use the following cues to ask questions about the pictures (Figs. 6–2 through 6–7). Add any necessary prepositions. Your classmate should respond to each question with a complete sentence or a short answer.

EXAMPLES   Look at Figure 6–1.
(what / the man / do?)
Student A: What **is** the man **doing?**
Student B: He'**s riding** in a race.

(he / win?)
Student A: **Is** he **winning?**
Student B: No, he **isn't.** He'**s losing.**

FIGURE 6–2

1. what / these children / do?
2. where / they / play?

FIGURE 6–3

3. what / the little blonde girl / do?
4. why / she / make a face?

FIGURE 6–4

5. what / the little boy / do?
6. what / the little girl / look at?

FIGURE 6–5

7. who / the little boy / talk to?
8. he / complain about / something?

FIGURE 6–6

9. what / they / do / here?

FIGURE 6–7

10. who / win / at the moment? (How do you know?)

CLOSE-UP   Prepositions with Verbs and Adjectives

A.   Combinations of verbs and prepositions

Here are some common verbs that need prepositions:

1. **complain ABOUT**   (*someone/something*)
    talk ABOUT   (*someone/something*)
    think ABOUT   (*someone/something*)

    The racers **are complaining about** the heat.
    The sportscaster **is talking about** the riders.
    The winner **is thinking about** the prize money.

2. **listen TO**   (*someone/something*)
    talk TO   (*someone*)

    I**'m listening to** the race on the radio.
    The reporter **is talking to** the winner.

3. **look FOR**   (*someone/something*)
    wait FOR   (*someone/something*)

    I**'m looking for** a seat with a good view of the race.
    The winner's family **is waiting for** him at the finish line.

B.   Combinations of adjectives and prepositions

Here are some adjectives that occur with prepositions:

1. be **excited ABOUT**   (*something*)
    be **worried ABOUT**   (*someone/something*)
    be **nervous ABOUT**   (*something*)

    The crowds **are excited about** the race.
    One of the riders **was worried about** his tires.
    Most of the riders **were nervous about** the big hills.

2. be **ready FOR**   (*someone/something*)
    be **responsible FOR**   (*someone/something*)

    The riders **are ready for** a cold drink!
    Who **is responsible for** the refreshments?

3. be **married TO**   (*someone*)

    The winner **is married to** my sister.

4. be **tired OF**   (*someone/something*)

    The winner **is tired of** the reporters' questions.

5. be **angry AT/WITH**   (*someone*)

    Some of the losers **are angry at** themselves.

You can find more combinations of verbs and adjectives with prepositions in Appendix C.

C.   Questions with preposition combinations

Include the *preposition* when using these verbs or adjectives in a question.

What are the racers talking **about?**

Who is the winner married **to?**

What are you looking **at?**

For whom are you waiting? (*very formal*)

PREPOSITION COMBINATIONS

*Use the following cues to ask questions about the pictures (Figs. 6–8 through 6–10).
Add any necessary prepositions. Your classmate should respond to each question with a
complete sentence or short answer. Use appropriate prepositions and articles in the
response.*

FIGURE 6–8

    a.   what / she / listen ?

    b.   what / she / think ?

    c.   who / she / angry ?

FIGURE 6–9

    a.   what / they / look ?

    b.   what / they / tired ?

    c.   what / they / complain ?

FIGURE 6-10

    a.   what / he / wait?

    b.   what / he / worried?

FOCUS 2   Contrasting the Simple Present Tense and the Present Progressive Tense

Answer the questions about the following examples.

FIGURE 6-11

    1.   Daniel is a university student.

        a. Does Daniel wear glasses?

        b. Is he wearing them now?

        c. Why not?

FIGURE 6–12

2. Dr. Johnson is a history professor.
   She often has to write articles about her research.

   a. What does Dr. Johnson do?
   b. What is she doing right now?

FIGURE 6–13

3. Dr. Johnson is at a cocktail party talking to her colleague, Dr. Schwartz.

   DR. SCHWARTZ: What's new with you?
   DR. JOHNSON: Well, right now, I'm writing an article about Algeria. I hope to finish it by the end of the month.

Indicate whether each of the following statements is true or false:

   a. Right now, Dr. Johnson is talking to Dr. Schwartz.
   b. Dr. Johnson started an article about Algeria sometime before the party.
   c. The article is finished.
   d. Dr. Johnson is still working on the article.

4. Jack usually drives to school. This week, however, he is taking the bus because his car is at the mechanic's.

    a. How does Jack usually get to school?
    b. How did he get to school today? Why?
    c. Do you think he ever plans to drive to school again? When?

A.   The simple present tense

The *simple present tense* refers to actions that are *not* limited to a specific time or current activity. The simple present tense refers to a habit, custom, or general fact.

> Daniel **wears** glasses. [*a general fact; he needs glasses*]
> Dr. Johnson **writes** articles about history. [*a general fact about her job*]
> Jack usually **drives** to school. [*a general habit*]

B.   The present progressive tense

The *present progressive tense* has a specific time focus: right now. It refers to activities that are limited to a specific time period. The activity started in the past, *is in progress right now,* and will end in the future. The activity is, therefore, *incomplete right now.* The present progressive tense can refer to single activities that are not complete or to activities that are repeating during a limited time period. The present progressive tense can also show that a change is in progress.

> Daniel **isn't wearing** glasses today. [*a temporary situation*]
> Dr. Johnson **is talking** to her colleague. [*one specific activity now*]
> Dr. Johnson **is writing** an article. [*a specific article not yet completed*]
> Jack **is taking** the bus this week. [*limited to "this week"*]
> More and more women **are working** nowadays. [*a change is taking place*]

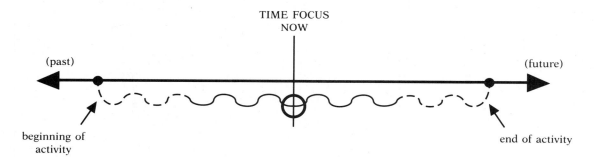

C.   Specific time expressions

The following time expressions refer to specific, limited time periods. These expressions often occur with the present progressive tense.

1. **today**

    I'm not feeling very well **today.**

2. **tonight**

    Wow! The wind is blowing awfully hard **tonight.**

3. **this** (morning/week/month/semester/year)

    This week we are studying progressive verbs.
    I'm taking several English courses **this semester.**

4. now/right now

Right now, Maria is doing a biology experiment.

5. at the moment

Dr. Johnson is working on an article **at the moment.**

6. currently

Dr. Johnson is **currently** working on an article about Algeria.

7. nowadays / these days

How are you spending your free time **these days?**

8. at present

At present, my sister is living at home, but she's looking for a house that she can afford to buy.

PRACTICE 2-1   General or Specific

Use the information about Mandy and the picture (Fig. 6–14) to answer the questions that follow.

Mandy is an engineering student at the university. Her courses are very difficult, and she has to study a lot every day. That's her guitar in the corner. She learned how to play the guitar several years ago. She enjoys playing her guitar as a way to relax.

FIGURE 6–14

1. Does Mandy play the guitar?
2. Does Mandy study a lot?
3. Does she study engineering?
4. Is she playing the guitar?
5. Is she studying her assignment?

PRACTICE 2-2   The Simple Present or Present Progressive Tense

*Use the following cues to make short dialogues. Use the **simple present tense** or the **present progressive tense**. Add necessary prepositions and articles.*

EXAMPLE   Pedro: you / take / difficult courses / this semester?
                      Are you taking difficult courses this semester?

              Millie: No, I . . .
                      No, I'm not.

1.   PEDRO: you / busy?
     MILLIE: Yes, I . . .
     PEDRO: what / you / do?
     MILLIE: I / read
     PEDRO: what / you / read?
     MILLIE: I / read / book about Martin Luther King, Jr.
     PEDRO: you / like to read / nonfiction?
     MILLIE: Yes, I . . . I / [often] read / books / famous people

2.   TINA: what / your father / do?
     ROLANDO: he / accountant
     TINA: where / he / work?
     ROLANDO: he / not work / at the moment. he / look / job

3.   CHARLENE: what / your father / do?
     MAGGIE: he / take / nap
     CHARLENE: he / [usually] take / nap / the afternoon?
     MAGGIE: Yes, he . . .

4.   DON: how / you / [usually] come / school?
     CARMEN: I / [usually] take / highway. But this week / I / drive
                through town
     DON: why / you / not take / highway / this week?
     CARMEN: they / repair / highway. traffic / slow

5.   SAM: where / you / [usually] study?
     KIM: I / [almost always] study / library // but / I / not study
             there / this week // because / they / paint

6.   KAREN: women in your country / [usually] work outside the home?
     MARIA: Not usually. But / more and more young women / start
               careers / nowadays

**GETTING
READY TO
FOCUS**   *Activities in the Past*

The Mysterious Demise of Alfred Malcom

Murder suspects and their alibis

Alfred Malcom was murdered last night. Someone poisoned him. The police
estimate the time of death to be 10:00 P.M. Here is a list of suspects.

Mary	Alfred's current wife
Alice	his ex-wife
George	his business partner
Edward	his brother

Alfred left a great deal of money to each of these people, so they all profit from his death. In the following conversation, a detective is questioning the suspects.

FIGURE 6-15

Detective:	Where were you last night at around ten o'clock, George?
George:	I was in a restaurant with some of my friends.
Detective:	Where were you, Mary?
Mary:	I was visiting my sister.
Detective:	Edward, what about you?
Edward:	Don't look at me! I was at home watching TV. You can ask my neighbors. They were watching with me.
Detective:	Were you at home last night, Alice?
Alice:	Yes, I was. I was reading a wonderful novel about World War II.
Detective:	Was anyone with you?
Alice:	No, I was alone all evening.

What were *you* doing at ten o'clock last night? Do you have an alibi? Who do you think poisoned Alfred Malcom?

FOCUS 3 The Past Progressive Tense

Last night at ten o'clock, Mary was visiting her sister, George was eating in a restaurant, Edward was watching TV, and Alice was reading a book.

What time did they start these activities?

What time did they finish?

A. Using the past progressive tense

Use the *past progressive tense* to talk about activities that were in progress at a specific past time in the past. The past progressive focuses on the activity at a specific time *in the middle of the activity.*

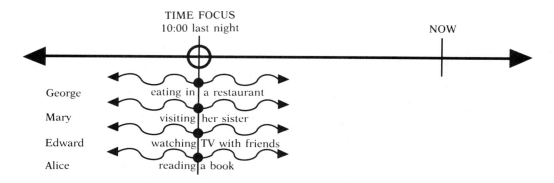

TIME FOCUS
10:00 last night

NOW

George   eating in a restaurant

Mary   visiting her sister

Edward   watching TV with friends

Alice   reading a book

B. Forming the past progressive tense

To form the **past progressive tense,** use the past tense of the auxiliary **BE (WAS, WERE)** with an **-ING verb.** To make the verb negative, add **NOT** after the auxiliary or use a negative contraction.

Subject +	BE (not) + -ING Verb +	Rest of Sentence
Edward	was watching	TV at ten o'clock last night.
His friends	were sitting	with him.
George	wasn't watching	TV.
He	was eating	in a restaurant.
I	wasn't doing	anything last night at that time.

C. Questions, answers, and short forms

To make a question, move the auxiliary **WAS** or **WERE** before the subject. Use the auxiliaries in short forms.

Were you **watching** TV with Edward at ten o'clock?   No, I **wasn't.**

Was Mary **visiting** her sister at that time?   Yes, she **was.**

Were George's friends **eating** with him?   Yes, they **were.**

What **was** Alice **doing** at the time of Alfred's death?   She **was reading.**

Where **were** George and his friends **eating?**   In a restaurant.

Who **was watching** TV with Edward?   His neighbors **were.**

You **weren't watching** TV at ten o'clock, **were** you?   No, I **wasn't.**

Alice **was reading** by herself, **wasn't** she?   Yes, she **was.**

Mary **wasn't sleeping** when Alfred died.   She **wasn't?**

George **was talking** to his friends.   So **was** Edward.

PRACTICE 3–1   Practice with the Past Progressive Tense

*Use the cues to find out what your classmate was doing at a particular time in the past. Use the **past progressive tense.** Your classmate should answer with a complete sentence.*

EXAMPLE   at 10:00 last night?

     Student A: What **were you doing** at 10:00 last night?
     Student B: I **was watching** television.

1. last Saturday at 3:00 P.M.?
2. around this time last year?

3. this morning at 7:30?
4. yesterday evening at 8:00 P.M.?
5. at midnight last night?

FOCUS 4 Time Clauses with **WHEN**

Look at Figure 6–16. Answer the questions about what was happening when the detective arrived.

FIGURE 6-16

1. What **was Mary doing** when the detective arrived?
2. What **were George and Edward doing** when the detective got there?
3. What **was Alice looking at** when the doorbell rang?

Now look at Figure 6–17. Answer the questions about what happened next.

FIGURE 6-17

1. What **did George and Edward do** when the detective came in?
2. What **did Mary do** when the detective came in?
3. What **did Alice do** when she saw the detective?

A time clause with **WHEN** shows the relationship between the action of the *main clause* and the action of the *time clause*.

A.   Activities already in progress when another action occurred

To show that one activity was already in progress at the time another action occurred, use the past progressive tense in the main clause and **WHEN** with the simple past tense in the time clause. The simple past tense verb of the time clause refers to a single event that happened in the middle of the other activity.

Main Clause: Past Progressive Tense	+	Time Clause: WHEN + Simple Past Tense
Mary **was crying**		when the detective **arrived.**
George and Edward **were talking**		when the detective **arrived.**

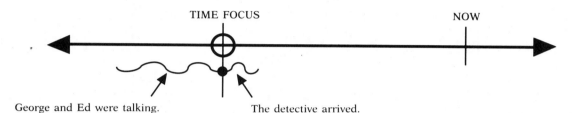

George and Ed were talking.   The detective arrived.

B.   Sequence of events: One action happening after another

To show that one action followed another action, use the simple past tense in both the main clause and in the time clause with **WHEN**. The action of the main clause occurred at the same time or immediately after the action of the time clause.

Main Clause: Simple Past Tense	+	Time Clause: WHEN + Simple Past Tense
Mary **stood up**		when the detective **came** in.
George and Edward **stopped** talking		when the detective **came** in.

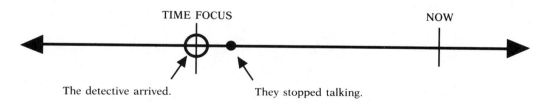

The detective arrived.   They stopped talking.

PRACTICE 4-1   Practice with the Past Progressive Tense

A.   Read each situation. Then use your imagination to answer the questions with complete sentences.

1. Dr. Johnson hurt her back yesterday.
   a. What **was she doing** when she hurt her back?
   b. What **did she do** when she hurt it?

2. Jenny was ten minutes late to class yesterday.
   a. What **were the other students doing** when she got there?
   b. What **was the teacher doing** when she got there?
   c. What **did the students do** when she came in?

B.   *Your classmate will tell you about a problem someone had yesterday. Ask a question with the past progressive tense to find out what was happening at that time. Then ask a second question using the simple past tense to find out what happened next. Use time clauses with* **WHEN.**

EXAMPLE   Student A: Jim broke his leg yesterday.
             Student B: He did?! **What was he doing when he broke it?**
             Student A: He was skiing.
             Student B: **What did he do when he broke it?**
             Student A: He started shouting for help.

1. I twisted my ankle yesterday.
2. Maria lost a contact lens yesterday.
3. Joel accidentally cut himself yesterday.
4. I dropped all my books and notebooks yesterday.

C.   *Your classmate will tell you about something that happened. Ask a question to find out* how *it happened. Your classmate will answer with a complete sentence using* **WHEN ALL OF A SUDDEN** *and any additional information that he or she wishes.*

EXAMPLE   Student A: Jim broke his leg yesterday.
             Student B: You're kidding! **What happened?**
             Student A: He was skiing **when all of a sudden** his ski fell off. When it came off, he fell and broke his leg.

1. When I flew to New York last weekend, our plane had to make an emergency landing.
2. Sylvie keeps all of her research data on her computer. Yesterday, she lost all the research information that was on her computer.
3. I almost had an accident on my way to school today.
4. David almost got a speeding ticket yesterday.

FOCUS 5   Time Clauses with **WHILE**

A.   **An action occurring during another activity**

WHILE is another connecting word for time clauses. **WHILE** refers to an activity or situation that has duration. Use **WHILE** in a time clause with the past progressive tense to mean *"during this activity."* A simple past tense verb in the main clause refers to an action that interrupted or occurred in the middle of the activity of the time clause.

Main Clause: Simple Past Tense	+	Time Clause: WHILE* + Past Progressive Tense
Jim **broke** his leg		while he **was skiing.**
Some friends **came** over		while I **was studying** last night.
I **ran into** an old friend		while I **was shopping** the other day.

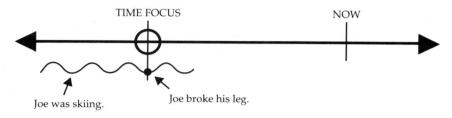

TIME FOCUS   NOW

Joe was skiing.   Joe broke his leg.

PRACTICE 5-1   Time Clauses with **WHILE**

*Combine the following pairs of cues to make sentences with **WHILE**. Use the simple past tense and past progressive tense. Add necessary articles and prepositions. Change nouns to pronouns as necessary. Fill in empty brackets with your own cues.*

EXAMPLES   a. Jim / break / leg
            b. Jim / ski

          Jim broke his leg while he was skiing.

          a. the politician / give / speech
          b. the politician / make / mistake

          While the politician was giving a speech, she made a mistake.

1.   a. I / fall asleep
     b. I / watch TV
2.   a. Jason / walk / on ice
     b. Jason / fall down
3.   a. Ruth / find / ten dollars
     b. Ruth / jog / park
4.   a. the patient / finish / magazine
     b. the patient / wait to see / doctor
5.   a. I / clean / house / yesterday
     b. [   ]

FOCUS 6   Stative Verbs and Activity Verbs

A.   **Introduction to stative verbs**

Certain types of verbs in English do not normally occur in progressive tenses. These verbs are called *stative verbs.* Verbs that have a stative meaning are describing a situation. They do not indicate any type of action. Stative verbs are usually formed with the *simple tenses,* even when the event they refer to occurs during a specific, limited time.

---

*It is also possible to use **WHEN** in time clauses with the past progressive tense: Jim broke his leg **when he was skiing.**

1. I **have** a headache at the moment.

   [In this sentence, **HAVE** is a stative verb. Use simple present tense even though the time focus is "at the moment."]

2. I **was** at home when Joe came in.

   [The verb **BE** is a stative verb. Use the simple past tense instead of the past progressive tense.]

B.   Examples of stative verbs

Here are some common verbs that normally have stative meanings. These verbs most often occur with the simple tenses. They do not normally occur with the progressive tenses.

   1. Verbs of description or appearance

be	I **am** tired at the moment.
resemble	With all those winter clothes on, you **resemble** a snowman.
seem	George **seemed** worried about something when I saw him today.
sound	Your idea **sounds** pretty good to me.

   2. Verbs of attitudes, opinions, and emotions

appreciate	We **appreciate** the help you are giving us.
believe	I **don't believe** a word that you are saying.
feel (= *"hold an opinion"*)	The teacher **feels** that the students are working very hard.
think (= *"hold an opinion"*)	The teacher **thinks** that the students are working very hard.
like	I **like** this song that they are playing on the radio.

   Other examples of stative verbs that express attitude, opinion, or emotion are:

   doubt, imagine, intend, mean, hate, love, want, wish, mind, matter, prefer

   3. Verbs of mental perception

know	I **don't know** what you are talking about!
realize	**Do** you **realize** what you're saying?
understand	I **didn't understand** what the professor was talking about.

   Other examples of stative verbs of mental perception are:

   forget, remember, guess, remind, recognize

   4. Verbs of measurement

cost	One English class **costs** a lot of money these days.
weigh	The last time Mary checked, she **weighed** 120 pounds.
equal	The money in this piggy bank **equals** $30.00.

   5. Verbs of possession, existence, or relationship

belong to	This car **belongs to** me now. John sold it to me yesterday.
consist of	This homework tonight **consists of** several workbook exercises.
have	We sure **have** a lot of homework today.

6. Examples of other common stative verbs include:

contain, exist, need, owe, own, possess

C. Verbs that can have a stative meaning *or* can refer to an activity

Some verbs occur as stative verbs with one meaning and as activity verbs with a different meaning. When these verbs have a stative meaning, they do not normally occur in the progressive tenses. However, when these verbs refer to an activity (a nonstative meaning), they can occur with the progressive tenses.

Verb	Stative Meaning	Nonstative (Activity) Meaning
think	*refers to an opinion*	*refers to an intentional mental activity*
	I **think** this is a nice city.	Please be quiet. I**'m thinking.**
	I **thought** the movie was interesting.	I **was thinking about** the test when you came in.
have	*refers to possession, existence, most illnesses, characteristics*	*occurs with idiomatic expressions*
	This room **doesn't have** heat today.	**have + (a meal, food, drink)**
	I **had** a headache when I saw you.	Sam **is having** lunch right now.
	Do you **have** the flu?	Sara **was** in the lobby **having** a cup of coffee when I saw her.
	I **have** a car.	**have + (an event)**
		It's noisy because the students **are having** a party.
		have a good time (a bad time, a hard time)
		I **was having** a wonderful time at the party when I had to leave.
		have fun
		Are you **having fun** here?
		have trouble (a problem, difficulty)
		John **is having** trouble with his car today.
Verbs of Sensation		
	describes something	*refers to an intentional activity*
look	Sam **looks** tired today.	Sam **is looking at** the blackboard.
feel	This cloth **feels** soft.	I **am feeling** the cloth.
smell	The soup **smells** wonderful.	Joe **was smelling** the soup when he burned himself.
taste	The soup **tastes** good too.	Joe **is** in the kitchen **tasting** the soup.
see*	*"be perceived by the eyes"*	*"to meet with" or "go out with"*
	I **see** what you are doing.	The doctor **is seeing** a patient in his office.
	Do you **see** that strange animal?	Joe and Susan **are seeing** a lot of each other.
hear*	*"be perceived by the ears"*	*refers to the presentation of a legal case*
	Do you **hear** something?	The judge **is hearing** a case at the moment.
	I **hear** a baby crying.	
Verbs of Measurement		
measure	*"to have a certain measurement or weight"*	*"to find out the measurement or weight"*
weigh		
	This room **measures** 10' by 12'.	The carpet layers **are measuring** the room.
	How much **does** your baby **weigh?**	The doctor **is weighing** the baby now.

*For an activity or nonstative meaning, use the verbs **LOOK (AT)** or **WATCH**. These verbs indicate that the activity is intentional and include the idea of "paying attention." *Examples:* I**'m watching** TV. The students **were looking at** some photographs when the teacher came in.

For an activity or nonstative meaning, use the verb **LISTEN (TO). This verb indicates that the activity is intentional and also includes the idea of "paying attention." *Examples:* I**'m listening,** but I don't hear anything. **Were** you **listening** when the teacher made the announcement about the test?

Simple and Progressive Tenses

Use the following cues to make short dialogues. Use appropriate verb tenses, and add any necessary articles or prepositions.

EXAMPLE

Rikka: where / you / go?

Norm: I / go / movies

Rikka: **Where are you going?**

Norm: **I'm going to the movies.**

1. BORIS: what / you / do?

   ROZ: I / fix / bicycle

   BORIS: what / happen?

   ROZ: I / ride / race // when / chain / break

   BORIS: oh no! / what / you / do?

   ROZ: I / drop out / race

   BORIS: that / too bad

   ROZ: I / upset // because / I / win // when / it / break. I / ahead of / other riders

   BORIS: who / win?

   ROZ: student / France

2. LANA: where / your roommate?

   CY: he / cut / grass

   LANA: your landlord / not [usually] cut / grass?

   CY: yes, but . . . my roommate / mow / lawn / this time // because / landlord / have / backache

   LANA: what / happen?

   CY: he / hurt / back // while / he / push / car / out of / ditch

   LANA: he / go [= *necessity*] / hospital?

   CY: no, he . . .

3. MANNY: what / you / do?

   FRANNY: I / look / cake / oven

   MANNY: how / it / look?

   FRANNY: it / look / great!

   MANNY: it / [certainly] smell / good!

Past Events

A.   Use the following pictures (Figs. 6–18 and 6–19) to tell a story about something that happened yesterday. In your own words, tell what happened. You will have to provide an ending to the story.

FIGURE 6–18

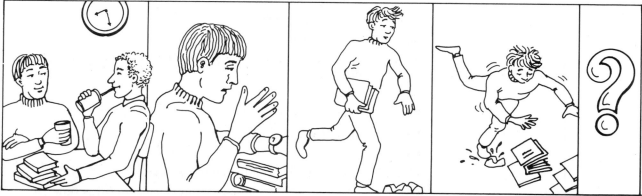

FIGURE 6–19

B.   Perhaps one or more of the experiences on the following list have happened to you. Tell your classmates about one such experience. Your classmates may wish to ask you questions.

1.   getting a speeding ticket
2.   having an accident
3.   getting lost
4.   doing something very embarrassing
5.   having a misunderstanding because of a communication problem

A WIDER ANGLE   Role Playing

In each situation, one person will play the role of a witness, and one person will play the role of a police officer. The police officer is interviewing the witness to get information for his or her report. The police officer should ask questions to find out what the witness saw. The witness should give as much information as possible.

1.   You are the only witness of an accident between a truck and a car at an intersection near your school.
2.   Two kids broke into your house last night. You caught a glimpse of them as they were running away.

Writing Practice

Write a short composition on one of the following topics.

TOPIC 1: Write about an accident or natural disaster that you witnessed or were involved in. Explain the circumstances leading up to the event, and then describe the sequence of events after the event.

TOPIC 2: Write a composition about a day when everything went wrong. Your composition can be true, or it can come from your imagination. You can write about yourself or about someone else.

Solution to the murder of Alfred Malcom:

Actually, Mary, George, and Edward all poisoned Alfred. Mary injected poison into his toothpaste before she went out. George substituted poison for Alfred's sleeping pills earlier in the day. Edward put poison in Alfred's cough syrup. The only one who did not try to kill Alfred was his ex-wife, Alice.

DEVELOPING YOUR SKILLS AND KNOWLEDGE

Chapter Exercises

EXERCISE 1 ## Questions and Answers

Complete the following exchanges by writing a question or a response in each blank. Use complete sentences.

1. (on the phone)

    SARAH: _____?
    CHEN: Yes, I am. I am *very* busy.

    SARAH: _____?
    CHEN: I'm washing all the windows in my house.
    SARAH: Washing windows! That doesn't sound like much fun. I

    never wash my windows._____

    _____?

    CHEN: I usually wash them twice a year.

    SARAH: _____?
    CHEN: I think I last washed them seven or eight months ago, so
           they're filthy.

2. SYD: Where's the director?

    PAT: _____.

    SYD: _____?
    PAT: He's talking to someone.

    SYD: Who _____?
    PAT: A new student.

    SYD: What _____?
    PAT: They're probably talking about the English language program.

EXERCISE 2 Simple Present Tense or Present Progressive Tense

*Fill in each blank with the **simple present** or **present progressive** form of the verb indicated.*

1. Sally is on vacation this week, so she _____ her
   (help)
   parents paint their house. During the semester, she

   _____ time to help them because she
   ([rarely] have)

   _____ a lot. They _____ anything
   (study [= *necessity*])   (not / paint)
   today because they _____ the first coat of paint to
                      (wait for)
   dry.

2. Frank _____ in the back row in chemistry class, but
         ([usually] sit)
   today he _____ in the front row because he forgot his
            (sit)
   glasses. The professor _____ chemistry equations on
                          (write)
   the blackboard with very small numbers and letters. Right now,

   Frank _____ to copy the formulas, but without his
         (try)
   glasses he _____ the blackboard very well, even from
              (not / read [= *ability*])
   the front row.

EXERCISE 3 Simple Past Tense or Past Progressive Tense

*Fill in each blank with the **simple past** or **past progressive** form of the verb indicated. If no verb is indicated, write an appropriate auxiliary or form of* be.

1. JOE: How _____ the weather when you

            _____ to this country?
            (get)
   PIERRE: It _____ terrible. When I

            _____ the plane, it _____,
            (get off)   (snow)
            and the wind _____ very hard. How about
                         (blow)
            when you arrived?

   JOE: I guess I _____ lucky. It

            _____ cold, but it _____.
                                           (not / snow)

2. My sister _____ her leg when she
                    (break)
_____ very young. She _____ down a
                                              (ski)
mountain when her ski suddenly _____ off, and she
                                          (come)
_____. When the safety patrol _____
        (fall)   (find)
her, she _____ in the snow.
              (lie)

EXERCISE 4   **Time Clauses**

*Use each of the following cues to make a sentence with a time clause. Use the
connecting time word WHEN or WHILE with the **simple past** or **past progressive**
form of the verb.*

   EXAMPLE   Jim / cut himself // he / shave

                   Jim cut himself **while** he was shaving.

                   (Jim was shaving **when** he cut himself.)

   1.   he / cut himself // he / scream
   2.   his wife / hear his scream // she / run to make sure he was all right
   3.   he / finish shaving // he / go into the kitchen for some coffee
   4.   he / pour his coffee // he / spill some on the counter
   5.   he / clean up the mess // he / knock over his coffee cup onto the
        floor

EXERCISE 5   **Mixed Verb Tenses**

*Fill in each blank with the appropriate form of the verb indicated. Use the **simple
present**, **simple past**, **present progressive**, or **past progressive** tense. If no verb is
indicated, write an appropriate auxiliary.*

   1.   ROD: What _____ rock music?
                           (you / think of)
        MICK: Sometimes I _____ it, but it
                                    (like)
                _____ like noise to me.
                    ([often] sound)
        ROD: _____ the song that they
                    (you / like)
                _____ on the radio right now?
                        (play)
        MICK: It _____ a nice rhythm, I guess. It's good for
                        (have)
                dancing.

   2.   GLORIA: _____ outside of the home in
                    (most women / [usually] work)
               your country?

INDIRA: Not most, but things _____. More and
(change)
more younger women _____ to establish
(begin)
their own careers. When my mother was young, women

_____ jobs outside the home. Nowadays,
([seldom] hold)
you can find women in many different professions.

3. JAN: _____ to go on the trip to Canada with the
(you / plan)
class?

SAL: No, I _____. I _____ enough
(not)   (not / have)
money. In fact, I _____ some money from Joe
(borrow)
last week. I _____ him thirty dollars. I
(owe)
_____ to spend any more money until I pay
(not / want)
him back.

JAN: Why _____ money from him?
(you / borrow)

SAL: I _____ to work last week when I
(drive)
_____ a flat tire. Joe _____
(have)   (ride)
with me at the time, so he _____ me some
(lend)
money to buy a new tire.

7 *Objects and Word Order*

Word Order Expectations

Sentence Puzzles

Puzzle 1

Read the following story. Fill in the missing information with anything that makes sense to you. You can use more than one word if you like.

Yesterday after _____, David went to the _____ to buy some

_____. When he got to the cashier, he took out his wallet and saw

that he didn't have any _____. He felt very _____. He couldn't

buy the _____. He said to _____, "Next time, I am going to be

sure to remember to _____."

How did you know what kinds of words or phrases to put in the blanks?

Puzzle 2

Look at the highlighted sentences. Do they seem strange to you? Why?

1. Jill: Where's your homework?
   Tom: **I gave.**

2. Elizabeth: I bought a new coat. **Do you like?**
   Patricia: No, **I don't like.**

3. Janice: Are my keys in the kitchen?
   Roberto: Yes, **I think you put them.**

Puzzle 3

Can you make a sentence from each of the following lists of words? Do not add, omit, or change the form of any words on the list.

1.	2.
mail carrier	David
dog	for
our	Karen
the	nice
yesterday	bought
bit	present
.	yesterday
	a
	.

Did you find more than one way to make a sentence? Did the meaning change?

You have just used your knowledge about *word order* in English to solve these sentence puzzles. Is the order of words in English different from or similar to the order of words in your language? In this chapter, you will focus on the word order patterns of different types of objects.

Objects of Verbs and Prepositions

When you hear certain verbs in English, you automatically expect a certain type of information to follow. For example, "I put" sounds very strange by itself. The listener expects to hear, "I put (something) (somewhere)."

A. Verbs with objects

Many verbs in English need to have an *object*. The *subject* of the verb performs the action. The action of the verb affects or happens to someone or something—the *direct object*.

Subject	+	Verb	+	Direct Object	+	Rest of Sentence
Our dog		bit		the mail carrier		yesterday morning.
David		didn't bring		his wallet		to the grocery store.
The teacher		can't remember		the students' names.		

The direct object comes immediately after the verb. If the verb has only one object, do not put another word or phrase between the verb and its object.

> Correct: I bought a car yesterday. Yesterday I bought a car.
>
> [MISTAKE: I bought yesterday a car.]

Here are some examples of verbs that usually need an object (*someone* or *something*).

buy	I **bought** *a new jigsaw puzzle* last week.
enjoy	Sam **enjoys** *crossword puzzles*.
do	**Do** you ever **do** *the crossword puzzle* in the newspaper?
find	**Can** you **find** *the answer* to this math puzzle?
get	Mary **got** *the game Monopoly* for her birthday this year.
hate	I **hate** *word games*.
have	**Do** you **have** *any interesting games* from your country?
like	Bill **doesn't like** *card games*.
want	Carol's mom **wants** *a new backgammon game* for Christmas.
would like	I'**d like** *a good book* about poker.

B. Objects of verbs with prepositions

Verb and preposition combinations also need an object. Here are some examples of *verb + preposition + object*.

listen to	**Do** you ever **listen to** *trivia games* on the radio?
talk about	Everybody'**s talking about** *interactive video games*.
wait for	I'**m waiting for** *a new game* that will be coming out soon.

PRACTICE 1-1 Using Objects

Use the cues to respond to each of the following questions with a complete sentence. If necessary, add a preposition.

EXAMPLE How did Sam get some extra money? (sell)

He **sold** his videocassette recorder.

1. What did Elizabeth do with the money that she won in the lottery? (buy)

2. Why couldn't Tony sleep well last night? (be worried)
3. Why did Mrs. Richards leave the concert early? (not / enjoy)
4. Where can I get information about today's weather forecast? (listen)

Pronouns as Subjects and Objects

A. Review of pronouns

Once a noun has been mentioned, it is possible to refer to the same noun with a *pronoun*. Like nouns, a *pronoun* can be the subject of a verb or the object of a verb or preposition.

Subject Pronouns	Object Pronouns	Reflexive Pronouns
I	me	myself
you	you	yourself (singular)
he	him	himself
she	her	herself
it	it	itself
we	us	ourselves
you	you	yourselves (plural)
they	them	themselves

B. Reflexive pronouns

What is the subject of the verb in each of the following sentences? What is the direct object?

Bill burned himself.   I cut myself.

If the object of the verb is the *same* as the subject of the verb, use a *reflexive pronoun* for the direct object.

Here are some special expressions with reflexive pronouns:

enjoy . . . self (*have a good time*)

I **enjoyed myself** at the party.
Did you **enjoy yourself** at the picnic?

by . . . self (*alone or without help*)

Bob did his homework **by himself.**
Terry lives **by herself.**

help . . . self, serve . . . self (*take, something that is offered without assistance*)

Help yourselves to the popcorn.
We **served ourselves** some iced tea.

PRACTICE 2-1 Using Pronouns

Complete each sentence with the appropriate pronouns.

1. TAMMY: Why is Jim upset with _____?

   JERRY: Because I spilled chocolate sauce all over

   _____.

2. MARIE: Did all of you enjoy _____ on the hike?

   JUDY: Yes. It was great, except that Mary fell down and hurt

   _____.

   MARIE: Did _____ have to go to the hospital?

   JUDY: Yes, _____ did. I took _____
   there.

3. MEL: Nobody lives with _____. I live by

   _____.

4. MR. PEREZ: Lisa, this is a buffet. There are no waiters or waitresses.
   You can go over to the serving table and help

   _____.

5. NELL: Tom cut _____ while _____
   was shaving.

FOCUS 3 Verbs with Two Objects

A. Introduction to indirect objects

Some verbs in English can occur with two objects: a *direct object* and an *indirect object*. The *indirect object* "receives" or is affected by the *direct object.*

FIGURE 7–1

Subject	+	Verb	+	Direct Object	+	Indirect Object
Jack		gave		the notebook		to Carol.

What did Jack give to Carol? The notebook.
Who did Jack give the notebook to? To Carol.

B. Word order patterns with direct and indirect objects

There are three different word order patterns for direct and indirect objects in a sentence. Different verbs require different patterns.

1. With the preposition **TO**: Direct object + **TO** + indirect object (Pattern 1)

Some verbs, particularly verbs of communication, require the preposition **TO** before the indirect object. Verbs that follow this pattern include: **announce, demonstrate, describe, explain, introduce, mention, repeat, say, speak, suggest**

Subject +	Verb +	Direct Object +	TO +	Indirect Object
I	will announce	the speaker	to	the audience.
My friend	described	her house	to	me.
The teacher	can explain	the lesson	to	the students.
Nobody	has mentioned	the problem	to	Mr. Smith.

2. With the preposition **FOR**: Direct object + **FOR** + indirect object (Pattern 2)

Certain verbs require the preposition **FOR** before the indirect object. Verbs that follow this pattern include: **answer,* cash, do, prescribe**

Subject +	Verb +	Direct Object +	FOR +	Indirect Object +	Rest of Sentence
The teacher	answered	some questions	for	the students	after class.
My neighbor	is doing	some yard work	for	me.	
The store	can't cash	a check	for	you	without proper identification.

3. No preposition: indirect object + direct object (Pattern 3)

With certain verbs, there is no preposition. In this case, the indirect object comes before the direct object. Verbs that follow this pattern include: **ask, cost, charge**

Subject +	Verb +	Indirect Object +	Direct Object +	Rest of Sentence
Some students	are asking	the teacher	a question.	
These books	cost	me	a lot of money.	
The mechanic	charged	Jim	five hundred dollars	to fix his brakes.

C.   Verbs that can use two patterns

1.   Pattern 1 and Pattern 3

Certain verbs can occur with or without the preposition **TO.** Many of the verbs in this group refer to movement of the direct object to the indirect object. Verbs in this group include: **bring, give, lend, mail, offer, owe, pass, pay, sell, send, show, take, teach, tell, write**

Pattern 1					Pattern 3			
Subject +	Verb +	Direct Object +	TO +	Indirect Object	Subject +	Verb +	Indirect Object +	Direct Object
I	gave	my notes	to	John.	I	gave	John	my notes.
You	owe	a dollar	to	Mary.	You	owe	Mary	a dollar.
He	took	a message	to	the teacher.	He	took	the teacher	a message.

---

*In conversational English, you may hear: "Answer me this . . ." or "Answer me something. . . ."

2.   Pattern 2 and Pattern 3

Certain verbs can occur with or without the preposition **FOR**. Many of the verbs in this group indicate that the direct object is created or obtained for the benefit of the indirect object. Verbs in this group include: **build, buy, cook, clean, find, fix, get, make**

Pattern 2					Pattern 3			
Subject +	Verb +	Direct Object +	FOR +	Indirect Object	Subject +	Verb +	Indirect Object +	Direct Object
I	bought	a vase	for	my mother.	I	bought	my mother	a vase.
Joe	fixed	some soup	for	himself.	Joe	fixed	himself	some soup.
Ted	made	dinner	for	Susan.	Ted	made	Susan	dinner.

D.   Special points about direct and indirect object word order

1.   Do not use a preposition if the indirect object comes before the direct object.

[MISTAKE: I bought ~~for~~ my mother a vase.]

2.   A question about an object may ask about either the direct object or the indirect object. This means that the question words **WHO** and **WHAT** can be the direct object or the indirect object of the verb in the question. If the question word is the indirect object, be sure to include the preposition.

I bought **something** for my mother.

What did you buy for your mother?

I bought a vase for **somebody.**

Who did you buy the vase for?

3.   If the direct object is a pronoun, it comes *before* the indirect object with the preposition **TO** or **FOR** (Pattern 1 or Pattern 2). In this case, do not use Pattern 3.

Direct object is a noun

I gave **a vase** to my mother. [pattern 1]
I gave my mother **a vase.** [pattern 3]

I bought **a present** for my mother. [pattern 2]
I bought my mother **a present.** [pattern 3]

Direct object is a pronoun

Question: What did you do with the vase?

    Answer: I gave **it** to my mother. [pattern 1]
        [MISTAKE: I gave my mother it.]

Question: Who is that present for?

    Answer: I bought **it** for my mother. [pattern 2]
        [MISTAKE: I bought my mother it.]

E.   Choosing which pattern to use

1.   The verb determines which word order patterns its direct and indirect objects take. You may simply have to learn which pattern(s) each verb takes.

2. If a verb allows two different patterns, use the pattern that puts the most important information or the new information as the <u>second</u> object.

Question: **Who** did you give your book to?

Answer: I gave it to **my roommate.**

["My roommate" (indirect object) is the new information.]

Question: **What** did you give to your roommate?

Answer: I gave him **my book.**

["My book" (direct object) is the new information.]

PRACTICE 3-1 Using Indirect Objects

Use the cues to respond to each of the following situations. Include a direct and indirect object in your response. For some items, there are two possible word order patterns.

EXAMPLE   John forgot to bring his wallet today. How did he pay for his lunch? (lend / some money)

His friend lent **him some money.**
His friend lent **some money to him.**

1. Luis went to Paris last year. What did he do for his parents when he came back?

   a. bring / some souvenirs
   b. show / his pictures
   c. send / postcards
   d. describe / the delicious food
   e. tell / some interesting stories

2. Ashley is ten years old. Yesterday was her mother's birthday. What did Ashley do to make her mother's birthday special?

   a. fix / breakfast in bed
   b. offer / a cup of coffee
   c. buy / a present
   d. make / a birthday cake
   e. draw / a picture

3. Last weekend, Rosa was cleaning out her attic when she found all kinds of things that she wanted to get rid of. What did she do with them?

   a. send / old photographs / her brother
   b. find / some old golf clubs / her sister
   c. give / baby clothes / her neighbor
   d. take / some old paperbacks / the local library

CLOSE-UP   **Separable Multiple-Word Verbs**

Quick quiz! In the column at the right, find the meaning of each highlighted verb.

1. Sam **filled out** his college applications yesterday.	a. extinguish
2. Please **put out** your cigarette.	b. give to the teacher
3. Henry usually **turns on** the TV as soon as he comes home.	c. complete
	d. fill up
4. I **threw away** some old notebooks.	e. get rid of
5. I have to **hand in** my homework.	f. take outside
	g. start the power

A. Introduction to multiple-word verbs

English has many common verb expressions that consist of more than one word:

verb + (prepositions / adverbs)

The preposition or adverb is part of the verb. A multiple-word verb has its own meaning, which is often different from the meaning of the verb alone.

EXAMPLES   **fill:** make a container full

fill out: complete a form

run: move quickly on foot

run into: meet someone by chance

B. Word order with separable multiple-word verbs

Some multiple-word verbs are separable. This means that the direct object can come after the two-word verb *or* between the verb and the preposition or adverb. A separable verb needs a direct object.

Sam **filled out** his application.

Sam **filled** his application **out**.

If the direct object of a separable verb is a pronoun, it *must* come between the verb and the preposition or adverb.

Correct: Sam filled **it** out.

[MISTAKE: Sam filled out **it**.]

C. Examples of separable verbs

Here are some common separable verbs. You can find many others in Appendix D. It is important to realize that many of these verbs have additional meanings.

hand in / turn in: submit something to a person who is collecting it
hand out / pass out: distribute

The students **hand** *their homework* **in** at the beginning of class.
The teacher **hands out** *the corrected homework* the next day.

take off: remove something, such as clothes
put on: dress oneself in something
have on: wear

Mary **took off** *her wet clothes* and **put on** *some dry ones.*
Now she **has** *dry clothes* **on.**

pick up: lift up or take hold of something
put down: stop holding something
put back: put something in its original place

When I **picked up** *the apple,* I saw that it was rotten, so I **put** *it* **back.**

pick up (at): get someone; give someone a ride
drop off (at): deliver someone or something to a place

> My friend **picked** me **up** at my house and **dropped** me **off** at the library.

write down / put down: make a note of

> Did you **put** "coffee" **down** on the shopping list?

turn on / switch on: start the power on a machine or appliance
turn off / switch off / shut off: stop the power
turn out (the lights): switch off or shut off

> I **turned on** the lights when I got home.
> I **turned** them **out** when I went out again.

turn up: increase the volume
turn down: decrease the volume

> Why did you **turn up** the TV? It's too loud. Please **turn** it **down** again.

take out / check out (of / from): borrow officially
take back (to): return

> Lisa **checked** a book **out** of the library. She has to **take** it **back** next week.

Close-Up

PRACTICE   **USING SEPARABLE VERBS**

Respond to each of the following questions with a complete sentence using the separable verb in the cue. You will need to provide the second part of the verb.

EXAMPLE   Question: Sally's library book is due next week. When does she have to return it? (take . . .)

Answer: She has to **take it back next week.**

1. What do most people do when the alarm clock rings? (turn . . .)
2. Where can students get books for research? (check . . .)
3. What do you have to do to apply to a university? (fill . . .)
4. How did Joe get to school this morning? (his roommate / drop . . .)
5. How did the students get the new activity schedule? (the teacher / pass . . .)
6. What do you do if the radio volume is too low? (turn . . .)
7. What did Dave do with his chewing gum before he entered the class? (throw . . .)

FIGURE 7–2

The child in Fig. 7–2 is running into the street in front of a car. What do you think the driver is saying to the child?

FIGURE 7–3

Your friend Roberto, in Fig. 7–3, is very nervous about the test he has to take today. What can you say to him to calm him down?

A.   Using imperative sentences

Imperative sentences ask someone to do something in a very direct way. Here are some of the different ways you can use the imperative. Keep in mind that the level of politeness depends a great deal on intonation of the speaker's voice.

   1. **to give a formal order or command**

      General: Fire your weapons!

      Dog owner: Sit, Spot! Sit!

   2. **to give instructions**

      Take the first street on your right.

      Open your books to page 116.

3. **to make requests**

   Please close the door.

   Please don't make me late.

4. **to give warnings**

   Watch out! There's a car coming!

   Don't be absent tomorrow. There's going to be a quiz.

5. **to express good wishes**

   Have a nice day!

   Have a safe trip!

B. Forming imperative sentences

To form an affirmative imperative sentence, use the base form of the verb; to form a negative imperative sentence, use **DON'T** with the base form of the verb. Do not include a subject; in an imperative sentence, the subject is always understood to be *"you."*

		Base Form Verb	+	Rest of Sentence
Affirmative:		**Watch**		out!
		Be		careful!
		Take		it easy!
Negative:	Don't	**go**		in the street!
	Don't	**be**		nervous!

PRACTICE 4-1   Using the Imperative

*You are very sick. You are in bed with a fever. What will you ask your roommate (or spouse) to do for you? Make requests using **imperative** sentences. Fill in empty brackets with your own cues.*

EXAMPLE   quiet

          Request: Please be quiet.

1. bring / some aspirin
2. give / more blankets
3. make / an appointment with the doctor
4. not / turn on / the stereo
5. [   ]

FOCUS 5   Polite Questions

If you are sick in bed with a fever, you could say to your roommate or spouse, "Please bring me some aspirin." Can you think of other ways to ask for aspirin?

If you are at your friend's house, and you need to use the phone, you could say, "I need to use your phone." Can you think of other ways to ask to use the phone?

A. Asking someone to do something

It is possible to make polite requests by using certain modal auxiliaries in questions. The subject in a request is usually **YOU.** To make a request negative, use **NOT** before the base form of the verb.

Auxiliary	+ Subject	+ Base Form Verb	+ Rest of Sentence	Possible Responses
Can*	you please	**be**	quiet?	Yes, of course.
Will	you please	**bring**	me some aspirin?	Sure. Here you are.
Could	you please	**wait**	for me?	I'm sorry. I can't.
Could	you please	**help**	me?	I'll be glad to.
Would	you please	*not* **be**	late?	Okay.
Would	you please	*not* **smoke**	here?	No problem. Sorry.

B. Asking for favors and permission

A polite question with the auxiliary **CAN, MAY,** or **COULD** can also be used to ask for *a favor* or to ask for *permission.* The subject in this type of question is often **I** or **WE.**

Auxiliary	+ Subject	+ Base Form Verb	+ Rest of Sentence	Possible Responses
Can*	I	**use**	your phone?	Certainly. Go right ahead.
Could	I	**borrow**	your pen?	I'm sorry. I'm using it right now.
May	I	**sit**	down?	Sure.

PRACTICE 5-1 Requests with Polite Questions

Change each of the following sentences to a polite question.

EXAMPLES   Please don't smoke here.
   Would you please **not smoke** here?

   I want something to drink.
   Could I have something to drink?

1. Please be quiet.
2. Don't make so much noise.
3. I need a pen.
4. Don't tell anybody my secret.
5. Hurry up!
6. I want to talk to you.
7. Don't smoke in my office.
8. Don't be late for class.
9. I would like to call you tonight.
10. Please speak louder.

---

*In polite questions, **CAN** is sometimes considered more informal than the other modal auxiliaries.

NOTE: You may also hear polite requests with the expression "Would you mind + (*gerund*) . . . ?" A *gerund* looks like an **-ING** verb. (You can study more about gerunds in Chapter 12.) Use the expression "Would you mind + (*gerund*)" to ask someone to do something for you. Because this expression means, "Would it bother you (*to do something*)?" you respond with a *negative* expression to indicate that you are willing to do what is asked.

EXAMPLES

Request: **Would you mind** bringing me some aspirin?
Response: **Of course not.** I'd be glad to.

Request: **Would you mind** meeting me after class?
Response: **Not at all.** I'll see you then!

Polite Questions and the Imperative in Situations

For each of the following situations, form an appropriate polite question or imperative sentence. Your classmate should respond.

EXAMPLE   You need a pen. Your classmate has two pens on his desk.

Student A: Could I borrow your pen?
Student B: Sure. Take this one.
Student A: Thanks.

1. Your roommate is dancing wildly in the living room. There is a glass lamp on the table nearby.
2. You are driving with your friend. He is going much faster than the speed limit. You feel very uncomfortable.
3. The teacher has just finished explaining *imperatives*. You still don't understand the lesson.
4. You have just called your friend's house. His or her roommate answers the phone and tells you that your friend isn't at home. You would like to leave a message.
5. You would like to borrow your classmate's pencil sharpener.
6. The sugar is on the table in front of your classmate. You would like to have some to put in your tea, but you can't reach it.

FOCUS 6   Noun Clause Objects from Questions

A.   Introduction to noun clause objects

Jill: Is Mr. Phillips in?
Secretary: No, I'm afraid he isn't here at the moment.
Jill: When can I call him?
Secretary: I'm sorry, but I don't know where he went or what time he plans to be back in the office. I'm not even sure if he plans to be back later today.

What information does Jill want?

Can the secretary give her the information? Why or why not?

The verb **KNOW** usually needs an object. What is the object of **KNOW** in each of the following sentences?

1. The secretary *doesn't know* **something.**
2. The secretary *doesn't know* **Mr. Phillips's schedule.**
3. The secretary *doesn't know* **if he plans to be back today.**
4. The secretary *doesn't know* **where Mr. Phillips went.**

In sentences 1 and 2, the object of the verb **KNOW** is a noun: *something, his schedule.*

In sentences 3 and 4, the object of the verb is an entire clause that comes from a question:

"Does he plan to be back today?" "Where did he go?"

The object is called a *noun clause* because an entire clause (a question) takes the position of a noun object in the sentence.

B. Forming noun clauses from questions

There are several points to notice about a noun clause that comes from a question.

1. Like other clauses, a noun clause has a subject and a verb phrase.
2. A noun clause from a question must be connected to the main clause by a connecting word or phrase.
3. If the noun clause comes from an information question, the connecting word is a question word or phrase. If the *noun clause* comes from a **YES/NO** question, the connecting word is **IF** or **WHETHER (OR NOT)**.
4. Although a noun clause comes from a question, it does not use question word order. The subject comes before the verb as it does in statements.

Subject +	Verb +	Object (Noun Clause)			
		Connecting Word(s) +	Subject +	Verb +	Rest of Clause
I	don't know	where	my books	are.	
I	don't know	why	John	didn't go	to the party.
I	wonder	what kind of ice cream	Sally	likes.	
I	don't know	who	—	has	my notebook.
I	have no idea	when	the movie	starts.	
I	don't know	how	Mike	got	here.
I	have no idea	whose car	that	is.	
I	wonder	if	Tom	eats	pizza or not.
I	don't know	if	we	have	a quiz this week.
I	don't know	whether or not	Lisa	is	absent.
I	wonder	whether	Pedro	has	a car or not.

PRACTICE 6-1 Noun Clauses

Respond to each of the following questions with a noun clause. Begin your response with one of these expressions:

I don't know . . .
I have no idea . . .
I'm not sure . . .   } + noun clause
I forget . . .
I can't remember . . .
I wonder . . .

EXAMPLE   Question: What's the president's middle name?
              Answer: I'm sorry. **I have no idea** what his middle name is.

1. Where is the mayor's office?
2. When is the next legal holiday here?
3. Are there any deserts in Canada?
4. How many people are there in this city?
5. Whose pencil is that student using?
6. Were there any good movies on TV last night?
7. Who was the second president of the United States?
8. What kind of TV shows does the president of the United States like?
9. Do they grow sugar cane in the United States?
10. How often does the American government print new money?
11. When did Hawaii become a state?

12. Does Colorado have much oil?

13. Where does the vice president of the United States live?

FOCUS 7 Polite Questions with Noun Clauses

Imagine that you are waiting for a bus. You aren't sure if you have missed the bus or not, because you don't know what time it is. There is another person near you who is also waiting for the bus. Which of these questions would you use to find out the time from the stranger at the bus stop?

"Excuse me. What time is it?"

"Excuse me. Could you tell me what time it is?"

For some people, the first form might seem strange because it is a direct question. To make the question "softer" or more polite, use the question as the noun clause object of a polite question.

Could you tell me *something?* **What time is it?**

Could you tell me **what time it is?**

Here are some different ways to ask for information with a polite question. The noun clause object contains the question the speaker wants to ask. However, because it is a noun clause, use statement, *not* question, word order.

Polite Question	+	Direct Object (Noun Clause)
Do you know		how much a new minivan costs?
Do you by any chance know		which car is better?
Do you have any idea		how I can get downtown from here?
Could you possibly tell me		where the bus station is?
Would you please tell me		if there is a bus stop near here?
I was wondering if you could tell me		where the closest bank is?

PRACTICE 7–1 Polite Questions for Information

*You are new in town. You need to stop strangers on the street to get the following information. Ask polite questions with **noun clauses.***

Unfortunately, the "stranger" does not have the information that you need. Your classmate should take the role of the stranger and respond to each of your questions with a noun clause.

EXAMPLE   *What street is this?*

Student A: Excuse me. Could you please tell me **what street this is?**

Student B: Sorry. I'm not sure **what street it is.**

1. Where is the nearest post office?
2. Where can I catch a taxi?
3. How much does it cost to take a taxi to the airport from here?
4. Did the Main Street bus just go by?
5. When does the bus usually stop here?
6. Is there a bus from here to the airport?
7. How long does it take to get to the airport from here?
8. Do I need exact change for the bus?

Situations

How would you react in each of the following situations? Use an imperative sentence or a polite question.

EXAMPLE   You would like to know the time. The man on the bus next to you has a watch.

Student: Excuse me. Could you tell me what time it is?

1.   You are walking with your friend's little boy. He is trying to pet a strange dog. You don't know if the dog is friendly or not.

2.   You are looking for Jason's Department Store, but you can't find it. Get directions from someone walking down the street.

3.   You are at a bank depositing money into your account. You can't remember today's date. Find out the date from the bank teller.

4.   You would like your friend to call you tonight.

A WIDER ANGLE

Role Playing

Your teacher will describe a situation to you. You and a classmate should pretend to be in that situation. You will start a conversation, and your classmate should respond.

Writing Practice

Choose one of the following topics.

TOPIC 1:   Your classmate would like to learn how to cook a dish from your country. Write a recipe with very clear directions for your classmate.

TOPIC 2:   Your classmate would like to come over to your house. Write the directions to your house from school. You can give directions for the bus or subway, for driving, or for walking.

TOPIC 3:   A student newspaper is collecting articles about games in different countries. Choose a simple game from your country. Write the instructions for playing this game.

DEVELOPING YOUR SKILLS AND KNOWLEDGE

Chapter Exercises

EXERCISE 1   Scrambled Sentences

Put each of the following groups of words in order so that they form a sentence that makes sense. Do not add or leave out any words. Pay attention to punctuation.

EXAMPLE   letter carrier   the
dog   yesterday
our   bit

Our dog bit the letter carrier yesterday.

1. very   night
   enjoyed   the
   I   last
   concert   much
        .

2. like   after
   some   would
   to   to
   we   music
   listen   dinner
        .

3. for   breakfast
   usually   strong
   my   family
   tea   has
        .

4. angry   get
   manager   the
   at   did
   who   yesterday
        ?

5. didn't   understand
   Paul   the
   new   well
   very   lesson
        .

EXERCISE 2 Pronouns

*Fill in each blank with a **subject pronoun** (I, you, she, etc.), an **object pronoun** (me, you, her, etc.), or a **reflexive pronoun** (myself, yourself, etc.).*

1. PAUL: What's the matter?

   JOAN: I burned _____ this morning.

   PAUL: Did _____ spill coffee on

   _____?

   JOAN: No, _____ didn't. I touched the coffee pot

   while _____ was still hot.

2. SAL: Did all of you enjoy _____ at the party last
   night?

   MINNIE: _____ sure did. _____ was
   a great party.

   SAL: Were Kim and Lena there?

   MINNIE: Yes, _____ were, but I didn't get the

   chance to talk to _____.

3. ALFREDO: When do you celebrate the New Year in your country?

   CONSTANTINE: _____ celebrate

   _____ according to the lunar calendar.

4. ALFREDO: Who does your mother work for?

   CONSTANTINE: Nobody. She and my father have their own

   business, so they work for _____.

EXERCISE 3 Direct and Indirect Objects

*Rewrite each sentence to include the **indirect object** in parentheses. In some sentences, there is only one place for the indirect object. In others, the indirect object can go in two different positions. If there are two possibilities, write both of them. Add any necessary prepositions.*

EXAMPLE   John bought some flowers. (his mother)

John bought some flowers for his mother.
John bought his mother some flowers.

1. Mark's tuition cost a lot of money this semester. (him)
2. His parents lent some money. (him)
3. Now he owes money. (his parents)
4. Mark explained his financial problems. (bank loan officer)
5. The loan officer asked a lot of questions. (Mark)

EXERCISE 4 Verbs and Objects

Use the cues to complete the following sentences. Add any necessary pronouns or prepositions. Do not repeat or add any nouns.

EXAMPLE   Toby: Does Mary have today's newspaper?

Julia: Yes, I _____ a few minutes ago.
                         (give)
Yes, I **gave it to her** a few minutes ago.

1. MARC: How did you get downtown this morning?

   EMIL: A friend _____ on his way to
                              (pick up)
   work and _____ downtown.
                        (drop off)

2. DON: Where did you get the money to pay for your car?

   NELSON: I _____ my parents. They
                        (borrow)
   _____ last week. I want to
                  (lend)
   _____ as soon as I can.
              (pay back)

3.   MARIE: How did you meet your wife?

          HENRY: My cousin _____ at a party. I
                                             (introduce)

                      _____ a few days later.
                          (ask out)

4.   The lights are on in my apartment. I guess I

      _____ before I left.
        (not / turn off)

5.   OLEG: Where are my new pants?

         CALVIN: Your sister _____.
                                (have on)

         OLEG: What? Why _____?!
                              (she / wear)

EXERCISE 5   Polite Questions

Change each of the following sentences to a polite question.

EXAMPLES   Don't be late.
               Would you please not be late?

               I want something to drink.
               May I have something to drink?

1.   Don't worry so much!
2.   I want to use your dictionary.
3.   Turn down the TV.
4.   I would like to ask you a personal question.

EXERCISE 6   Noun Clauses

Fill in each blank with an appropriate noun clause.

EXAMPLE   Ms. Weng: Where is the new student from?
               Millie: I'm not sure <u>where he's from.</u>

1.   CECIL: What time does the movie start?

     FRANCIS: I forget _____.

2.   VINNIE: Are there any nice nightclubs in this neighborhood?

     JUNE: I'm new here. I don't know

     _____.

3.   TALIA: Does our teacher have any pets?

     MENDY: I have no idea _____.

4.   NADINE: Can whales breathe underwater like fish?

     NORBERT: I'm not sure _____.

5.   TED: Who did Mike sell his car to?

     ALICE: Ask Mike. He can tell you _____.

6.   JACQUES: Why doesn't Carol ever eat in the cafeteria?

      TAMIL: Why don't you ask her _____.

7.   MIDGE: How often does it snow in Boston?

      FREDDIE: I don't know _____.

8.   BEN: Where is the main post office?

      ALEXANDER: I'm sorry. I'm afraid I have no idea

      _____.

9.   ED: Where does the governor live?

      MARIO: I can never remember _____.

EXERCISE 7   Polite Questions

Complete each of the following conversational exchanges by writing an appropriate question or response. In some situations, the speaker is asking for information. In others, the speaker is making a request or asking for permission.

1.   BOB: _____?
      SUE: Yes, of course. Go right ahead. It's in the kitchen.

2.   TOM: Excuse me. I think I'm lost. _____?
      GAS STATION
      ATTENDANT: Sure. Just get back on the highway and go north for another five miles. You'll see the sign.

3.   SECRETARY: Good morning.

      MR. KIM: Hello. I'm not sure if I'm in the right place or not. I

      need to talk to Dr. Kraus. _____?

      SECRETARY: Yes, of course. It's the third office on the left.

4.   BRAD (ON THE
      PHONE):   Hello?

      ED: Hi. This is Ed Rufus. _____?

      BRAD: I'm sorry. He isn't here right now. _____?

      ED: Yes, please. _____ that Ed Rufus called?

      BRAD: Sure.

8 *Future Situations*

THE BIG PICTURE

Uses of **WILL** and **BE GOING TO**

Future Use of Present Verbs

Time Clauses

Future Real Conditions

The Future Progressive Tense

Future Possibilities

Expectations

AT A GLANCE

A Glimpse of the Future

"Seeing" the Future

Are there people in your country who claim—either seriously or just for fun—that they can "see" or predict the future? What are some of the traditional methods of making predictions or telling fortunes in your country? Has anyone ever told your fortune? What did he or she predict for you?

Predictions for the Twenty-First Century

Here are some predictions that scientists and scholars have made regarding travel and transportation in the twenty-first century.*

1. Most vehicles will use hydrogen for fuel. The widespread use of this fuel will solve our current energy problems and will eliminate a great deal of pollution.

2. The average citizen will be able to travel to the moon, to space stations, and to other planets by space shuttle.

Source: David Wallechinsky, Amy Wallace, and Irving Wallace. *The People's Almanac Presents the Book of Predictions* (New York: William Morrow and Company, Inc., 1980), pp. 216–218, 228.

3. Automated highways will come into widespread use. Vehicles will enter an approach ramp and enter their destination into a highway computer. The highway will take them to the appropriate exit, where the drivers will once again resume control of the car. Traffic on highways will move quickly without accidents or traffic jams.

4. People will travel to other countries and continents in rockets that fly outside the earth's atmosphere.

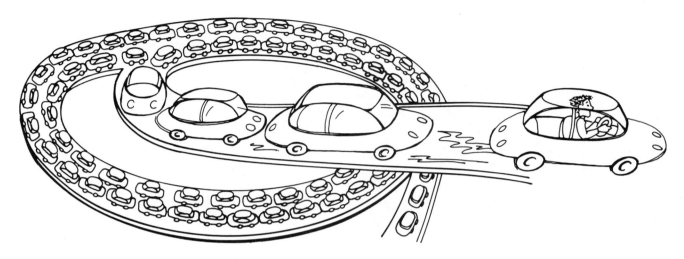

Do you agree with these predictions? Do you have any other predictions about transportation and travel in the future?

> **In this chapter, you will practice talking about future events and situations. You have probably already learned to use the auxiliary WILL to refer to future events. In this chapter, you will practice a number of different ways to talk about plans, predictions, and future situations.**

FOCUS I   Future Using **WILL**

A. Uses of WILL

The modal auxiliary **WILL** can mean "future." As a future auxiliary, it has two basic uses:

1. To talk about future events and facts

> George **will be** at the party tonight.
> We **will have** a test on Chapter 8 next week.

2. To offer predictions for the future

> In the twenty-first century, people **will go** to the moon for their honeymoon.
> Hydrogen **will become** a widely used fuel.

In both situations, the future events seem definite to the speaker. If speakers want to indicate that they do not feel 100 percent sure about their predictions, they can use expressions such as the following:

maybe	**Maybe** fossil fuels will become obsolete.
probably	Transportation will **probably** be much faster in the future.
I think	**I think** people will be able to travel easily in space.
it is possible	**It is possible** that we will all drive electric cars.

B. Forming sentences with WILL

Like other modal auxiliaries, **WILL** has only one form for all subjects. It must be the first auxiliary in the verb, and it is always followed by the base form verb or base form auxiliary.

1. Affirmative and negative statements

I **will be** out of town next week.	I **will not be** in class all week.
Sam **will graduate** next year.	He **will not stay** after graduation.
Cars of the future **will use** hydrogen fuel.	They **will not use** gasoline.

2. Contractions

a. **WILL → 'LL**	I**'ll be** out of town next week.
b. **WILL NOT → WON'T**	I **won't be** in class all week.

3. Questions and answers

Will you **be** in class tomorrow?	Yes, I **will.**
Will Sam **stay** here after graduation?	No, he **won't.**
What **will** he **do** after graduation?	He**'ll get** a job back home.
Who **will hire** him?	His uncle probably **will.**
Future cars **will use** hydrogen fuel, **won't** they?	Yes, they **will.**
They **won't use** gasoline, **will** they?	No, they **won't.**

4. Auxiliary reactions

Statement:	I**'ll be** absent all next week.
Reaction:	You **will?!**
Question:	Who **will be** in class tomorrow?
Answer:	I **won't,** and neither **will** Ivan.

C. Ability and necessity in the future

Ability

	Subject +	WILL / WON'T "future" +	BE ABLE TO "ability" +	Base Form Verb
Fifty years from now,	doctors	will	be able to	cure cancer.
In the future,	people	won't	be able to	own a lot of land.

Necessity

	Subject +	WILL / WON'T "future" +	HAVE TO "necessity" +	Base Form Verb
Fifty years from now,	people	will	have to	conserve water.
In the future,	people	won't	have to	work 40 hours a week.

Predictions with **WILL / WON'T**

The adverb **PROBABLY** means "almost certain" (not 100 percent certain, but almost).

The adverb **PROBABLY** often occurs in predictions. It usually occurs after the auxiliary **WILL** but before the auxiliary **WON'T**.

> Scientists **will** *probably* **be able to predict** earthquakes in the future.
> They *probably* **won't be able to prevent** earthquakes.

A. *Give your predictions for the twenty-first century. Use the cues to make sentences with* **WILL** *or* **WON'T**.

EXAMPLE   there / [probably] a lot of pollution

> There **will probably be** a lot of pollution in the future.
> (There **probably won't be** much pollution.)

1. people / [probably] have large families
2. the incidence of cancer / [probably] increase
3. the average citizen / [probably] travel [= *ability*] / other planets
4. the world / [probably] be dependent on oil
5. everyone / [probably] speak the same language
6. scientists / [probably] change [= *ability*] / seawater into drinking water easily and cheaply
7. people / [probably] get [= *necessity*] / their water from the sea

B. *Use* **WILL** *or* **WON'T** *to give your predictions on the following topics.*

1. Scientists are continually making new advances in space technology. What do you think people will be able to do in space 100 years from now?
2. The growing world population is a big problem. If the population gets very large, what are some things that people won't be able to do in the future? What are some things that people will have to do?

FOCUS 2   Special Uses of **WILL**: Willingness

Think about things that you are willing to do and things that you are not willing to do.
Is there any food that you are not willing to eat?
Have you seen any new hair or clothing fashions that you might be willing to try?
Are there any current fashions that you are not willing to follow?

The modal auxiliary **WILL** often carries a meaning that is not simply "future." It can give information about the attitude of the subject toward an action. The auxiliary **WILL** can indicate whether the subject is ready and willing to do something or not. Use **WILL** or **WON'T** to show willingness in the following situations.

1. Use **WILL** or **WON'T** to make a promise.

> Mrs. Perez: Have a safe trip to the United States, and study hard!
>
> Anita: I **will.** I **will make** you proud of me.
>
> Mrs. Perez: You've never been on your own before, so please be careful!
>
> Anita: Don't worry, Mom. I **won't do** anything foolish. **I'll take** good care of myself.

2. Use **WILL** to volunteer or offer to do something.

> Jim: I would like to know my horoscope for today.
>
> Fortune teller: **I'll tell** you your horoscope.
>
> Jim: You **will?** Thanks. I appreciate it.

3. Use **WILL** to make a request in a polite question.

> Mr. Smith: **Will** you **call** me when you arrive in Canada?
>
> Selma: Yes, of course. **I'll be** glad to.

4. Use **WON'T** to show a refusal to do something.

> Babysitter: This little girl is driving me crazy!
>
> Friend: How come?
>
> Babysitter: She **won't do** anything I tell her!

5. Use **WON'T** to show that something is not functioning properly.

> Emily: What's the matter?
>
> Ruth: This pen **won't write.**

PRACTICE 2-1   Willingness

A.   *How does the meaning differ in each of the following pairs of sentences?*

    1. Mike doesn't play soccer with us.

      Pete won't play soccer with us.

    2. This soda machine doesn't give change.

      This soda machine won't give me my change.

B.   *Respond to the following questions or statements using* **WILL** *or* **WON'T.**

EXAMPLE   Donald: I'm dying for a cup of coffee, but I don't have any change.

        Joe: **I'll buy** you a cup of coffee.

          (**I'll give** you some change.)

    1.   Please don't call me after 10:00 P.M.

    2.   This bag is too heavy for me to carry.

    3.   What's wrong with your car?

    4.   The phone's ringing, but I can't answer it!

    5.   It's not a good idea to walk alone at night.

    6.   Why are you kicking that vending machine?

C.   *Answer the following questions.*

    1.   What are some things that you **will gladly do** for a friend?

    2.   What are some things that you **won't do,** not even for a good friend?

The verb expression **BE GOING TO** + (verb) is another common way to talk about the future.

A.   Uses of BE GOING TO + (verb)

There are three basic uses of the future expression **BE GOING TO**:

1.   To ask for and give information about plans and intentions:

Kati: What **are** you **going to do** during your next vacation?

Marie: **I'm going to visit** my uncle and aunt in New York.

2.   To talk about future events:

Marie: My cousin **is going to be** in New York too.

3.   To make predictions about events that seem sure to happen, often in the near future:

Fred: Look at those dark clouds. Let's go inside. It**'s going to rain.**

B.   Forming sentences with BE GOING TO + (verb)

Subject	+	BE (NOT)	+	GOING TO	+	Base Form Verb
I		am		going to		**cook** dinner tonight.
Kati		isn't		going to		**stay** here.
You		are		going to		**see** Kati at the wedding.

C.   Questions and answers

Are you **going to visit** your uncle?	Yes, I **am.**
Is your brother **going to go** with you?	No, he **isn't.**
Who **is going to go** with you?	Nobody **is.**
You **aren't going to drive, are** you?	No, I'm **not.**
How long **are** you **going to stay** there?	About two weeks.
Who else **is going to be** there?	My aunt **is,** and so **are** my cousins.

PRACTICE 3–1   Future Plans

A.   Use the following cues to find out about a classmate's future plans. First, ask a YES/NO question with BE GOING TO. If your classmate answers NO, ask a second question to get more information about his or her plans.

EXAMPLE   you / go to Alaska for your next vacation?

Student A: **Are** you **going to go** to Alaska for your next vacation?

Student B: No, I'm not.

Student A: Where **are** you **going to go?**
(What **are** you **going to do?**)

Student B: **I'm going to stay** here.

1.   you / take a Caribbean cruise on your next vacation?
2.   you / watch a late night talk show on TV tonight?
3.   you / write about your homework in your next letter home?
4.   you and your friends / have a party tonight?

5. you / eat at McDonald's on your next birthday?

6. your best friend / do your laundry for you this weekend?

B. *Report back the information that you got from your classmate.*

EXAMPLE   Chang isn't going to go to Alaska for his next vacation. He's going to stay here.

CLOSE-UP   **Future Time Expressions**

Can you think of different ways to answer the following question?

When are you going to leave?
I'm going to leave _____.

Here are some time expressions for the future.

IN (+ period of time): refers to a point in time after a specific time period (**IN** + time period is different from other uses of **IN**)

in a little while, in two weeks, in a year

I am going to leave **in a month.**
I am going to leave **in four days.**

THIS: refers to the future time period closest to now

this summer, this evening, this Christmas

THIS COMING: refers to the next occurrence of a particular time period. It is most often used with days of the week, holidays, and seasons

this coming summer, this coming Monday, this coming Thanksgiving

I'm going to leave **this weekend.**
I'm going to leave **this coming January.**

TOMORROW: refers to the day after today

tomorrow morning, tomorrow afternoon, tomorrow evening, tomorrow night, the day after tomorrow

I'm going to leave at noon **tomorrow.**
I'm going to leave **the day after tomorrow.**

NEXT: * refers to the time period just after the current one

next Tuesday, next weekend, next week, next month, next year, next semester

I'm going to leave **next Monday.**
I'm going to leave **next month.**

*Do not use prepositions or the article **THE** to indicate a future point in time.
[MISTAKE: I'm going to leave ~~in~~ next month. I'm going to leave ~~the~~ next month.]

AFTER NEXT: refers to the time period just after the next one

the month after next, the year after next

I'm going to leave **the weekend after next.**
I'm going to leave **the Monday after next.**

IN THE NEXT + (period of time): refers to an event that will occur during a time period that goes from now to a future time

in the next few days, in the next couple of months, in the next 50 years

Technology will probably change rapidly **in the next 100 years.**
I'm going to buy a car **in the next two or three months.**

(period of time) + **FROM** + (point in time): refers to a future event that will occur at the end of a specified time period that begins at a specified point in time

a week from today, several years from now, two weeks from tomorrow

I'm going to leave **three weeks from Monday.**
I'm going to leave **a year from now.**

LATER: refers to a point in time after now

later, later this morning, later today, later this week

I'm going to leave **later this month.**
I'm going to leave **later this year.**

SOON: refers to the near future

soon, pretty soon, fairly soon, very soon

I'm going to leave **soon.**

SOMETIME / SOMEDAY: refer to an unspecified future time

sometime, sometime today, sometime this week, someday

I'm going to leave **sometime soon.**
Someday, I'm going to be famous.

IN THE FUTURE: refers to an unspecified future time period. The expression often indicates a contrast with the present. To be a little more specific, you can say: **IN THE NEAR FUTURE** or **IN THE DISTANT FUTURE.**

In the future, people will probably stop eating meat.
Scientists will probably develop an economical electric car **in the near future.**

This expression can also mean "starting from now; from now on."

You were late to class today. Please come on time **in the future.**

Close-Up

PRACTICE **FUTURE TIME EXPRESSIONS**

Use BE GOING TO with the following cues to ask about a classmate's future plans. Begin your question with When . . . ? Your classmate should answer with a complete sentence. Fill in empty brackets with your own cues.

EXAMPLE   you / go back to your country?

Student A: When **are** you **going to go** back to your country?
Student B: I**'m going to go** back to my country next year (in a month, this summer).
             (I**'m** never **going to go** back to my country.)

1. the people here / elect a new leader?
2. you / get a haircut?
3. you / write some letters?
4. the teacher / give the next test?
5. [?]

FOCUS 4 Future Plans with Present Tenses

*Answer these questions about the verbs in the following conversational exchanges: What form is each verb? Is the verb talking about a **future** action, an action **now**, or a **general fact**? How do you know?*

Tom:	What **are** you **doing?**
Sue:	I**'m trying** to fix my bicycle.
Kim:	What **are** you **doing** this coming weekend?
Bob:	I**'m going** to my uncle's house for dinner.
Lisa:	When **does** John usually **leave** for school?
Jean:	He usually **leaves** at around 8:30.
Dirk:	When **does** the next bus to Greenwood Mall **leave?**
Carla:	It **leaves** in fifteen minutes.

A.   The present progressive tense as a future form

The present progressive tense can refer to future events if *both* of these conditions are true:
1. There is a future time expression in the context.
2. The action refers to definite plans or intentions.

Use the present progressive tense to express a firm commitment to the action or to indicate that some kind of arrangements for the action have already been made. Verbs of motion (**GO, COME, LEAVE, BRING, TAKE,** and so on) often occur with this future use of the present progressive.

> Kati **is flying** to New York *next month*. [*She already has her ticket.*]
>
> Marie **isn't going** anywhere *during the break*. [*She made a firm decision about this.*]

Notice that in the following sentence, it is *not* possible to use the present progressive tense to talk about the future.

> [MISTAKE: It is raining tomorrow. (*It is not possible to plan the rain. This is a prediction, not a plan.*)]

B.   The simple present tense as a future form

The simple present tense can refer to future events if *both* of these conditions are true:
1. There is a future time expression in the context.
2. The action refers to an event that is on an official or fixed schedule that the speaker does not control.

Verbs of scheduling (**BEGIN, START, END, FINISH, ARRIVE, DEPART, LEAVE, BE,** and so on) often occur with this future use of the simple present tense.

The concert **is** *tomorrow.*

My bus **leaves** *in ten minutes.*

We **have** a test *next week.*

Notice that in the following sentences, it is *not* possible to use the simple present tense to talk about the future.

[MISTAKE: It rains tomorrow. (*It is not possible to schedule rain.*)]

[I study tonight. (*My studying is not part of an official schedule.*)]

PRACTICE 4-1   Using Present Tenses with Future Meaning

A.   *Here is a list of things that Sheila has decided to do this coming weekend.*

Saturday A.M.		**Saturday P.M.**	
do laundry		1:00	meet Rick; go to soccer game
clean house		2:00	start of the soccer match
go to post office		5:30	early dinner with Rick downtown
		7:00	movie at theater downtown

Sunday A.M.		**Sunday P.M.**	
10:00–11:00	church	1:30	meet Barbara at library
11:30	meet friends for brunch	6:00	have dinner with parents
		9:00	watch the movie on Channel 8

Use the following cues to ask about Sheila's upcoming weekend. Use only **simple present tense** *or* **present progressive tense.** *Your classmate will use the information from the list to answer with a complete sentence. Add any necessary articles. Keep in mind that Sheila's list is not an official schedule.*

EXAMPLE   what / Sheila / do / on Saturday morning?

Student A: What **is** Sheila **doing** on Saturday morning?

Student B: She **is doing** laundry.

when / the soccer game / start?

Student A: When **does** the soccer game **start?**

Student B: It **starts** at two o'clock.

1. where / Sheila / go / on Saturday morning?
2. what else / she / do / on Saturday morning?
3. who / she / meet / in the afternoon?
4. what time / they / meet?
5. where / they / have dinner?
6. what / they / do / after dinner?
7. what time / the movie?
8. what / Sheila / do / on Sunday morning?
9. what time / church services / begin?
10. when / church / over?
11. who / she / have brunch / after church this Sunday?
12. what / [   ]?
13. what time / [   ]?

*B.   Use the cues with the **simple present** or **present progressive tense** to get information about future plans and scheduled events. (Although **BE GOING TO** + [verb] is also possible here, just practice using the present tenses.) Your classmate should answer each question with a complete sentence.*

EXAMPLE   when / this semester / end?

Student A: When **does** this semester **end?**

Student B: It **ends** in December.

1.   what time / your last class / finish today?
2.   what time / you / go home today?
3.   what / you / have for dinner tonight?
4.   what / you / do tonight?
5.   when / the next school term / begin?
6.   when / your passport / expire?
7.   when / the next grammar test?

FOCUS 5   Future Time Clauses

A future time clause can give information about a specific point in the future.

Ralph: When are you going to take a vacation?

Norma: We are going to take a vacation **as soon as this semester is over.**

There are two points to remember about future time clauses.

1.   The verb in the main clause usually has a future verb tense form: **BE GOING TO / WILL.**
2.   The verb in the time clause must have a present tense verb form. Although the meaning is future, do not use **WILL** or **BE GOING TO** in the time clause.

Main Clause		Time Clause	
Future Verb	**+**	**Time Word +**	**Present Verb**
John**'s going to buy** a car		**before**	he **starts** graduate school.
You **won't be able to go** home		**until**	you **take** your final exams.
I**'ll try** not to call you		**while**	you **are studying.**
We**'re going to have** a party		**after**	the semester **is** over.
Are you **going to go** home		**as soon as**	you **finish** your exams?
John**'s going to celebrate**		**once**	the semester **ends.**

PRACTICE 5-1   Future Time Clauses

A.   David is going to go back to his country the day after tomorrow. Here are some of his plans and predictions. Combine the phrases to make sentences with future time clauses, using the time words in parentheses. Fill in empty brackets with your own cues.

EXAMPLE   (before) give his apartment key to the landlord // go to the airport

David is going to give his apartment key to the landlord **before** he goes to the airport.

(**Before** he goes to the airport, he is going to give his key to the landlord.)

1.	[before]	call his friends // leave
2.	[as soon as]	get to the airport // check his luggage
3.	[after]	take a long nap // eat dinner on the plane
4.	[until]	sleep // the plane / land
5.	[ ]	hug his mother // get off the plane

B. *Use the following cues to ask a classmate about his or her future plans. Your classmate should answer each question with a complete sentence using a time clause.*

EXAMPLE when / have a party?

Student A: When are you going to have a party?

Student B: I'm going to have a party **as soon as** I pass the TOEFL.*

1. when / watch TV today?
2. when / go to the grocery store?
3. when / buy a new car?
4. when / do your homework?
5. how long / continue to study in this English program?

C. *What did you find out about your classmate?*

EXAMPLE Arturo is going to have a party as soon as he passes the TOEFL.

FOCUS 6 Future Real Conditions

What will happen if hydrogen becomes a common fuel?

If hydrogen becomes a common fuel, there will be less pollution in our atmosphere.

If hydrogen becomes a common fuel, we won't have an energy shortage.

A future sentence with an **IF clause** talks about future results of *possible* future situations. This type of sentence is called a *future real condition.*

A. Forming future real conditions

A *future real condition* consists of a main clause with a future verb and a conditional clause that consists of a connecting word and a present tense verb form. One of the most common connecting words for a conditional clause is **IF**. In a future real condition, the **IF clause** describes a possible future situation; the main clause talks about the future result of that situation. The most common future verb form in conditions is **WILL**.

Main Clause: Future Verb +	Conditional Clause: Present Verb
There **will be** less air pollution	**if** we **use** hydrogen fuel in the future.
We **won't have** an energy crisis	**if** hydrogen **is** inexpensive and plentiful in the future.
We **will have** an energy crisis	**if** we **don't find** new sources of energy.

The **IF** clause frequently comes before the main clause. When the **IF** clause comes first, it must be followed by a comma.

If we don't find cleaner fuels**,** air pollution will become worse and worse.

---

*TOEFL stands for the Test of English as a Foreign Language.

B. Connecting words for conditional sentences: IF and UNLESS

Both **IF** and **UNLESS** can be connecting words in real conditions. These connecting words indicate a relationship between the possible future condition and the possible future result.

1. **IF** indicates that if the condition is true, the result in the main clause will also be true.

If the weather is nice tomorrow,	I will play tennis.
(*When condition is true,* →	*this will happen; this result will also be true.*)
(*When this condition is NOT true,* →	*this will NOT happen.*)

2. **UNLESS** indicates the one condition that will *prevent* the situation of the main clause. If it turns out that the condition in the **UNLESS** clause is true, then the result in the main clause will *not* be true.

I will play tennis tomorrow	unless it rains.
(*This will happen only if* →	*this condition is NOT true.*)
(*This will NOT happen if* →	*this condition is true.*)

Here are some more examples of sentences with **UNLESS:**

> Many animal species will become extinct in the future **unless** we protect them.
> We will have an energy shortage in the future **unless** we find new energy sources.
> George won't be in class tomorrow **unless** he feels better.

PRACTICE 6-1 Future Conditions

*Your classmate will ask a question about future plans. Answer each question with two possibilities. Use future real conditions with **IF** clauses to explain the two possibilities. Fill in empty brackets with your own cues.*

EXAMPLE Student A: what / Lisa / wear to the football game next weekend?
Student B: a. very cold // winter coat
b. not too cold // new sweater

Student A: What is Lisa going to wear to the football game next weekend?
Student B: a. **If** it's very cold, she'**ll wear** her winter coat.
b. **If** it's not too cold, she'**ll wear** her new sweater.

1. STUDENT A: what / Ben / do tonight?
   STUDENT B: a. good movie on TV // watch it
   b. not anything good on TV // read a book

2. STUDENT A: where / Jack and his friends / have lunch tomorrow?
   STUDENT B: a. school cafeteria / not crowded // eat there
   b. cafeteria / too crowded // eat at MacDonald's

3. STUDENT A: what / Carol / do after class tomorrow?
   STUDENT B: a. weather / nice // go jogging
   b. rain // work out in the gym

4. STUDENT A: what / you / do this coming weekend?
   STUDENT B: a. [?]
   b. [?]

IF and UNLESS

A.   *Sarah needs to get a student loan from the Financial Aid Office in order to study at the university next year. Complete the following sentences about Sarah using* **IF** *or* **UNLESS**.

1.   Sarah will be able to attend school next semester

_____ she can get a loan.

2.   She won't be able to attend school next semester

_____ she can't get a loan.

3.   She won't be able to attend school next semester

_____ she gets a loan.

4.   She won't be able to attend school _____ they refuse to give her a loan.

5.   She will attend school next semester _____ they refuse to give her a loan.

B.   *Complete the following sentences.*

1.   I will watch TV tonight if . . .
2.   I will watch TV tonight unless . . .
3.   I will eat breakfast tomorrow if . . .
4.   I will eat breakfast tomorrow unless . . .
5.   I won't eat breakfast tomorrow unless . . .
6.   I won't eat breakfast tomorrow if . . .

More Practice with **UNLESS**

Now look back at the situations in Practice 6–1. For each situation, discuss the two possible future conditions using **UNLESS** *and* **IN THAT CASE**.

EXAMPLE   Lisa will wear her new sweater to the football game next weekend **unless** it's very cold. **In that case,** she will wear her winter coat.

1.   Ben . . .
2.   Jack and his friends . . .
3.   Carol . . .
4.   [   ]

WHAT IF . . .?

Read the following conversation. What does the phrase **WHAT IF . . .** *mean?*

Molly: I'm going to buy a car this month.
Max: Really? What color car are you going to buy?
Molly: I'm going to get a red one.
Max: **What if** they don't have a red car?
Molly: If they don't, I'll try to get a blue one.

In conversation, the question **WHAT IF . . . ?** is the short informal form of these questions: *What will happen if . . . ?* and *What will you do if . . . ?*

A.   Use the cues to ask your classmate about future plans. Then find out what will happen to these plans in different possible future conditions. Add necessary articles and prepositions. Fill in empty brackets with your own cues.

EXAMPLE   Student A: do / this weekend?
                                 What are you going to do this weekend?
                    Student B: go camping
                                 I'm going camping with some friends.
                    Student A: what if // rain?
                                 What if it rains?
                    Student B: [   ]
                                 If it does, I guess we'll stay here.

1.   STUDENT A: who / John / invite to the movie tomorrow night?
      STUDENT B: he / invite / Sandra
      STUDENT A: what if // busy?
      STUDENT B: [   ]

2.   STUDENT A: who / give you a ride to the airport next weekend?
      STUDENT B: my roommate
      STUDENT A: what if // car / break down?
      STUDENT B: [   ]

3.   STUDENT A: what / you / write about in your research paper?
      STUDENT B: different ethnic groups in my country
      STUDENT A: what if // not find [= *ability*] / enough information?
      STUDENT B: [   ]

4.   STUDENT A: what / you / do this coming weekend?
      STUDENT B: [   ]
      STUDENT A: what if // [   ]?
      STUDENT B: [   ]

B.   Now use the information from Part A to complete the following sentences.

EXAMPLE   (Student B) is going to go camping next weekend unless **it rains.** In that case, **s/he won't go.**

1.   John is going to take Sandra to the movie tomorrow night unless. . . . In that case, . . .
2.   (My classmate's) roommate is going to give him or her a ride to the airport unless . . . In that case, . . .
3.   (My classmate) isn't going to write about different ethnic groups unless . . .
4.   (My classmate) is going to . . . this coming weekend unless . . . In that case, . . .

FOCUS 7   The Future Progressive Tense

Tammy Wilson watches the evening news on TV from 6:30 to 7:30 every evening.

What **was** she probably **doing** at around 7:10 yesterday evening?
It's 7:10 right now. What **is** she probably **doing**?
What **will** she probably **be doing** at around 7:10 tomorrow evening?

A. Using the future progressive tense

1. Use the future progressive form to focus on an activity that will be in progress at a specific time in the future.

> Don't call me *at midnight.* I'**ll be sleeping** then.

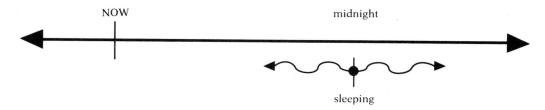

2. Future progressive can also refer to an activity that will continue over a period of time from now into the future.

> I'**ll be living** here *for another three years.*
> Yuri **will be living** here *for three more years.*
> Chang **will be living** here *until he gets his Ph.D.*

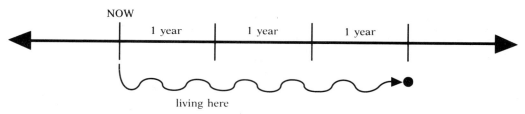

B. Forming the future progressive tense

1. Affirmative and negative statements. The future progressive verb tense consists of **WILL / WON'T + BE + -ING** verb.

Subject +	WILL/WON'T "future" +	BE + -ING Verb "In progress" +	Rest of Sentence
Tammy	will	be watching	the news tomorrow evening at 7:00.
She	won't	be watching	a comedy.

2. Questions

> **Will** you **be studying** at home tonight? Yes, I **will.**
> What **will** you **be studying?** I'**ll be studying** math.
> Jack **will be studying** with you, **won't** he? You're right. He **will.**

3. Special questions

Use the question phrase **HOW LONG . . . ?** to find out the time period of a future activity.

> **How long** will you be living in that apartment? For one semester.
> Until I graduate.

Use the question phrase **HOW MUCH LONGER . . . ?** to find out how long a future activity will continue, starting from now.

> **How much longer** will Chang be working on his Ph.D.? For another six months.
> For six more months.

Activities in Progress

A. *Find out what your classmate will be doing at the following times. Ask a question with the future progressive form. Your classmate will answer with a complete sentence. Fill in empty brackets with your own cues.*

EXAMPLE   7:00 tonight?

Student A: What will you be doing at 7:00 tonight?
Student B: I'll probably be washing the dinner dishes.

1.   this coming Sunday morning at 7:00 A.M.?
2.   a year from now?
3.   at around 10:00 this evening?
4.   [?]

B. *Find out what the following people are doing now. Then find out how much longer they will be doing that. Fill in empty brackets with your own cues.*

EXAMPLE   what / do?
            eat dinner

Student A: What are you doing?
Student B: I'm eating dinner.
Student A: How much longer will you be eating?
Student B: I'll probably be eating for another 10 minutes.

1.   STUDENT A: what / John / do?
     STUDENT B: play basketball
2.   STUDENT A: who / support / Daniel?
     STUDENT B: his parents
3.   STUDENT A: where / you / live / at the moment?
     STUDENT B: [   ]

FOCUS 8   Possibilities in the Future

Use the modal auxiliaries **MAY** and **MIGHT** instead of **WILL** to make predictions about possibilities in the future. **MAY** and **MIGHT** mean almost the same thing and can be used in the same situations. These auxiliaries are always followed by the base form of a verb or an auxiliary. To make the verb negative, add **NOT** after the auxiliary **MAY** or **MIGHT**.

Maybe scientists will find life on other planets someday.
Scientists **might** (may) **find** life on other planets someday.

Someday, maybe there won't be enough space on this planet for everyone.
Someday, there **might** (may) **not be** enough space on this planet for everyone.

Here are some additional examples of future possibilities:

Are you going to go to the international potluck dinner party?

I **might.** It depends if I can get a ride or not.
I'm not sure. I **might not.** My sister **might be coming** into town then.
Yes, I am. And I **may bring** a friend.
I don't know. I **may not be able to go** because I **might have to work** then.

Future Possibilities

*Answer each of the following questions with different possibilities using **MIGHT** or **MAY**.*

EXAMPLE   What will people wear in the future?

They might wear disposable clothes.
(They might wear very light, loose clothes.)

1.   Where will people have to live if the earth becomes too crowded?
2.   How will people travel to work 200 years from now?
3.   What kind of food will people eat in the future?
4.   What are some things that doctors will be able to do in the future?
5.   What will be different in your country 50 years from now?

FOCUS 9   Logical Expectations

Reprinted by permission of Leo Michael
FIGURE 8–1

Does the student in Fig. 8–1 think that it will be difficult to decide what to wear? Why?

The modal auxiliary **SHOULD** can be used to make a prediction about the future. Use **SHOULD** to express *a logical expectation* for the future.*

The speaker uses **SHOULD** to indicate that there is every reason to believe that something will probably happen. **SHOULD** is always followed by the base form of a verb or an auxiliary. To express a negative expectation, add **NOT** after **SHOULD**. The contraction for **SHOULD NOT** is **SHOULDN'T**.

---

*For information about a different meaning of **SHOULD** (advice), see Chapter 10.

Here are some more examples of logical expectations with **SHOULD**:

> Secretary: Will this package arrive in Seattle by Friday?
>
> Postal employee: It **should.** Today is Monday; five days **should be** enough time. It **shouldn't take** longer than that.

> Dean: Do you think the students will have enough time to finish this test?
>
> Professor: Yes, I do. They **should be able to answer** 50 questions in an hour.

> Tanya: Are our guests here yet?
>
> Cal: No, but they **should be arriving** any minute now.

PRACTICE 9-1 Expectations with **SHOULD**

A.   How does the meaning differ in the highlighted sentences in the following conversations?

1. CAROL: Do you know when Jill is going to get here?

   MALCOLM: Yes. **She will get here at around nine o'clock.**

2. CAROL: Do you know when Jill is going to get here?

   MALCOLM: I'm not sure. **She might get here at around nine.** When I talked to her earlier, she wasn't sure what time she would be ready to come over.

3. CAROL: Do you know when Jill is going to get here?

   MALCOLM: Well, I just called her house. She's already left. It will probably take about 20 minutes to get here, so **she should get here at around nine.**

B.   Change the sentences that begin with I (DON'T) EXPECT . . . to sentences with SHOULD.

EXAMPLE

> Secretary: When will my package arrive in Seattle?
>
> Postal employee: I expect that it will get there by Friday.
>
> **It should get there by Friday.**

1. TAMMY: Do you think I will be able to recognize Jim when he arrives?

   JERRY: I expect that you will be able to recognize him.

2. MARCUS: What time do you think Uncle James will be arriving in New York?

   CLEO: I expect that he will be arriving at around four o'clock.

3. ALBERT: Do you think it will take Sonia a long time to get a new ID card?

   MEGAN: I don't expect that it will take very long.

A WIDER ANGLE

Group Project: A Utopian Society

*A **utopia** is a perfect society, one without any problems. Form a small group with some of your classmates. Your group's job is to plan the perfect society for the future. Discuss what your perfect society will be like and how it will be different from today's society. Your plan does not have to be real or even possible. Use your imagination!*

You might want to consider the following topics: **marriage and the family, technology, schools, recreation,** *and* **entertainment.**

Writing Practice

Write a short composition on one of the following topics.

TOPIC 1:   Write a description of a perfect future society—your idea of a utopia.

TOPIC 2:   Describe your hometown (or your country) 50 years from now. Write about your predictions and your hopes for its future.

TOPIC 3:   What will your life probably be like 15 years from now? Make predictions about your future.

TOPIC 4:   Imagine the day that you return to your country. Describe how you imagine your arrival and your first few days back home.

DEVELOPING YOUR SKILLS AND KNOWLEDGE *Chapter Exercises*

EXERCISE 1   Predictions with WILL

Use the following cues with **WILL** *or* **WON'T** *to give your predictions about life one hundred years in the future.*

EXAMPLE   there be / (probably) peace everywhere

There will probably be peace everywhere.

(There probably won't be peace everywhere.)

1.   scientists / [probably] change [= *ability*] / deserts into fertile farmland
2.   we / [probably] get a lot of food from the sea
3.   there / [probably] be a third world war
4.   agriculture / [probably] very important in my country
5.   doctors / [probably] perform [= *ability*] / brain transplants
6.   my great-grandchildren / [probably] know [= *necessity*] / a lot about computers

What other predictions do you have for the future?

7.   (Won't) . . .
8.   (Will) . . .

EXERCISE 2   Willingness

A.   **Promises:** *Sonia is about to leave for the United States to study. Her mother is, of course, a little nervous because her daughter has never traveled alone before. Complete Sonia's promises to her mother with sentences using* **WILL** *or* **WON'T.**

MOTHER: I want you to write to me at least every other week.

SONIA: OK, Mom. _____.

MOTHER: Study hard.

SONIA: Don't worry. _____.

MOTHER: And don't lose a lot of weight! You are already much too thin!

SONIA: _____.

MOTHER: I'm so afraid that you will get homesick.

SONIA: _____.

MOTHER: Well, have a great time!

SONIA: Thanks. _____.

B.   *Refusals:* Complete each sentence using **WON'T** to show a refusal or malfunction.

1.   CHAD: What's the matter with your key?

      LISA: I don't know. It _____.

      CHAD: Maybe it's the wrong key.

2.   DOM: I'm having some problems with the horn in my car.

      MISSY: What's the matter?

      DOM: The horn _____.

3.   FRANNY: I don't think you should give that pink shirt to David for his birthday.

      TIMOTHY: How come?

      FRANNY: He _____. He doesn't like pink.

EXERCISE 3   Be Going To

Answer each of the following questions with a complete sentence.

1.   What holiday are the people of this country going to celebrate next?
2.   Who's going to cook your dinner tonight?
3.   What are you going to have for dinner?
4.   Where are you going to be at 9:00 this evening?

EXERCISE 4   Future Time Expressions

Write one word to complete each sentence with a future time expression.

1.   Marge and Tom are going to get married _____ a couple of months.

2.   Pierre is going to finish his master's degree two years _____ now.

3.   What are you going to do _____ coming Saturday?

4.   I can't talk right now. Can you call me back _____ a few minutes?

5.   Luis is going to go to Venezuela the month after _____.

EXERCISE 5 **Different Meanings of Present Tense Verbs**

Look at the verbs in the following conversations. Decide if the action is taking place ***now***, *is going to take place in the* ***future***, *or is referring to a* ***general situation***.

EXAMPLE

Bob:	Hi, Jill. Are you busy?	
Jill:	Yes, I am. **I'm working** on a computer program.	**now**
Bob:	**Are** you **going** to the lecture on computer graphics tomorrow?	**future**
Jill:	Of course. I **go** to all of Dr. Kroll's lectures.	**in general**

1. SAM: What **are** you **doing** tonight? _____

   SUE: **I'm going** dancing. _____

2. LIZ: Hi, Jack. What **are** you **doing**? _____

   JACK: **I'm trying** to fix my car. _____

   LIZ: What's the problem? _____

   JACK: The brakes **aren't working** very well. _____

3. MR. GIBSON: **We're having** a barbecue this Saturday. _____

   We'd like to invite you to come.

   MR. PROWITT: Thanks, Pete. Unfortunately, **I'm going** to New York this weekend for our annual national meeting. _____

   MR. GIBSON: When **does** your flight **leave?** _____

   MR. PROWITT: Supposedly at 7:00 P.M., but it rarely **leaves** on time. _____

EXERCISE 6 **Future Time Clauses**

Fill in each blank with the appropriate tense of the verb indicated.

According to Jeane Dixon's* predictions, someday soon scientists

_____ the oceans into fish farms. She believes that while
     (turn)

they _____ the deepest waters of the Pacific, they
          (explore)

_____ large numbers of gigantic squid. Once they
     (discover)

_____ about the existence of the squid, they
     (know)

_____ their meat as a valuable and inexpensive source of
   (use [= *ability*])

protein. She also believes that scientists of the future

_____ plants to predict changes in nature. For example,
     (grow)

_____

*Jeane Dixon is an American astrologer who is famous for her predictions about the future.

they _____ plants that are sensitive to earth tremors. When
         (have)
these plants _____, scientists _____ that an
                 (react)   (know)
earthquake _____ soon.
                (occur)

Source: Jeane Dixon, *Yesterday, Today, and Forever* (New York: William Morrow and Company, Inc., 1975).

EXERCISE 7   Future Real Conditions

A.   Use the information in the situation to complete each sentence with **IF** *or* **UNLESS.**

The U.S. presidential elections are coming up in a few months. Before citizens can vote in an election, they must register by the registration deadline. The deadline is tomorrow. Pamela hasn't registered yet.

1. She won't be able to vote _____ she doesn't register by tomorrow.

2. _____ she registers today or tomorrow, she won't be able to vote.

3. _____ she registers by tomorrow, she will be able to vote.

4. She will be able to vote _____ she forgets to register by tomorrow.

5. In the United States, people cannot vote _____ they register first.

B.   Use the information in each situation to form a future condition. Use **IF** *or* **UNLESS** *as the connecting word.*

EXAMPLE   In the future, maybe scientists will find intelligent life on other planets. In that case, many people will be surprised.
If scientists find intelligent life on other planets, many people will be surprised.

1. Maybe there will be an energy problem in the future. In that case, we will have to find new sources of energy.
2. Maybe scientists will invent an economical electric car. In that case, people won't need gasoline for their cars.
3. Maybe people won't have smaller families in the future. In that case, there will be a food shortage.

EXERCISE 8   Future Progressive Tense

Answer the questions with a complete sentence.

1. Where will you be living one year from now?
2. How much longer will you be studying English?
3. How long will you be living in this city?
4. How much longer will you be living at your current address?

Future Possibilities

Rewrite each sentence using the auxiliary MIGHT instead of the adverb MAYBE.

> **EXAMPLE**   Maybe I'll eat out tonight.
> **I might eat out tonight.**

1. Maybe the teacher will give a test next week.
2. Maybe the test won't be difficult.
3. Maybe I will have to be absent next week.
4. Maybe I won't be able to go to class.
5. Maybe I will be visiting my aunt and uncle in Florida.

EXERCISE 10   **Logical Expectations**

Read each situation and answer the question using SHOULD.

> **EXAMPLE**   It usually takes a week for an airmail letter to reach Japan from here.
> If I send a letter tomorrow, when will it get to Japan?
> **It should get there a week from tomorrow.**

1. It usually takes Wendy twenty minutes to get to school. She left her house five minutes ago. When will she get to school?
2. Carlos is planning to study English for the next two years. During that time, he will be living with an American family. How good do you think his English will be in two years?
3. David has just used a car wax that is guaranteed to last at least three months. Will he have to wax his car next month?

EXERCISE 11   **Talking about the Future**

Choose the answer that best completes the following sentences. Be prepared to explain your choice.

1. JOSÉ: Where are you going to be tonight at around 8:00?

   MARIA: I'm not sure. I _____ at the student center.

   a. am going to be   b. might be   c. will be   d. am

2. MIGUEL: What time do you think we will be arriving in Cleveland?

   JULIA: According to the schedule, we _____ at around 6:00, but you can never know for sure! The weather around the Great Lakes can change suddenly.

   a. are going to arrive   b. might arrive   c. should be arriving   d. will be arriving

3. TING: Do you have any plans for this evening?

   HEITOR: Yes. I _____ to a movie with some friends.

   a. might go   b. should go   c. am going   d. may be going

4. AHMED: I don't see how I will ever understand English verb tenses!

    YOSHI: Calm down. I _____ them to you.

    a. might explain   b. should explain   c. explain   d. will explain

5. ANGIE: Let's call Ted and Lynn at 7:00 tomorrow morning.

    CATHY: We'd better not. That's awfully early in the morning. They _____ then.

    a. might be sleeping   b. may sleep   c. are going to sleep

    d. will sleep

9 Events and Experiences Related to the Present

┌─────────────────────────────────┐
│ **THE BIG PICTURE** │
└─────────────────────────────────┘
The Present Perfect Tense
The Present Perfect Progressive Tense

AT A GLANCE

Connecting the Past and the Present

Photography: A Wide-Angle Shot

What kind of picture can a photographer take with:

    a. a very fast shutter speed?
    b. a telephoto or "zoom" lens?
    c. a wide-angle lens?

Photographers use a **wide-angle lens** when they want to focus on a large area in a single photograph.

English has a verb tense that allows the speaker to focus on two periods of time with one verb. This verb tense is called the *present perfect tense.* The present perfect tense can focus on the past (before now) and the present (now) at the same time.

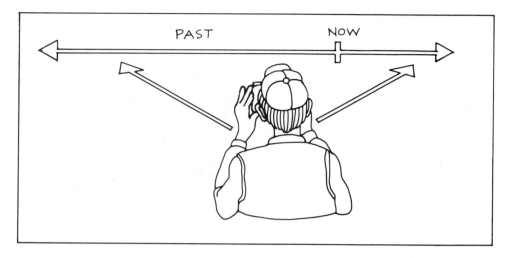

Past Events Connected to Now

The woman in the following cartoon is visiting her husband in the hospital. She is the person who is talking.

©1981 Universal Press Syndicate   4-23

"Oh no! I've broken my nail."

Why is the woman upset at the moment?
When did she break her fingernail?
When did she notice that it was broken?

In this chapter, you will practice the present perfect tenses to talk about past events and experiences that are connected in some way to the present time.

FOCUS 1   Introduction to the Present Perfect Tense: Indefinite Past Time

The grammar explanations and examples for this section are based on the following situation:

> When Anita first came to study in the United States, she lived in Cleveland, Ohio. She studied English there for one year. When she finished her English studies, she moved to Bloomington, Indiana, to get a degree in music at Indiana University. She is in Indiana pursuing her music degree now.

A.   Review of the simple past tense

Anita **saw** the Ohio Ballet twice when she was a student in Cleveland.

1.   When did Anita see the Ohio Ballet?
2.   Is she still a student in Cleveland?

Use the *simple past tense* to focus on an event that happened at a specific past time. Events in the simple past happened at or during a time period that is also completed.

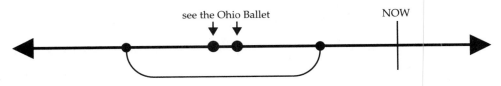

She was a student in Ohio.

B.   Present perfect

Anita **has seen** the Indiana University Ballet perform three times.

1.   When did she see the Indiana University Ballet?
2.   Is she still a student at Indiana University?

Use the *present perfect tense* (**HAS / HAVE + past participle**) to talk about events that happened before now, but at an unspecified past time. The action is completed, but the time period is <u>not</u> completed. Because the time period is not yet complete, there is the possibility that the action might take place again in the future. The present perfect tense <u>cannot</u> occur with a specific past time.

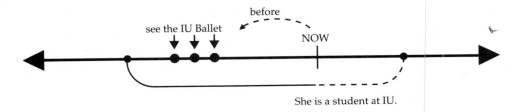

She is a student at IU.

Understanding the Time Reference

*Look at the verbs in the following sentences. Did the action in each sentence take place at a **specific past time**, or did it happen at an **indefinite time before now**?*

EXAMPLE   I visited Niagara Falls last month.

(time = **specific:** last month)

I have visited Niagara Falls.

(time = **indefinite:** before now)

1. John **has gone** to Florida on vacation several times. (time =

_____)

2. He **went** there last winter. (time = _____)

3. While he was there, he **got** a terrific tan. (time =

_____)

4. I **have never gone** to Florida. (time = _____)

5. I **have gone** to a tanning spa twice. (time = _____)

Complete and Incomplete Time Periods

Following are two conversations. During what time period did the action in each of the sentences occur? Choose the appropriate verb form to complete the sentence, and explain why you chose it.

1. LOUIS: When _____ back from your trip to
                        a. did you get
                        b. have you gotten
            California?

   KAREEM: The day before yesterday.

   LOUIS: _____ a good time?
                     a. Did you have
                     b. Have you had

   KAREEM: Oh yes! It was very interesting.

   LOUIS: _____ to Hollywood?
                     a. Did you go
                     b. Have you gone

   KAREEM: No. I _____ enough time.
                       a. didn't have
                       b. haven't had

   _____ there?
                   a. Did you go
                   b. Have you gone

   LOUIS: Yes. It's very interesting.

2. TYRONE: _____ in a foreign country?
                   a. Did you ever live
                   b. Have you ever lived

   KEN: Yes. I _____ in Zaire from 1988 to 1990.
                 a. lived
                 b. have lived

TYRONE: Really? How interesting! _____ the chance
                                      a. Did you have
                                        b. Have you had

to see any mountain gorillas?

KEN: Yes. During one of my vacations, I _____
                                        a. took
                                        b. have taken

a hiking trip to see the gorillas.

TYRONE: Wow! You're lucky. I _____ in a foreign
                                        a. never lived
                                        b. have never lived

country, and I _____ any animals in the
                                a. never saw
                                b. have never seen

wild like that. Maybe I'll try to go on a safari some time

after I graduate!

FOCUS 2   Forming the Present Perfect Tense

A. Forming the present perfect tense

The present perfect tense consists of the auxiliary **HAS** or **HAVE** and a past participle. Add **NOT** to the auxiliary to make the verb negative.

Past participles for regular verbs take the **-ED** ending. They have the same spelling and pronunciation as regular simple past verbs (see Appendix A). Many common verbs have irregular past participles (see Appendix B).

Subject	+ Auxiliary "before now"	+ Past Participle	+ Rest of Sentence
The woman	has	broken	her fingernail.
The man	has	had	an accident.
It	has not	rained	recently.
I	have not	been	to Washington yet.
We	have	seen	the movie several times.
You	have	made	a wonderful dinner!
They	have not	arrived	yet.

B. Contractions

Have	→	've	**I've broken** my fingernail.
Has	→	's	He**'s had** an accident.
Have not	→	Haven't	I **haven't been** to Washington yet.
Has not	→	Hasn't	It **hasn't rained** recently.

C. Questions and answers

Have you **had** dinner yet?	No, I **haven't.**
Has Tony **seen** that movie?	Yes, he **has.**
How many times **has** he **seen** that movie?	He**'s seen** it twice.
What **have** you **done** to your hair?	I**'ve gotten** a permanent.
Who **has been** to Miami before?	Sam and Don **have.**
Who(m) **have** you **met** so far?	We**'ve met** some teachers.

Tony**'s seen** that movie, **hasn't** he?   Yes, he **has.**
You **haven't seen** it, **have** you?   No, I **haven't.**
Lisa**'s had** lunch, **hasn't** she?   I think she **has.**

D. Ability

The modal auxiliary **CAN** does not occur in the present perfect. Use the present perfect form of **BE ABLE TO** to talk about ability before now or continuing up to now:

Subject +	HAS / HAVE (NOT) *"before now"* +	BEEN ABLE TO *"ability"* +	Base Form Verb
John	has	been able to	**make** a lot of friends here.
I	haven't	been able to	**practice** my English very much.

OTHER EXAMPLES

> I **have never been able to get** a good tan.
>
> **Have** you **been able to get** in touch with Sam yet? No, I **haven't.**

E. Necessity

The modal auxiliary **MUST** does not occur in the present perfect. Use the present perfect form of **HAVE TO** to talk about necessity before now or continuing up to now:

Subject +	HAD / HAVE (NOT) *"before now"* +	HAD TO *"necessity"* +	Base Form Verb
The city	has	had to	**raise** taxes twice this year.
I	haven't	had to	**go** to see a doctor here.

OTHER EXAMPLES

> Jim **has never had to cook** for himself.
>
> **Have** you **had to go** to a dentist for any reason? Yes, I **have.**

PRACTICE 2–1   Forming the Present Perfect Tense

A.   *Complete each sentence with the present perfect form(s) of the verb indicated.*

     1.   (change) Computers _____ the way we live.

     2.   (use) I _____ a computer, but my roommate

         _____ .

     3.   (make) Computer engineers _____ a lot of progress with computer robots.

     4.   (invent) But nobody _____ a computer that has emotions.

B.   *Use the following cues to make true sentences about yourself. Do not mention a specific time; use the present perfect form to talk about actions "before now."*

EXAMPLE   fly in an airplane // fly in a helicopter

> I **have flown** in an airplane before, but I **haven't flown** in a helicopter.

(I **have flown** in an airplane before, and I **have flown** in a helicopter too.)

(I **haven't flown** in an airplane, and I **haven't flown** in a helicopter either.)

1. drive a car // drive a truck
2. ride a horse // ride a camel
3. take a bus in this town // take a taxi
4. have spaghetti // make it
5. taste apple cider // taste carrot juice
6. go cross-country skiing // go sledding

C. *Report what you found out about your classmates.*

EXAMPLE   Henry has flown in an airplane, but he hasn't flown in a helicopter.

FOCUS 3 Experiences

Is there a famous place in your country that you have never visited in your life?
Is there a famous place in your country that you have visited many times in your life?
Look at the sentences below. When did these actions happen?

> I **have never seen** Mt. Rushmore.
>
> **Have you ever been** to Niagara Falls?
>
> My brother **has driven** over the Golden Gate Bridge **many times.**

The present perfect tense is often used to talk about experiences in our lives. A past experience is something that:

1. happened *before now*
2. happened during our lives (an incomplete time period)

A.   Experiences: EVER / NEVER / NOT EVER

The adverb **EVER** means "at any time" and **NEVER** means "at no time." They can occur with different verb tenses.

Simple present: "at any time in general"

> **Do** you **ever smoke?**
>
> No, I **never do.** I **hate** it.
> (Yes, I **do.** I sometimes **have** a cigarette after dinner.)

Simple past: "at any time during a past time period"

> **Did** you **ever smoke** in high school?
>
> No, I **never did.** I **never wanted** to smoke then.
> (Yes, I **did.** I **smoked** a lot back then.)

Present perfect: "at any time before now"

> **Have** you **ever smoked?**
>
> No, I **never have.** I **have never been** interested in trying it.
> (Yes, I **have.** I **tried** it once when I was very young.)

Future: "at any time in the future"

Will you **ever start** smoking?

No, I **never will.**

The adverb **EVER** is used with the present perfect tense to ask questions about experiences. Put **EVER** in the middle position: after the subject in the question.

The adverb **NEVER** (or **NOT EVER**) occurs in statements about experiences that have not happened. Put **NEVER** or **NOT EVER** in the middle position: after the auxiliary and before the past participle.

I **have never been*** to Paris. **Have** you **ever been** there?

No, I **haven't ever been** to Paris.

B.   Experiences: (number of) TIMES

The present perfect tense can also occur with the **number of times** an experience has happened during a person's life so far. Once again, do not mention the specific times the experiences took place.

Use the question phrase **HOW MANY TIMES . . . ?** with the present perfect tense to ask about the number of times an experience has taken place. Use the question word **WHEN . . . ?** with the simple past tense to ask for a specific past time.

Present Perfect	Simple Past
I **have been** to Europe three times.	I **went** to Europe last year.
How many times **have** you **seen** this film?	When **did** you **see** this film?
We **have gone** to the museum twice.	We **went** to the museum a month ago.

PRACTICE 3-1   Opinions Based on Experience

Ask your classmates if they like the following things. If they have had experience with the item, they will give you their opinion. If they have never had any experience with it, they will tell you so.

EXAMPLE   music by Frank Sinatra?

Student A: Do you like music by Frank Sinatra?

Student B: **I don't know. I've never listened to it.**
              (I've never heard of him.)

Remember: Do not give an opinion if you have never had experience with the item.

1.   hot cereal?   5.   Thai food?
2.   the actress Sally Field?   6.   Egyptian movies?
3.   the TV show *60 Minutes*?   7.   the rock group The Beach Boys?
4.   to play racquetball?   8.   to watch Japanese sumo wrestling?

PRACTICE 3-2   Past Experiences

Use the present perfect tense with the following cues to talk about the number of times you have had these experiences.

***HAS / HAVE BEEN TO** + (place) means "have visited" or "have gone to" a place.

EXAMPLE   go to Disney World

I have never gone to Disney World.
I have gone to Disney World twice.
I have gone to Disney World many times.

1.	buy a lottery ticket	9.	use a computer
2.	win a lottery	10.	lose your passport
3.	ride a roller coaster	11.	find money on the sidewalk
4.	fly a kite	12.	leave your books in the classroom
5.	fall asleep in class	13.	forget your homework at home
6.	feel homesick here	14.	rent a car
7.	catch a cold here	15.	lend money to a classmate
8.	get a speeding ticket		

PRACTICE 3-3   Questions about Experiences

A.   *Find out if your classmate has had the following experiences by asking a question with **HAVE YOU EVER . . . ?** Your classmate will respond with a short answer and an echo question. You should then respond to the echo question.*

EXAMPLE   go to Disneyland?

Student A: **Have** you **ever gone** to Disneyland?
Student B: No, I **haven't. Have** you?
Student A: Yes, I **have.**
              (I **haven't** either.)

1. drive in snow?
2. eat Mexican food?
3. hear of the singers Simon and Garfunkel?
4. play golf?
5. cut class?

B.   *Now use this information to compare your experiences with your classmate's. Use **AND SO, AND NEITHER,** or **BUT** with an auxiliary.*

EXAMPLE   My classmate has never gone to Disneyland, **and neither** have I.
                     My classmate has gone to Disneyland, **and so** have I.
                     My classmate has never gone to Disneyland, **but** I have.

PRACTICE 3-4   Conversation Starters

English speakers often use the question **"HAVE YOU EVER . . . ?"** to introduce a topic of conversation. The person who asks this question may need information about the topic and is trying to find someone who has experience. Or, the speaker may have had an interesting experience that he or she would like to talk about.

Joe: **Have you ever been** to Epcot Center?
Sue: Yes, as a matter of fact, **I have.** I went there last year for vacation.
Joe: Really? I might go there for spring vacation. How was it?
Sue: It was a lot of fun.

Mary:	**Have you ever been** to Epcot Center?
Dave:	No, **I haven't.** Why do you ask?
Mary:	I went there last month.
Dave:	You did? How was it?
Mary:	It was incredible!

Imagine that you are having something to drink with your classmate. Choose one of the following topics to start a conversation with "HAVE YOU EVER . . . ?" Or, you can make up your own topic. Continue the conversation. You and your classmate should give only true information. Fill in empty brackets with your own cues.

1. get lost in this city?
2. visit a local family here?
3. be in a car accident?
4. go to a disco in this city?
5. break any bones in your body?
6. meet somebody famous?
7. [   ]?

FOCUS 4   Adverbs: **SO FAR, YET, STILL, ALREADY**

Pedro and Ampol are studying English. Last Friday, the teacher assigned five different exercises for homework. Today is Saturday. The exercises are due on Monday.

Pedro:	**Have** you **done** your English homework **yet?**
Ampol:	Not all of it. But I **have started** it.
Pedro:	How many exercises **have** you **done?**
Ampol:	I**'ve done** two of them **so far.** What about you?
Pedro:	I **still haven't started** the assignment.
Ampol:	What about your roommate?
Pedro:	He**'s already finished** the entire assignment!

When did the students get the assignment? When do they have to finish the assignment? How much more time do they have to complete the assignment?

Why do you think they use the present perfect tense?

The adverbs **SO FAR, YET, STILL,** and **ALREADY** are often used with the present perfect* tense to talk about actions that have occurred before now during a time period that has not yet ended.

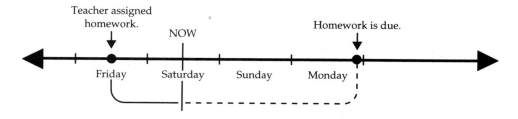

*In informal conversation you may hear native English speakers use the simple past tense with these adverbs instead of the present perfect tense.

EXAMPLE   How many exercises **did** you **do** so far? I already **started** the assignment.

However, in this chapter, we will focus on using the present perfect tense, **not** the simple past tense, to talk about actions completed before now during a time period that has not ended yet.

A. SO FAR

We've had six tests **so far this semester.**
So far, I've gotten over 85% on all of the tests.
Have you done all of the homework **so far?**

Use **SO FAR** with the present perfect tense to talk about actions completed *before now.* The time period is not finished yet, and it is reasonably expected that the action will be repeated before the time period ends. **SO FAR** usually goes at the end of the sentence, but it can also go at the beginning.

Pedro *has visited* six different states **so far.**
So far, Pedro *has visited* six different states.

SO FAR usually goes before the adverb for the time period:

How much money have you made **so far** *this month?*

B. YET and STILL

Have you *applied* to a university **yet?**
No, I **still** *haven't picked* up an application.
Have you *paid* your rent **yet this month?**
John *hasn't paid* the rent **yet this month.**
John **still** *hasn't paid* his rent.

Use **YET** and **STILL** with the present perfect tense to talk about actions that are expected to happen during a certain time period that is not completed.

1.   Other aspects of **YET**

YET occurs with the present perfect in **YES / NO** *questions* and *negative* sentences.

Has Karl called you **yet?**
No, I haven't heard from him **yet.**

YET usually goes at the end of the sentence.

Has the professor corrected our exams **yet?**
No, she hasn't given our exams back **yet.**

YET usually goes before the adverb for the time period:

I haven't paid the rent **yet** *this month.*

2.   Other aspects of **STILL**

Use **STILL** with the present perfect to emphasize that the subject is waiting for an action to take place.

STILL occurs with the present perfect in *negative* statements.

Jorge **still** hasn't arrived.

STILL occurs before a negative auxiliary.

We took that test two weeks ago, and we **still** *haven't gotten* our scores.

C. ALREADY

Mrs. Cox: Please don't forget to send in our income tax form. Today is the deadline.
Mr. Cox: I've **already** mailed it. I sent it last night.

Use **ALREADY** with the present perfect tense to show that an action happened *before now*. The adverb **ALREADY** gives the idea that the action happened sooner than expected.

ALREADY usually occurs with the present perfect in *affirmative* sentences.

ALREADY often goes in the middle position for adverbs, after the auxiliary **HAVE**.

> I've **already** mailed it.

ALREADY can also go at the end of the sentence.

> I've mailed it **already**.

PRACTICE 4-1   Using **SO FAR**

Use the following cues to form questions with SO FAR. Your classmate should respond to each question with a complete sentence.

EXAMPLE   how many times / you / call home / this month?

        Student A: How many times have you called home **so far this month?**

        Student B: I've called home **twice so far.**

                (I haven't called home at all **so far this month.**)

  1.   how many times / you / late to class / this week?
  2.   how many letters / you / receive / this month?
  3.   how many letters / you / write / this month?

PRACTICE 4-2   Using **YET** and **STILL**

A.   Look at the following sentences. How does each pair differ in meaning?

  1.   a. Have you **ever** tried pizza?
      b. Have you tried pizza **yet?**
  2.   a. I have **never** used a computer.
      b. I haven't used a computer **yet.**
  3.   a. I **still** haven't seen your house.
      b. I have **never** seen your house.

*B.   Read the following situations. Use the cues to ask questions with **YET**. Your classmate will give negative responses using **STILL** with the cues. Be sure to add any necessary articles, pronouns, objects, or prepositions.*

EXAMPLE   Your passport is going to expire in a month.

        Student A: [yet] you / renew / passport?
        Student B: [still] not have / time
        Student A: Have you renewed your passport yet?
        Student B: No, I still haven't had time to do that.

  1.   We are going to study the past perfect tense sometime this term.

      STUDENT A: [yet] the teacher / teach the past perfect tense?
      STUDENT B: [still] we / not learn

2. George is planning to get an undergraduate degree at a Canadian university.

    STUDENT A: [yet] George / start / undergraduate degree?

    STUDENT B: [still] he / not pass / English entrance test

3. Your classmate is going to buy a new car.

    STUDENT A: [yet] you / buy / new car?

    STUDENT B: [still] I / not save / enough money

PRACTICE 4-3   Practice with **ALREADY**

Answer each question using the verb indicated and **ALREADY** *in the middle position. Fill in the empty brackets with your own cues.*

    EXAMPLE   Why doesn't Miguel want any coffee? (drink)
                        Because he's already drunk three cups.

1. Why don't Eli and Ruth want to go to the movie with us? (see)
2. Why don't you feel like having breakfast with me now? (have)
3. Why doesn't the Davis family want to go to New York for vacation?
   [   ]
4. Why doesn't Melina need to take the TOEFL again? [   ]

CLOSE-UP   **Present Tenses with YET, ALREADY, STILL**

Use the verb cues to complete each sentence with the appropriate verb tense.

    Jim took the International TOEFL earlier this month.

    Sam: Hey, Jim! How did you do on the TOEFL earlier this month?

    Jim: I [not / know] _____.

            I [wait] _____ for my score.

            I [not / receive] _____ it.

Now go back and add the adverb **STILL** *to each of these sentences. Did the verb tense change?*

The adverbs **YET, ALREADY,** and **STILL** can occur with all of the present tenses. The adverb does not change the time focus of the verb.

1. Use the *simple present tense* with these adverbs to talk about general facts or states (*be, know, have,* and so on).
2. Use the *present progressive tense* with these adverbs to talk about activities that are currently in progress and are limited to a specific time.
3. Use the *present perfect tense* with these adverbs to talk about single actions that were (or were not) completed before now.

YET: Use in **YES / NO** *questions* and *negative* sentences.

Simple present:

    Jim **doesn't have** a job **yet.**

Present progressive:

Jim **isn't working** for anyone **yet.**

Present perfect:

Jim **hasn't found** a job **yet.**

ALREADY: Use in *affirmative* sentences.

Simple present:

He **already needs** a loan.

Present progressive:

He **is already getting** low on cash.

Present perfect:

He **has already spent** his savings.

STILL

Simple present: Use in *negative* or *affirmative* sentences.
Jim **still doesn't have** a job.
He **still needs** a job.

Present progressive: Use in *affirmative* sentences.
He **is still looking** for a job.

Present perfect: Use in *negative* statements.
He **still hasn't found** a job.

Close-Up

PRACTICE   **ADVERBS WITH PRESENT TENSES**

*Read the following situations. Respond to the questions using the cues with the adverbs in parentheses. Add the verb BE if necessary. Use the **simple present, present progressive,** or **present perfect tense.** Do <u>not</u> use the simple past tense.*

EXAMPLE   Bruce looks terrible. How come?

[still] he / sick
He**'s still** sick. (state verb)

[yet] he / not recover from the flu
He **hasn't recovered** from the flu **yet.**
(event not completed before now)

[still] he / recover from the flu
He**'s still recovering** from the flu.
(action in progress)

1. Sally looks worried. What's the matter?

   a. [yet]   she / not get money from her parents / this month
   b. [still]   the money / not arrive
   c. [still]   the money / not here
   d. [still]   she / wait for a check from home
   e. [still]   she / not have any money
   f. [yet]   she / not pay the rent

2. Dave wants to borrow my calculator again. Why?

   a. [yet]   he / not buy one of his own
   b. [yet]   he / not have one of his own
   c. [still]   he / try to solve a calculus problem
   d. [already]   his new batteries / die

FOCUS 5   JUST with the Present Perfect Tense

JUST

1. **JUST** can show that an action happened a short time before now. It occurs with the present perfect tense to emphasize that there is a current result.

   Don't walk on that floor! I have **just** waxed it! It's wet!

   We aren't hungry now. We've **just** eaten.

2. **JUST** can also occur with the simple past tense with almost no difference in meaning.

   I **just** waxed the floor.

3. **JUST** occurs in the middle position for adverbs.

   We have **just** eaten.

PRACTICE 5-1   Using **JUST** with the Present Perfect Tense

*Read the following situations. Use the present perfect tense to describe what **has just happened**.*

EXAMPLE   Mr. Smith's hand is on the alarm clock. It's 7:00 A.M. Mr. Smith doesn't look very happy.

His alarm **has just rung.**

1. Maria is laughing, jumping up and down, and screaming something about the lottery.
2. Diane and Sam are coming out of a church. Diane is wearing a long white dress and carrying flowers. Everyone is throwing rice at them.
3. Fred is holding an envelope in his hand. He looks very happy.

"I can always tell when you two have been watching afternoon soaps!"

Thinking about Recent Activities

Who has just come home in the cartoon above?

Who is meeting him at the door?

What were they doing shortly before he came home?

Are they watching soaps* on TV now?

How does the man know what they were doing?

Thinking about the Time Focus

Look at the following sentences. What is the time focus for the activity in each sentence?

They **are watching** TV.

They **were watching** TV when I got home.

They **have been watching** TV.

A.   Using the present perfect progressive tense

The *present perfect progressive tense* refers to activities that were in progress or that continued during a recent time period. The adverbs **LATELY** and **RECENTLY** often occur with the present perfect progressive tense.

---

*A "soap" is a soap opera, a type of TV show that continues from day to day or from week to week. Soap operas focus on the problems, romances, and lives of the characters.

I haven't been sleeping well **recently.**

Joe's been feeling sick **lately.**

The present perfect progressive does not usually occur with most stative verbs (see Chapter 6, Focus 6).

B. Forming the present perfect progressive tense

The **present perfect progressive tense** has two auxiliaries:

HAS / HAVE + BEEN + -ING verb.

To make the verb negative, add **NOT** after **HAS** or **HAVE.**

Subject	+	HAS / HAVE (NOT) "before now"	+	BEEN "in progress"	+	-ING Verb	+	Rest of Sentence
They		**'ve**		**been**		**watching**		TV.
I		**haven't**		**been**		**doing**		well in my classes.
You		**have**		**been**		**playing**		tennis.
We		**haven't**		**been**		**having**		very nice weather recently.
Joe		**'s**		**been**		**working**		hard lately.
Sue		**hasn't**		**been**		**sleeping**		well recently.
It		**has**		**been**		**raining.**		

C. Questions and answers

To form a question in the present perfect progressive, move **HAS** or **HAVE** before the subject. Use **HAS** or **HAVE** for short forms.

Have you **been doing** well in your classes?	Yes, I **have.**
Has it **been raining?**	No, it **hasn't.**
How **have** you **been feeling** recently?	I**'ve been** fine.
What **has** your roommate **been doing** lately?	He**'s been** traveling.
Who**'s been helping** you with your work?	Joe **has,** and so **have** some other friends.
It**'s been snowing, hasn't** it?	Yes, it **has.**
We **haven't been getting** much rain, **have** we?	No, we **haven't.**

PRACTICE 6-1 Present Perfect Progressive Tense

Use the following cues to ask questions with the present perfect progressive tense. Your classmate should answer each question with a complete sentence.

EXAMPLE   where / you / eat lunch recently?

Student A: Where **have** you **been eating** lunch recently?

Student B: **I've been bringing** my lunch from home.

1. what / happen / your country recently?

2. what / they / talk / the news lately?

3. what changes / the government of _____ / try to make recently?

4. how late / you / stay up recently?

Use the cues to complete the following conversations. Use appropriate verb forms, and add any necessary articles and prepositions.

1. Mike is in the cafeteria. Pedro has just come in.

   MIKE: hi, Pedro! you / look hot!

   PEDRO: we / [just] finish / exciting soccer match

   MIKE: your team / win?

   PEDRO: no, we _____. we / lose / 4 to 3

   MIKE: I / not know how to play soccer. I / [never] play it. you / teach me how to play sometime?

   PEDRO: sure! I / play soccer quite a bit / lately. I / glad to teach you

2. Lucy and Tony are talking in the kitchen.

   LUCY: where / you // when / I / call / last night?

   TONY: I / library / study.

   LUCY: you / [always] study / library?

   TONY: well, I / study / there a lot / recently // because / I / do some research

   LUCY: how late / you / stay there last night?

   TONY: I / there / about three hours

GETTING READY TO FOCUS *Up to Now*

Time Lines

A. Christophe

Christophe is a student from Haiti. He has been in the United States for three years. He studied English for one year, and then he began his undergraduate program in Mechanical Engineering. He has finished his freshman and sophomore years and has just started his junior year.

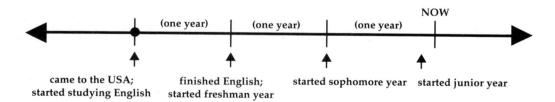

True or false?

1. Christophe is in the United States now.
2. He is studying English.

3. He finished studying English two years ago.
4. He is a junior.
5. He has finished two years of his undergraduate program.
6. He has been studying Mechanical Engineering for two years.
7. He came to the United States two years ago.

B. Miklos and Katia

Miklos has been married since 1993. He met his wife in 1992 at work.

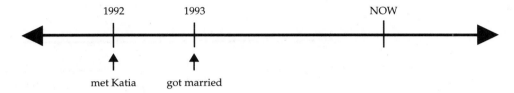

Complete the sentences.

1. Miklos met Katia in 19 _____.

2. They have known each other since 19 _____.

3. He met her _____ years ago.

4. He has known her for _____ years.

5. Katia and Miklos got married in 19 _____.

6. They have been married since 19 _____.

7. They got married _____ years ago.

8. They have been married for _____ years.

You have seen that the *present perfect tense* can refer to completed actions and that the *present perfect progressive tense* can refer to recent activities. In the next section, you will practice a different use of these two tenses.

FOCUS 7 Situations Continuing Up to Now

A. Introduction

The present perfect tense and the present perfect progressive tense often occur with the time expressions **FOR** or **SINCE**.

Christophe **has been studying** engineering *for two years*.

When did he start studying engineering?

Is he still studying engineering?

Miklos and Katia **have been** married *since 1993*.

When did they get married?

Are they still married?

The combination of the time expressions **FOR** and **SINCE** with these perfect tenses indicates two things:

1. It indicates when the situation began in the past.

    (Christophe started studying engineering two years ago.)

    (Miklos and Katia got married in 1993.)

2. It indicates that the situation continues up to now.

    (Christophe is still studying engineering.)

    (Miklos and Katia are still married.)

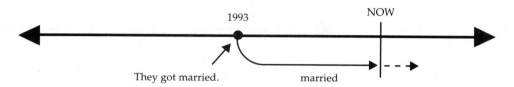

Use either of the two present perfect forms with **FOR** and **SINCE** to talk about a time period that began in the past and continues up to the present. Other verb tenses cannot have this time reference.

> I came here two months ago. I am still living here now.

Correct:	I **have been living** here *for two months.*
	I **have lived** here *for two months.*
[MISTAKE:	I am living here for two months.
	I live here for two months.
	I lived here for two months.
	I was living here for two months.]

If the time period or the situation has *not* continued up to the present, do *not* use a present perfect tense.

> Tomas studied English from 1993 to 1994.

Correct:	He **studied** English for one year.
[MISTAKE:	He has studied English for one year.
	He has been studying English for one year.
	He has been studying English since 1993.]

B.   Choosing the present perfect or the present perfect progressive tense

Both the present perfect and the present perfect progressive can occur with the expressions **FOR** or **SINCE** to indicate a situation continuing up to now.

1.   Use the **present perfect progressive** tense with repeated actions and continuing activities.

> Somebody **has been knocking** on the door for five minutes.
>
> We'**ve been driving** since seven o'clock this morning.

2.   Use the **present perfect** tense for stative verbs.

> Jim **has had** his car for several years.
>
> I **have known** Christophe since 1985.

3.   Some common activity verbs can occur with **FOR** and **SINCE** in *either* the present perfect or the present perfect progressive tense with almost no difference in meaning. These activity verbs include **FEEL**, **TEACH**, **STUDY**, **WORK**, **LIVE**, **STAY**, and **WEAR**.

The sentences in the following pairs have basically the same meaning.

I've **been feeling sick** since yesterday.
I've **felt** sick since yesterday.

Joe's **been working** here for years.
Joe's **worked** here for years.

Sue **hasn't been teaching** here for very long.
Sue **hasn't taught** here very long.

PRACTICE 7-1 Understanding the Present Perfect Tenses

Read each situation and answer the questions that follow.

1. Debbie has had a headache since she woke up.

   a. Does Debbie still have a headache?
   b. When did she first notice it?

2. Dr. Robinson worked in Pakistan for two years. He moved back to the United States in 1985, and he's been working here ever since.

   a. Where does Dr. Robinson work?
   b. Where did he use to work?
   c. Has he ever lived in Pakistan?
   d. When did he go to Pakistan?
   e. How long did he live there?
   f. When did he return to the United States?

FOCUS 8 Time Expressions Up to Now

A. Time expressions

The time words **SINCE** and **FOR** can occur with the present perfect tenses to refer to a situation that began in the past and continues up to now.

1. **SINCE** focuses on the beginning point of a time period that continues up to now. The beginning point can be a specific past time expression or a time clause.

Subject + Present Perfect (progressive) + SINCE + Specific Point in Time			
Bob	's been wearing glasses	since	last year.
Janis	has been working	since	she graduated from high school.
I	haven't seen either of them	since	high school.

2. **FOR** focuses on the length or duration of the time period.

Subject	+	Present Perfect (progressive)	+	FOR	+	Time Period
Bob		's been wearing glasses		for		a long time.
Janis		has been working		for		ages. (*"a very long time"*)
I		haven't seen either of them		for		two years.
Teddy		has been in Africa		for		ten months.

It is possible to omit **FOR**.

> He's been wearing glasses a long time.
> He's had his car ten months.

3.   **THE LAST / THE PAST + time period** refers to a time period that includes now, *not* a specific past time. Use the time word **FOR**.

> It's been raining **for the last five days.**
> [*It started raining five days ago, and it is still raining.*]
> I've been looking for an apartment **for the past month.**
> [*I started looking for an apartment a month ago, and I'm still looking.*]

4.   The present perfect tenses can also occur with time expressions with **ALL**.

> We've been studying hard **all year.** [*this year*]
> I've had a cold **all week.** [*this week*]
> You've been nervous **all morning.** [*It is still morning.*]

B.   Questions with HOW LONG . . . ?

Use **HOW LONG . . . ?** with the present perfect tenses to ask about a time period that began in the past and continues up to now.

> **How long** *have you been living* here? For three years.
> **How long** *have you had* that car? Since last January.

Keep in mind, however, that **HOW LONG . . . ?** can occur with different verb tenses to talk about different time periods.

1.   *Simple past:*

> How long **did** you **live** in Paris?
> I **lived** there for one year. [*The time period is finished. I don't live there anymore.*]

2.   *Present perfect:*

> How long **have** you **lived** here?
> I**'ve lived** here for one year. [*The time period is not finished. I'm still here.*]

3.   *Future:*

> How long **will** you **be living** here?
> I**'ll be living** here for five years. [*The time period will end in the future.*]

PRACTICE 8-1   Using **FOR** and **SINCE**

*Use the following time expressions to answer the question about Ruth. Use **FOR** or **SINCE** where appropriate.*

How long has Ruth lived here? She's lived here _____.

EXAMPLE   (five years) She's lived here **for five years.**

1. (1980)	6.	(the beginning of the year)
2. (a few years)	7.	(last year)
3. (ages)	8.	(the last year)
4. (quite a while)	9.	(the past few months)
5. (she got married)	10.	(all semester)

HOW LONG . . . ?

A.   *Choose one of the following cues to ask your classmate a question with HOW LONG . . . ? and the **present perfect** or **present perfect progressive** tense. Do not ask about something that does not continue up to now! Your classmate will answer with a complete sentence. Fill in the empty brackets with your own cues.*

EXAMPLE   play tennis

Student A: **How long have you been playing tennis?**
Student B: I have been playing tennis **for four years.**

be married   have a moustache
know _____ [*classmate*]   study English
play [*a sport*]   have pierced ear(s)
attend this school   [   ]

B.   *Now find out about your classmate's family. First, use the following cues to ask a question about a current situation, using the **simple present** or **present progressive** tense. Once you find a classmate who answers "YES," ask a question with HOW LONG . . . ?*

EXAMPLE   play a musical instrument

Student A: **Does anyone in your family play a musical instrument?**
Student B: Yes, my father does. He plays the guitar.
Student A: Really? **How long** has he been playing?
Student B: He's been playing as long as I can remember!

1.   be afraid of dogs   5.   own a business
2.   live alone   6.   wear glasses
3.   play a sport very well   7.   use a computer
4.   know how to drive

Interviews

Interview a classmate using the following cues. Your classmate should answer each question with a complete sentence.

INTERVIEW 1
1.   where / live / at the moment?
2.   how long / live there?
3.   you / like it? Why?
4.   how much longer / live there?
5.   where / live // before / move there?
6.   how long / live there?
7.   you / like it? Why?

INTERVIEW 2
1.   who / the leader of your country?
2.   the leader of your country / a king?
3.   how long / he (she) / the leader?
4.   who / the leader of your country before him (her)?
5.   when / he (she) / become the leader?

INTERVIEW 3

1. how long / you / wear your hair this way?
2. how much longer / you / think // you / keep this hairstyle?
3. what kind of hairstyle / you / have / before this one?
4. how long / you / wear your hair that way?
5. why / you / change your hairstyle?

INTERVIEW 4

1. you / have a job / at the moment?
2. where / you / work?
3. how long / you / work there?
4. you / like it? Why?
5. how much longer / you / continue to work there?
6. you / [ever] have any other jobs?
7. where / you / work / before this one?
8. how long / you / work there?
9. how / you / like it?

PRACTICE 8–4 Mixed Verb Tenses

*Work with one of your classmates to make a conversation from the following cues.
Choose appropriate verb forms, and add any necessary articles and prepositions.*

SALLY: I / sorry // that / I / call you so late last night. you / sleep?

JANE: no, I _____. I / read

SALLY: really? what / you / read?

JANE: I / read / novel by James Michener

SALLY: Michener? I / [never] hear / him

JANE: he / very popular. I / read / quite a few of his books

SALLY: what kind of books / he / [usually] write?

JANE: he / write historical novels

SALLY: what book / you / read now?

JANE: I / read / *Poland.*

SALLY: it / any good?

JANE: I / not know yet. I / [just] start it. I / read only 30 pages so far

SALLY: how long / you / read his novels?

JANE: oh, I / read them // since / I / high school. what about you, Sally? you / like to read?

SALLY: yes, I _____. But / I / not read [= *ability*] / very much so far this term. I / very busy. I / write [= *necessity*] / four papers since the beginning of the semester!

JANE: I / give you this book // when / I / finish it. you / have [= *possibility*] / more time later on

SALLY: Thanks. That would be great!

Job Interview

*Your teacher will hand out a job description for a position open in a school, company,
or organization. Several students will take the role of applicants for this position. The
rest of the class will take the role of an interviewing committee. It is the committee's
job to interview the applicants and hire one of them for the position. After the
committee members have interviewed the candidates, they will discuss who should get
the job.*

Writing Practice

Write a composition on one of the following topics.

TOPIC 1: As part of the application procedure, many universities require students
to write an autobiographical sketch. Write a short autobiography for the
admissions office at a university. Your composition should include information
about:

> a. your educational background
> b. your work experience
> c. your special interests
> d. your future plans and goals

TOPIC 2: We live in a time of rapid change. Write a short composition about the
recent changes in the world, your country, or your hometown. How has it
changed? How have people's lives been changing recently? What other changes do
you predict for the future?

Chapter Exercises

Forming the Present Perfect Tense

*Fill in each blank with the **present perfect** form of the verb indicated. Remember: you
need to use the auxiliary HAS or HAVE with the past participle. In some blanks, you
will need to write only the auxiliary.*

1. BETTY: _____ a lot of money since you
        (you / spend)
    came here?

    PETER: Yes, I _____. _____ you?

    BETTY: So _____ I.

2. GINGER: _____ sick recently?
        (Gary / be)
    WILLY: Yes, he _____, and his roommate _____ too.

3. CHUCK: You _____ my keys by any
                              (not / see)
           chance, _____ you?

   CORNELIA: I'm afraid I _____.

4. RUPERT: _____ yet?
                      (the mail / arrive)
   NAOMI: I think it _____.

5. AVIVA: _____ the TOEFL before?
                         (you / take)
   STAN: No, I _____. _____ you?

   AVIVA: Neither _____ I.

EXERCISE 2 Simple Past or Present Perfect Tense

*Complete each sentence using the **simple past** or **present perfect** form of the verb indicated. If there is no verb cue, use an appropriate short form or form of the verb BE.*

JOE: _____ a roller coaster?
              (you / [ever] ride)
SUE: Yes, I _____. I _____ roller coasters
                                              (ride)
     many times.

JOE: I _____ one for the first time last
                   (ride)
     weekend.

SUE: Where _____ it?
                      (you / ride)
JOE: I _____ the roller coaster in a nearby
                   (ride)
     amusement park.

SUE: _____ you afraid?

JOE: Yes, I _____. But I _____ it too. I
                                              (enjoy)
     can't wait to write to my brother about it. He

     _____ one.
              ([never] ride)

EXERCISE 3 Experiences

Answer each question with a short answer. Then give additional information.

EXAMPLE   Have you ever been to New York?

               Yes, I have. I went there last month.
               (No, I haven't. But I hope to go there next year.)

1. Have you ever seen a volcano?
2. Have you ever gone swimming in the Mediterranean Sea?

3. Has anyone in your family ever traveled overseas?
4. Have you ever made a snowman?

EXERCISE 4 Using Adverbs with the Present Perfect Tense

A. *Answer the questions with complete sentences.*

1. How many movies have you seen so far this month?
2. When did you last see a really good movie?
3. How often do you go to the movies?
4. How many letters have you received so far this week?
5. How many letters have you written so far this month?

B. *Use the cues with the **present perfect** tense to answer the following questions. Make the verb negative if necessary. In each of your answers, include one of the following adverbs: STILL, YET, ALREADY.*

EXAMPLE   Manoli: It's 1:30. Why is Christos hungry? (have lunch)

Tanya: He hasn't had lunch **yet.**

(He still hasn't had lunch.)

1. There is a trip to an art museum next week for any interested students. Why isn't Kate planning to go on this trip? (go there)
2. The deadline for applications to Wilson College is next Monday. If Georgetta isn't careful, she might not be able to attend. How come? (send in her application)
3. Tom is telling his roommates about an exciting movie he's just seen. They have just asked him not to tell them the ending. Why don't they want him to continue talking about the film? (see it)

EXERCISE 5 Adverbs with Mixed Verb Tenses

*Read the situation. Then use the cues to answer the questions that follow. Use the **simple present**, **present progressive**, or **present perfect** tense.*

EXAMPLE   Bruce looks terrible. How come?   [still] sick
He's still sick.

Representatives from two countries are having a meeting to discuss trade between their nations. Originally, the meeting was supposed to last only two days. However, the talks started three days ago, and the representatives haven't left yet. How come?

1. [still]   discuss the trade problem
2. [yet]   not finish discussing everything
3. [already]   make some progress
4. [yet]   not find solutions to all of the problems
5. [already]   reject several proposals
6. [still]   want to find a good solution

EXERCISE 6 Mixed Verb Tenses

Complete the conversation by writing an appropriate form of the verb indicated.

JACK: Where _____?
                              (you / be)
              I've been waiting for two hours!

MARK: I _____ at Sally's new apartment.
                     (be)

JACK: New apartment? When _____?
                                 (she / move)

MARK: She _____ yesterday. But she
                   (move)
           _____ some help moving furniture
                 (need)
           earlier so I _____ over for a little while.
                               (go)

JACK: Why _____?
                   (she / move)

MARK: Her previous landlord _____ the rent
                               (raise)
           last month. She _____ to pay it.
                       (not / afford [= *ability*])

JACK: How _____ her new apartment?
                (be)

MARK: It _____ nice. The landlord _____
          (be)   ([just] / paint)
           the entire apartment so everything _____ nice and clean.
                                  (be)

JACK: _____ moving everything in yet?
               (she / finish)

MARK: Almost. She _____ all of her furniture
                   ([already] move)
           and books, but she _____ all of her
                         (not / bring)
           clothes over yet. She _____ that later
                           (do)
           today. When I _____, she
                       (leave)
           _____ on the floor unpacking boxes of
                 (sit)
           books.

EXERCISE 7 Present Perfect Progressive

Answer each question with a complete sentence or a short answer with new information.

1. What have you been doing in the evenings lately?
2. What have you and your classmates been studying in your other classes recently?
3. How has the weather been lately?
4. Have you been thinking about buying anything recently? What? (Or, why not?)

EXERCISE 8 Time Expressions

A. *Fill in each blank with **FOR** or **SINCE**.*

1. Margie! I haven't seen you _____ ages! What have you been up to?

2. Patricia has been getting strange phone calls _____ the last month.

3. Ben has had a cold _____ he went camping last weekend.

4. Rudy and Mary have been living in Maryland _____ they got married.

5. Dr. Kroll took a teaching position at a university in New Jersey in 1984. He's gotten several pay raises _____ then.

B. *In each of the following pairs of sentences, use the information from the first sentence to complete the second sentence. Use an appropriate time expression with one of the following time words: **FOR, SINCE, LAST,** or **AGO**.*

EXAMPLE   Tom bought his car two years ago.
       He's had it **for <u>two years</u>.**

1. John has had glasses for three years.

   He started wearing glasses _____.

2. I've been looking for my keys for the last 24 hours.

   I lost them _____.

3. Mr. and Mrs. McNaught got married in 1979.

   They've been married _____.

4. The Johnsons have lived in Arizona for ten years.

   They moved there _____.

5. Rick moved to Boston when he quit his first job.

   He's been living there _____.

EXERCISE 9 Mixed Verb Tenses

Complete each sentence with an appropriate form of the verb indicated.

1. Maria is a professional photographer. Her specialty is wildlife. She

   _____ photographs of wild animals. She
   (take)

   _____ at least 20 of her pictures to different
   (sell)

   magazines since she _____ a wildlife photographer.
                        (become)

   Right now, she _____ on a project for *National*
                    (work)

   Geographic. For the past few weeks, she _____ photos
                                              (take)

of bears in the Rocky Mountains. Last week, while she

_____ a mother bear with her baby bear cubs, she
         (study)

_____ several snakes, so she _____
         (see)   (take)

some pictures of them too. As soon as she _____ her
                                                    (complete)

project on the bears, she _____ to Africa to take
                                    (go)

pictures of elephants.

2. Joe _____ a lot of trouble with his car recently. In
              (have)

fact, he _____ some trouble with his car just last
              (have)

week. He _____ home from school when it
              (drive)

_____, and he _____ it to a garage.
    (break down)   (take [= necessity])

They _____ it the next day. Now, the car
          (fix)

_____ very well. He _____ any
          (run)   (not / have)

trouble since they _____ it. However, Joe is afraid
                          (repair)

that he _____ car troubles next winter, so he
           (have [= possibility])

_____ a new one before the weather
          (buy)

_____ bad.
          (get)

–

10 *Suggestions and Advice*

THE BIG PICTURE

Modal Expressions

AT A GLANCE

Ask Ann Landers

Do newspapers in your country carry advice columns? Have you ever written a letter to a newspaper asking for advice? Have you ever read an advice column? The following letter (Fig. 10–1) was written to a famous American advice columnist, Ann Landers.

ANN LANDERS

DEAR ANN: I have a beautiful daughter who goes to the University of Illinois. She is 21 and has been seriously dating a fellow who is 22.

"Ralph" is a nice enough person, but he is at least three inches shorter than my daughter.

This does not seem to bother them. But it bothers me.

I have tried to explain to my daughter that they make a very odd-looking couple. Whoever said "love is blind" was certainly right. She thinks I am foolish and has no idea what I am talking about.

This young woman has everything going for her—looks, brains and personality. Many tall fellows have shown an interest in her. But she insists on throwing herself away on this runt.

How can I make her understand that Ralph's height may not bother her now, but it could make her very unhappy later on in life?—Concerned Mom in Chicago

Dear Mom: Why don't you just mind your own business? It's obvious that your daughter has a lot more sense than you. I can't think of anything dumber than to dump a guy because he is short—except maybe to go with a guy because he is tall.

FIGURE 10–1

Source: "Ann Landers," News America Syndicate, April 17, 1986.

What is this woman's problem? What advice does she want from Ann Landers? What advice can you give her? Do you agree or disagree with the advice Ann Landers gave?

Ask Snoopy

What role is the dog Snoopy playing in the following cartoon (Fig. 10–2)?

FIGURE 10–2

Source: "Peanuts," Charles Schulz, United Feature Syndicate, Inc., January 12, 1986.

What is this person's problem? What does "Dr. Snoopy" suggest? Do you have any other advice to give this person?

> **In this chapter, you will practice different ways to make suggestions and to give advice.**

FOCUS 1 Suggestions

A. Asking for advice and suggestions

Use the modal auxiliaries **CAN, SHALL,** and **SHOULD** to ask for suggestions or advice.

> How **can** I relieve the stress of driving home at rush hour?
>
> What **can** I do to relax when I drive home?
>
> Where **shall** we go for dinner tonight?
>
> What **should** the woman do about her daughter's short boyfriend?

B. Making suggestions

There are a variety of ways to offer suggestions in English. Here are a few of the ways to suggest something to someone.

Problem:

> How can I relieve the stress of driving in rush-hour traffic?

Suggestions:

1. **WHY DON'T** + subject + base form verb + rest of sentence

    Why don't you listen to classical music?
    Why don't you eat some ice cream?

2. **HOW ABOUT / WHAT ABOUT** + noun / -ING verb?

    How about some ice cream?
    What about listening to some classical music?

3. Subject + **COULD** + base form verb + rest of sentence

    You **could** listen to some classical music.
    We **could** eat ice cream.

4. **LET'S* (NOT)** + base form verb + rest of sentence

    Let's eat ice cream.
    Let's not listen to loud music.

C. **Responding to suggestions**

Ashley: I don't have anything to do tonight.

What suggestions can you give to Ashley? If she likes your suggestion, what will she say? What if she doesn't like your suggestion?

Here are some examples of ways to offer suggestions and possible responses:

Suggestions	Affirmative Responses	Negative Responses
Let's go bowling.	O.K.	I have a better idea.
Why don't we go bowling?	(That's) Fine with me.	We could, but . . .
We **could** go bowling.	(That) Sounds good.	I don't really feel like it.
What about bowling?	All right.	Maybe. I'll think about it.
How about going bowling?	Fine.	Let's not.
Why don't you go bowling?	Good idea.	I'd rather not.
I **could** take you bowling.	Great! I'd love to.	Thanks, but I don't think so.

PRACTICE 1–1   Offering Suggestions

A classmate will use the following cues to describe situations or problems. Make a suggestion for each situation using:

WHY DON'T YOU? / YOU COULD / HOW (WHAT) ABOUT? / LET'S

Your classmate will respond to your suggestion.

EXAMPLE   Situation: a messy roommate

Student A: My roommate is very messy. I like to live in a clean, neat place. What can I do?

Student B: **Why don't you find another roommate?**

Student A: I could, but I really like my roommate!

***LET'S** is the contraction for "let us." Speakers use **LET'S** to make a suggestion for a group that includes themselves.

Student B: Well, **you could talk to your roommate about the problem.**

Student A: That's a good idea. I think I will.

SITUATIONS

1. no friends here
2. a friend who always wants to copy homework
3. no quiet place to study at home
4. not learning English quickly enough
5. homesick

FOCUS 2   Expressing Preferences

The modal expression **WOULD RATHER** means "prefer."

Kenny: Let's go bowling.

Martha: Let's not. I **would rather rent** a video. (I prefer to rent a video.)

A.   Forming sentences with WOULD RATHER

Subject +	WOULD RATHER (NOT) +	Base Form Verb +	Rest of Sentence
I	would rather not	go	bowling.
We	would rather	rent	a video.
John	would rather	see	a movie at a theater.

Subject +	WOULD RATHER +	Base Form Verb "Preferred Alternative" +	THAN +	Base Form Verb
I	would rather	rent a video	than	go bowling.
John	would rather	go out	than	rent a video.

B.   Contractions

The contraction for **WOULD** is **'D.**

I'd rather rent a video.

You'd rather not go out to a movie.

C.   Questions and answers

Would you **rather go out** than **stay** here? No, I **wouldn't.**

John **would rather go out, wouldn't** he? Yes, he **would.**

What **would** you **rather do: go** bowling or **see** a movie? **I'd rather** see a movie.

Why don't we go bowling? **I'd rather not.**

PRACTICE 2-1   Preferences with WOULD RATHER

Use the cues with WOULD RATHER to ask your classmates about their preferences between two choices.

EXAMPLE   watch a soccer match // play in a soccer match?

Howard: **Would** you **rather watch** a soccer match or **play** in a soccer match?

Pete: **I'd rather play** soccer.

1. cook dinner // do the dishes?
2. go to a restaurant // eat at home?
3. drive a car // be a passenger?
4. To get exercise, [   ] // [   ]?
5. On Saturday nights, [   ] // [   ]?

FOCUS 3 Advice and Obligation

Concerned Mom: My daughter's boyfriend is too short. I don't think she **should go out** with him. I think she **should go out** with a taller man. How can I convince her to break up with him?

Ann Landers: Height doesn't make any difference where love is concerned. You **shouldn't try** to break them up. You **should mind** you own business. You **ought to worry** about more important things.

A. Using SHOULD and OUGHT TO

A speaker uses **SHOULD** or **OUGHT TO** to give his or her opinion about what is best in a situation. **SHOULD** and **OUGHT TO** have the same meaning.

1. *Giving advice*

   You **should mind** your own business.

   You **shouldn't worry** about your daughter.

2. *Giving an opinion about what is right or wrong*

   She **shouldn't go out** with a short man. [*The speaker thinks it's wrong or a bad idea.*]

   A mother **ought to respect** her daughter's choices. [*The speaker thinks it's a mother's obligation.*]

B. Forming sentences with SHOULD and OUGHT TO

SHOULD and **OUGHT TO** are followed by a base form verb or auxiliary. However, **OUGHT TO** is almost never used in questions and is only rarely used in negative sentences. Use **SHOULD** for questions; use **SHOULDN'T** for negative opinions.

Subject	+	Auxiliary "opinion/advice"	+	Base Form Verb	+	Rest of Sentence
I		**ought to**		**study**		hard.
You		**should** (not)		**stay**		at home all the time.
She		**ought to**		**talk**		to her teachers about her problem.
They		**should** (not)		**eat**		at that restaurant.

C. Questions and answers

To make a question, move the auxiliary **SHOULD** before the subject. Use the auxiliary **SHOULD** in short forms.

Should I **say** anything to my daughter about her boyfriend? No, you **shouldn't.**

Should I **leave** her alone? Yes, you **should.**

What **should** I **say** to her? You **shouldn't say** anything.

Who(m) **should** she **go out** with? With whomever she wants.

I **should let** her decide, **shouldn't** I? Of course you **should.**

I **shouldn't say** anything about it, **should** I? No, you **shouldn't,** and neither **should** your husband.

D. Contrast between necessity and advisability

HAVE TO or MUST indicates that an action is *necessary;* there is no choice.

You **have to take** a test before you can get a driver's license.

DOESN'T or DON'T HAVE TO indicates that an action is *not necessary.*

You **don't have to go** to driving school to get a license.

SHOULD indicates the opinion that an action is a *good idea.*

You **should get** your license soon.

SHOULDN'T indicates the opinion that an action is a *bad idea.*

You **shouldn't try** to take the written test without studying first.

PRACTICE 3-1 Advice and Opinions

Complete the following sentences with your opinions.

1. If you want to learn English well, you ought to _____.

2. If you want to learn English well, you shouldn't _____.

3. If you want to get in shape, you should _____.

4. If you want to stay in shape, you shouldn't _____.

PRACTICE 3-2 Advisability and Necessity

A.   One of your friends is planning to join you here in this country to study English. You have had some experience here, so you can give your friend some information and advice about things to do before coming here.

Complete the following sentences with **YOU SHOULD** *or* **YOU HAVE TO.**

1. _____ get a student visa.

2. _____ fill out an application for the school.

3. _____ buy your airplane ticket as soon as possible.

4. _____ bring your money in traveler's checks.

5. In addition, you should _____.

6. And you have to _____.

B.   Your friend has just arrived in this country. Give your friend some advice about living and studying here.

Complete the sentences with **YOU DON'T HAVE TO** *or* **YOU SHOULDN'T.**

1. _____ sign anything without reading it carefully.

2. _____ carry a lot of cash.

3. _____ be a citizen in order to get a driver's license.

4. _____ eat at school if you don't want to. You can bring your lunch.

What other information can you give your friend?

5. You don't have to. . . .
6. You shouldn't. . . .

FOCUS 4   Opinions and Advice after the Fact

Paul: I think I failed the economics quiz this morning.
Terri: You're kidding! It was so easy!
Paul: I know, but I didn't study last night. Instead, I went out with some of my friends.
Terri: You **shouldn't have gone out** without studying first!
Paul: I know. **I should have studied,** but I didn't feel like it.

What did Paul do last night? Does he regret it now? Why? What is Terri's opinion about what he did?

A.   Understanding opinions given after the fact

To make a judgment or to give an opinion about a past situation, use **SHOULD (NOT) HAVE** with the past participle.

Terri communicates two things when she says: *You shouldn't have gone out.*

1. Paul *did* go out.
2. She thinks this was a bad idea.

Paul communicates two things when he says: *I should have studied.*

1. He *didn't* study.
2. He regrets this. It was a good idea to study.

B.   Forming sentences with past opinions

Situation	Subject	+	SHOULD (NOT) "opinion"	+	HAVE "past"	+	Past Participle
Paul didn't study last night.	He		should		have		studied.
Paul went out with his friends.	He		shouldn't		have		gone out.

C.   Contrasting past necessity and past advisability

HAD TO indicates that something happened because it was necessary. There was no choice.

I **had to take** Nick to the emergency room last night.

DIDN'T HAVE TO indicates that an action in the past was not necessary. In some cases, it happened anyway; in other cases, it didn't happen.

Chrys: We parked in the parking garage.
Alix: You **didn't have to park** there. There's a special parking lot for emergency room patients.
Chrys: Really? I didn't know that. Well, at least we **didn't have to wait** very long in the waiting room.

SHOULD HAVE with a past participle indicates that the appropriate action did not take place.

> I **should have called** Nick's mother, but I just didn't think about it.

SHOULDN'T HAVE with a past participle indicates that the action that took place was *not* an appropriate action.

> I **shouldn't have told** Nick's girlfriend about it because it made her worry.

PRACTICE 4–1   Understanding the Situation

Read each of the following dialogues and answer the questions.

1. AMY: Where have you been? We've been worried about you!
   SUE: I'm sorry I'm late. I know I **should have called,** but I just didn't think about it.

   a. Is Sue late?
   b. Did she call to say that she was going to be late?
   c. What two things is she sorry about?

2. TOM: I ran out of gas on the highway last night.
   LIZ: How did that happen?
   TOM: My gas gauge is broken, so I didn't know how much gas I had.
   LIZ: You **should get** that fixed!
   TOM: I know.
   LIZ: So what did you do?
   TOM: I walked home.
   LIZ: Why didn't you go to a gas station?
   TOM: I didn't have any money.
   LIZ: You **should have called** me!
   TOM: I didn't want to bother you.

   a. True or False:
      Tom ran out of gas last night.
      Tom called Liz for help.
      Liz is glad that Tom didn't call her.
   b. What advice does Liz give Tom for the future?

PRACTICE 4–2   Making Judgments about the Past

*A.   Read the situations to find out what really happened. Then give your ideas about what **should have happened**.*

EXAMPLE   Paul didn't study for the test, so he got a low score.
                 He **should have studied** for the test.

1. I didn't water my plants, and now they are dead.
2. I'm afraid I've forgotten Mary's phone number because I didn't write it down.

3. Paul bought a used car and has had nothing but trouble with it ever since.

4. Last night, Pat drove home from a party when he was dizzy.

5. A van with a group of students in it had to stop suddenly, and some people got hurt because they didn't have on their seatbelts.

B. *State your opinion about the decisions that were made in the following situations.*

EXAMPLE   Peter found a wallet in the library. He took the money out and threw the wallet away.

OPINION   I don't think he should have kept the money.
                I think he should have taken the wallet to the university police.

1. Gerald accidentally backed into a brand-new sportscar as he was leaving the parking lot. He got out and saw that he had made a giant dent in the door of the other car. He quickly got back in his car and drove away.

2. Christopher was planning to study for a test last night. At around ten o'clock, his cousin and some other friends dropped by and ended up staying until after midnight. Christopher did not tell them about his test. After they left, he was too tired to study. As a result, he did not do well on the test.

C. *Answer the following questions.*

1. Think about your teenage years. Is there anything that you did or didn't do as a teenager that you wish you could change now? Tell your classmates something that you should have done or shouldn't have done during your teenage years.

2. Now that you are in this country, can you think of anything that you should have brought with you? Is there anything that you shouldn't have brought with you?

3. Think about last weekend. Tell about something that you should or shouldn't have done last weekend.

PRACTICE 4-3   Contrasting Necessity and Advisability in the Past

Read the situations. Complete the sentences with **HAD / DIDN'T HAVE TO** *or* **SHOULD(N'T) HAVE** *and the appropriate form of the verb indicated.*

1. Larry's rent is due on the first of every month. This month, he paid the rent 10 days late. The landlord was very kind and didn't make Larry pay the late fee.

   a. Larry _____ the rent at the beginning of the
                    (pay)
      month.

   b. He _____ the rent so late.
          (pay)

   c. He was lucky. He _____ a late fee.
                          (pay)

   d. Larry didn't pay the rent on time because he was broke. In fact,

      he _____ money from a friend in order to pay his
              (borrow)
      rent.

2. Carmen got a parking ticket for parking her car in front of a fire hydrant. The fine for the ticket was $50.00. She paid the ticket in court.

a. Carmen _____ to court to pay the fine.
   (go)

b. She _____ to jail.
   (go)

c. She _____ her car in front of a fire hydrant.
   (park)

d. She _____ a different place to park.
   (find)

FOCUS 5   Warnings and Strong Advice

A.   Using HAD BETTER

The modal expression **HAD BETTER** gives strong advice or a warning. It indicates that there might be a negative consequence if the advice is not followed.

> It looks like rain. I**'d better take** my umbrella.
>
> [*If I don't take it, I might get wet.*]
>
> We**'d better not be** late for class.
>
> [*If we are late, we might miss the quiz.*]

HAD BETTER offers a warning for the future or for now. It does not usually occur in questions.

B.   Forming sentences with HAD BETTER

HAD BETTER is always followed by a base form verb.

Subject	+	HAD BETTER (NOT)	+	Base Form Verb	+	Rest of Sentence
We		had better not		be		late for class.
You		had better		call		your parents.
I		had better		take		an umbrella.

C.   Contractions

The contraction for **HAD BETTER** is **'D BETTER**.

> We**'d better** not **be** late.
>
> You**'d better call.**
>
> I**'d better take** an umbrella.

D.   Consequences with HAD BETTER

Here are some ways to indicate a negative result with **HAD BETTER.** Notice the punctuation.

Warning	Negative Consequence
You**'d better take** an umbrella,	**or else** you'll get wet.
You**'d better take** an umbrella.	**If you don't,** you'll get wet.
You**'d better take** an umbrella.	**Otherwise,** you'll get wet.
We**'d better not be** late to class,	**or** we might miss the quiz.
We**'d better not be** late to class.	**If we are,** we might miss the quiz.

Warnings and Consequences

*Give warnings or strong advice to the people in the following situations. Use **HAD BETTER (NOT)**. Be sure to include the negative consequence.*

EXAMPLE

Tom smokes three packs of cigarettes a day.

He**'d better** stop smoking, **or** he might develop heart trouble.
He**'d better** stop smoking. **If he doesn't,** he will ruin his lungs.
He**'d better** quit, **or else** he might get cancer.

1. There is a factory that has been dumping toxic waste chemicals into the river for the past four years.
2. Park isn't planning to buy any health or medical insurance during his next five years here as a student.
3. Tina and Sarah are thinking about breaking their lease and moving out of their apartment three months early.
4. It's nighttime. William wants to ride his bike to the store. His bike doesn't have any lights or reflectors.

FOCUS 6   Prohibition

What do the following signs mean (Fig. 10–3)?

FIGURE 10–3

These signs give information about something that is prohibited. *Prohibited* means "not allowed."

There are two negative modal auxiliaries that indicate prohibition: **MUST NOT** and **CANNOT**. Both auxiliaries are followed by a base form verb.

A.   MUST NOT / MUSTN'T

The contraction for **MUST NOT** is **MUSTN'T**. This negative auxiliary communicates two similar ideas.

1.   The action is not allowed; it is *prohibited.*

> You **mustn't park** here. There's a NO PARKING sign.

2.   It is *necessary* that you *not* do something.

> You **mustn't make** noise. The baby is sleeping.

B.   CANNOT / CAN'T

CANNOT or **CAN'T** can indicate that something is *not allowed.*

> You **can't smoke** here. There's a NO SMOKING sign.

C.   Contrasting NOT HAVE TO and MUST NOT

Both **HAVE TO** and **MUST** indicate that something is necessary. However, their negative forms have very different meanings.

DOESN'T / DON'T HAVE TO indicates that something is not necessary.

> You **don't have to put out** your cigarette. You can smoke in here. [*It is not necessary to put out your cigarette.*]

MUSTN'T indicates that it is necessary that you *not* do something.

> You **mustn't smoke** here. There's a NO SMOKING sign. [*Something is necessary: no smoking. It is necessary that you not smoke.*]

PRACTICE 6–1   Prohibition

Explain the following signs (Figs. 10–5 through 10–8) using **YOU MUSTN'T** *or* **YOU CAN'T***. Follow the example given for Figure 10–4.*

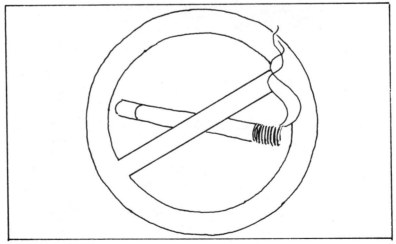

FIGURE 10–4

EXAMPLE   You **mustn't smoke** here.
             (You **can't smoke** here.)

FIGURE 10–5

FIGURE 10–6

FIGURE 10–7

FIGURE 10–8

PRACTICE 6-2   Contrasting **NOT HAVE TO** and **MUST NOT**

A.   Here is a list of activities that are related to people in the military service. Give information about soldiers using HAVE TO / NOT HAVE TO or MUSTN'T.

EXAMPLES   have short hair   A soldier **has to have** short hair.

take drugs   A soldier **mustn't take** drugs.

pay for their clothes   Soldiers **don't have to pay** for their clothes.

1.   disobey orders from their commanding officers
2.   be in good health
3.   pay for medical expenses
4.   get up early
5.   leave town without permission
6.   pay for room and board

B.   *Here is a list of activities related to obtaining a driver's license. Give information about getting a driver's license here or in your native country. Use* **YOU HAVE TO / YOU DON'T HAVE TO,** *or* **YOU MUST NOT.**

1. pay a lot of money
2. pass a vision test
3. show that you can parallel park
4. pass a written test
5. pass a driving test
6. drive without a seatbelt during the driving test
7. drive on the highway during the test
8. go over the speed limit during the test
9. bribe bureau officials
10. go to driving school first
11. get a physical examination by a doctor

FOCUS 7   Expectations with **BE SUPPOSED TO**

What are "manners"? What is etiquette? "Miss Manners" is famous for her column about manners and etiquette in different situations. Here is an example of a question asked by one of her readers:

TODAY'S COLUMN

Who takes first bite at dinner?

Miss Manners

DEAR MISS MANNERS: Is it true that when guests are invited to one's house for dinner, nobody is supposed to eat until the first bite has been taken by the hostess, or by both the host and the hostess?

Is this true of buffet dinners, as well as dinners which the hostess serves? Is it also true when guests are invited to a picnic?

What if the host and hostess expect the guests to take the first bite? Is this a breach of etiquette?

Is it appropriate for me, as a guest at a buffet dinner, to mention that I am waiting for the host and hostess to start eating, so that I can eat?

Gentle Reader: There is no difficulty making buffet guests wait to eat. No matter how hard the hostess tries to get them to take that first

step of serving themselves, they all stand around like fools, refusing to budge.

However, the rule about waiting for the hostess to eat the first bite applies only to the dinner table. Buffet guests and picnickers may begin as soon as they have found a place to sit and mopped up whatever they spilled while putting their plates on their laps.

At the dinner table, the hostess starts things by lifting her own fork or, if the first food served is congealing while some plates are still empty, by saying, "Oh, please go ahead and begin."

Derelict hosts may be prompted by a guest's staring woefully at his filled plate and saying, "Oh, this looks delicious."

United Feature Syndicate

Miss Manners reprinted by permission of UFS, Inc.

In the United States, the hostess **is supposed to** take the first bite.

Think about rules of etiquette at a formal dinner in your country. Who starts eating first at a formal dinner? The guest? The oldest person? The oldest male? The hostess?

A.   Using **BE SUPPOSED TO**

The expression **BE SUPPOSED TO** with a base form verb indicates someone else's expectation.

1. The expectation can come from a plan or agreement.

> I'm **supposed to pick up** my brother at school today. [*He is expecting me because we made a plan.*]

2. The expectation can come from a group or society in the form of "social rules."

> The hostess **is supposed to take** the first bite at the dinner table in the United States. [*People expect this because it is the accepted social custom.*]

3. The past tense of **BE SUPPOSED TO** expresses an expectation about the past. It does not indicate what actually happened; it talks about what was expected. In fact, it often refers to actions that did *not* happen.

> Chuck: Where were you yesterday? We **were supposed to have lunch** at noon!
>
> Lena: Oh, that's right. I'm so sorry. I forgot. [*The action was expected, but it didn't happen.*]

B.   Forming sentences with BE SUPPOSED TO

BE SUPPOSED TO is followed by the base form of a verb. To make the expression negative, use a negative form of the auxiliary **BE**. To talk about past expectations, use **WAS** or **WERE**.

Subject	+	BE (NOT)	+	SUPPOSED TO	+	Base Form Verb	+	Rest of Sentence
You		aren't		supposed to		start		eating before the hostess.
We		are		supposed to		wait		for the hostess.
Hank		was		supposed to		tell		Mr. Fritz about the meeting.
I		wasn't		supposed to		know		anything about the surprise.
They		were		supposed to		call		us about the change in plans.

C.   Questions and answers

Use the auxiliary **BE** with **SUPPOSED TO** to make questions.

> What **am I supposed to do** with this application form?
> **Am I supposed to give** it to the admissions office? Yes, you **are**.
> Where **was** Jim **supposed to meet** us this morning? In my office.
> You **aren't supposed to eat** ice cream on your diet, **are** you? No, I'm **not**, and **neither are** you.

PRACTICE 7–1   **BE SUPPOSED TO**

*A.   Respond to the questions using the cues with appropriate forms of **BE SUPPOSED TO**.*

EXAMPLE   Why is Lisa in such a big hurry?

(be at a meeting / three minutes)

She **is supposed to be** at a meeting in three minutes.
(She **was supposed to be** at a meeting three minutes ago.)

1.   JULIA: Why is Tom upset?

BELIN: (his roommate / clean / house / this morning / but . . .)

2. JOANIE: Why did Sylvie get in trouble with her embassy?
   CLEM: (renew / passport / last month)
3. TERESA: Why did Tony get upset with his friends?
   CLAUDIA: (they / meet him / 8:00 / but / not get there / until 9:30)

B. *Answer the following questions about driving in this country.*

1. What are drivers supposed to do when they see or hear an ambulance nearby?
2. What are you supposed to do if you want to change lanes?
3. What are you supposed to do when you want to turn left at an intersection, and there is oncoming traffic?

A WIDER ANGLE

Different Customs—Class Discussion

Discuss the following topics with your classmates.

TOPIC 1: Weddings and Marriage Customs
In many cultures, a wedding is a big event. There are different customs and expectations that accompany a wedding. Discuss the "social rules" connected with a wedding in your country. If you wish, you can compare a traditional wedding to a contemporary wedding.

You should consider the following topics in your discussion:

a. *The finances:* Who is supposed to pay for various things (the rings, the bride's dress, the wedding party, the honeymoon)?
b. *Gifts:* Who is supposed to give gifts? What kind of gifts?
c. *Legal considerations:* What does the couple have to do in order to be legally married?
d. *Special customs:* What does the groom have to do? What about the bride? What about their families? Is there anything that they shouldn't do?

TOPIC 2: Eating Customs
Think about eating customs in your country. What are some of the expectations about what people are supposed to do? What are some things people shouldn't or mustn't do? Give information about eating customs that might be useful for someone who is planning to visit your country.

Writing Practice

Choose one of the following topics.

TOPIC 1:   One of your American friends is planning to travel to your country next month. Your friend has never traveled outside of the United States before. Write a letter giving your friend advice about what to do and information about what to expect. You should explain any customs that might seem unusual to your friend.

TOPIC 2:   Your young cousin (or nephew or niece) does not care about school. As a result, he or she is not doing very well. You know that education is very important. Write a letter to convince him or her that school is important.

EXERCISE 1 **Suggestions**

Complete the following conversations.

1. ORSON: I'm starving, and I still have two more classes before I can eat lunch.

    KATE: _____?

    ORSON: Good idea. I think I will.

2. DONNY: I don't know what to get my sister for her birthday.

    LUCY: _____?

    DONNY: No, that's a nice idea, but it's out of my price range.

    LUCY: _____.

    DONNY: I think she already has one.

    LUCY: _____?

    DONNY: I gave her some last year.

    LUCY: _____.

    DONNY: That's a perfect gift! Thanks!

EXERCISE 2 **Preferences**

Use the following cues to make sentences regarding your preferences for cars. Write three sentences with WOULD RATHER . . . THAN and three sentences with WOULD RATHER NOT.

EXAMPLES   I **would rather be** a passenger in a large car **than** in a small car.

In winter, I **would rather drive** a car with four-wheel drive **than** a car with rear-wheel drive.

I **would rather not drive** a compact car on the highway.

I **would rather not buy** a used car.

a used car	a large car
a new car	a compact car
a sports car	a midsize car
a two-door car	a car with four-wheel drive
a four-door car	a car with front-wheel drive
a truck	a car with rear-wheel drive
a minivan	a [ ] car
a foreign car	a car with [ ]
a domestic car	[ ]

EXERCISE 3   Expressing Opinions and Advice

Read each situation. Then complete the sentences that follow.

1. Elena is feeling very frustrated these days. When she first started studying English, her English improved rapidly. Nowadays, she doesn't notice much improvement even though she continues to study hard. She feels a little discouraged.

    a. She shouldn't _____ because _____
       _____.

    b. If she feels bad about her English, she ought to _____
       _____.

2. Toshio has gained a lot of weight since he came here, and none of his clothes fit him anymore.

    a. He should _____.

    b. He also ought to _____.

    c. He shouldn't _____.

EXERCISE 4   Necessity and Advisability

Complete each sentence by combining the verb indicated with the appropriate form of
HAVE TO *or* **SHOULD**. *Make the verb negative if appropriate.*

1. The law in Ohio requires everyone in a car to wear seat belts. If you

   drive in Ohio, you _____ a seat belt.
                          (wear)

2. Serious injuries can be prevented by wearing seat belts. You

   _____ a seat belt when you are in a car.
      ([always] wear)

3. In some places, senior citizens _____ full price for a
                                           (pay)

   movie. Instead, they get a discount.

4. Tony's father is supporting him while he is a student. Tony is lucky.

   He _____ himself.
         (support)

5. If you want to learn English quickly, you _____ afraid
                                                    (be)

   of making mistakes. You can learn a lot from mistakes.

EXERCISE 5   Opinions about the Past

A.   Read each situation. Then write two sentences using the verb cues with
SHOULD(N'T) HAVE.

EXAMPLE   Fred bought a very impractical car.

                  a. buy a sports car   He **shouldn't have bought** a sports car.
                  b. get a practical car   He **should have gotten** a practical car.

1. Jerry came to class yesterday even though he had a fever.

   a. come to class
   b. stay in bed

2. Claudia sent her parents a postcard. They were a little disappointed because they wanted to hear more news.

   a. send a postcard
   b. write a long letter

3. My roommates and I had a big party last night. We made so much noise that our neighbors called the police.

   a. make so much noise
   b. be more considerate of our neighbors

B. *Read each situation. First complete the verb, using the appropriate form. Then complete the rest of the sentence. The auxiliaries are provided for you.*

1. Heather wore her new leather jacket to the football game. During the game, it started to rain very hard. Her jacket got ruined.

   a. Heather shouldn't have _____ _____.
   (verb)
   b. As a result, she had to _____ _____.
   (verb)
   c. She should have _____ _____.
   (verb)

2. Against the advice of her friends, Karen bought a used car. Since she got the car, it has been in and out of the garage for repairs.

   a. Karen should have _____ _____.
   (verb)
   b. She shouldn't have _____ _____.
   (verb)
   c. She's had to _____ _____ recently.
   (verb)
   d. She should probably _____ _____
   (verb)
   as soon as possible so that she won't have to _____
   (verb)

   _____.

EXERCISE 6 **Warnings**

A. *Complete each warning with a possible consequence.*

EXAMPLE   You'd better be careful with your coffee, or . . . you're going to spill it.

1. I'd better do my laundry soon, or . . .

2. Michelle had better renew her visa. If she doesn't, . . .

3. We'd better stop and get gas. Otherwise, . . .

4. Frank had better not stay up all night, or . . .

5. You'd better not be late for class again. If you are, . . .

B.   *Complete each sentence with a warning using **HAD BETTER (NOT)**.*

EXAMPLE   <u>You'd better be careful,</u> or you're going to spill your coffee.

1. _____ because they might be sleeping.

2. _____, or I'm going to get fat.

3. _____. If he doesn't, he'll regret it.

4. _____. Otherwise, no one will be able to understand you.

5. _____. If I don't, no one will be able to read it.

EXERCISE 7   Prohibition

Here are some common warnings found on different products. Complete the sentences to explain the meaning of the warning labels in your own words.

1. The label on a bottle of cleaning liquid says, "Harmful if swallowed."

   You mustn't _____ this substance.

2. The label on a can of insecticide says, "Keep out of reach of children."

   You must _____.

   Children mustn't _____.

3. The label on a bottle of cough syrup says, "Caution: Federal law prohibits dispensing without a prescription."

   A pharmacist cannot _____ this medicine

   unless _____.

EXERCISE 8   Contrast NOT HAVE TO and MUSTN'T

*Complete the sentences with **MUSTN'T** or **DON'T / DOESN'T HAVE TO**.*

1. This cake mix is very easy! You _____ add anything except water!

2. If you add water to this chemical, it will produce a dangerous gas.

   You _____ add water to this chemical.

3. That medicine is very strong. You _____ leave it where children can get into it by accident.

4. I'm terrible at learning foreign languages. Fortunately, I am a

   chemistry major, so I _____ take a foreign language.

EXERCISE 9 **Different Modal Expressions**

Read each situation. Then add appropriate verbs to complete the sentences that follow. The auxiliaries are provided for you.

1. Roz and Jacques made plans to meet at his house at ten o'clock this morning. Unfortunately, Roz had a flat tire on the way to school. She didn't get to Jacques's house until eleven o'clock.

   a. Roz was supposed to _____

   _____.

   b. Jacques was angry because he had to _____

   _____.

   c. Roz was late because she had to _____

   _____.

   d. Roz had a good excuse for being late, but she should have

   _____.

2. Jim failed the history test this morning because he answered only the questions on the front of each page. He didn't notice that there were questions on the back too.

   a. Jim didn't realize that he was supposed to _____

   _____.

   b. The teacher was sad because she had to _____

   _____.

   c. Jim should have _____

   _____.

   d. When taking tests, students should always _____

   _____.

   e. The next time, he'd better _____,

   or _____.

11 Relationships between Past Events

The Sequence of Past Events

Trouble in the Kitchen

Steve and his wife, Angie, take turns doing the shopping. This week it was Steve's turn. The following pictures (Figs. 11–1 and 11–2) show what happened when Steve got home with the groceries.

FIGURE 11–1

FIGURE 11–2

Look at the pictures. Then number the following list of events in the order in which they happened. What happened first? Second? Third? Fourth?

_____ Angie saw the mess on the floor.

_____ Steve was carrying in the groceries.

_____ Angie heard a noise in the kitchen.

_____ The grocery bag broke.

Did Angie see Steve carrying in the grocery bags? Did she see the groceries fall? What did she see? What happened before she came into the kitchen? What was Steve doing when the bag broke? What did he do when it broke?

In this chapter, you will practice talking about the relationship between different past actions. You will see how to use verb tenses to show which actions happened first.

FOCUS I   Introduction to the Past Perfect Tense

A.   Review of present perfect time focus

The time focus for the *present perfect tense* is now. The present perfect tense refers to an action that occurred sometime **before now.**

Steve **has** just **dropped** a bag of groceries.

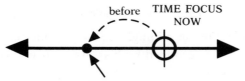

Steve dropped the bag

B.   Introduction to past perfect time focus

The past perfect (**HAD** + past participle) is similar to the present perfect tense in that it communicates the idea of "before." However, the time focus for the past perfect is a specific past time. The *past perfect tense* refers to an action that occurred **before a specific past time focus.**

Steve **had** just **dropped** a bag of groceries <u>when Angie came into the kitchen.</u>

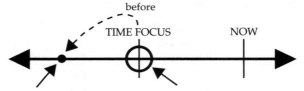

Steve dropped the bag.   Angie came in.

The past perfect tense first focuses on a specific past time and then "jumps back" to something that happened before that time. Because the past perfect tense means "before," it must relate a past event to another past event or time.

Notice the relationship of the verb to the time focus in the following examples:

I **saw** a good movie on TV last night. [simple past: at a specific past time]

I **have seen** some good movies recently. [present perfect: before now]

I didn't watch the movie on NBC last night because I **had seen** it. [past perfect: before last night]

Sequence of Events

A.   Look at the highlighted verbs in each sentence. Which event or situation occurred first: A or B?

1.   The teacher **got** upset because the students **hadn't studied** for the
        (A)   (B)
test.

2.   I **had gone** to bed when my roommate finally **came** home.
        (A)   (B)

3.   The movie **had started** when we **got** to the theater.
                    (A)   (B)

B.   Look at the highlighted past perfect verbs. For each sentence, give the past time focus and tell what had happened before the time focus.

EXAMPLE   The movie **had started** when we got to the theater.

Time focus: . . . when we got to the theater
What had happened before: The movie had started.

1.   I called Jim at midnight last night, but he **had already gone** to sleep.

2.   Mr. Smith dropped by his wife's office yesterday afternoon at around four-thirty, but she**'d left.**

3.   Elizabeth was starving in calculus class this morning because she **hadn't eaten** breakfast.

FOCUS 2   Forming the Past Perfect Tense

A.   Forming sentences with the past perfect tense

To form the *past perfect,* use the auxiliary **HAD** with a past participle. To make the verb negative, add **NOT** after **HAD.**

Bill dropped by at around ten-thirty last night.

Time Focus +	Subject +	HAD (NOT) "before the time focus" +	Past Participle +	Rest of Sentence
At that time, . . .	I	had	gone	to bed.
	we	had	had	dinner.
	you	had not	finished	your homework.
	Bill	had not	eaten	anything.

B.   Contractions

HAD→'D

I**'d gone** to bed when Bill came over.
We**'d had** dinner when he got there.

HAD NOT→HADN'T

You **hadn't finished** your work when he came over.
He **hadn't eaten** dinner before he came over.

C. Questions and answers

To form a question, move the auxiliary **HAD** before the subject. Use **HAD** and **HADN'T** for short forms.

> **Had** Mrs. Wu ever **eaten** pizza before she came here?
> No, she **hadn't.**
>
> **Had** you ever **tasted** pizza before?
> Yes, I **had.**
>
> How many times **had** you **eaten** it before you came here?
> Only once.
>
> Why **hadn't** Mrs. Wu **had** pizza before?
> She**'d** never even **heard** of it. They don't eat pizza in her country.
>
> You**'d had** thin-crust pizza before, **hadn't** you?
> Yes, I **had.**
>
> You **hadn't eaten** Chicago-style pizza, **had** you?
> Yes, I **had.**
> You **had?!**

D. Ability and necessity

1. To talk about **ability** before a past time, use the *past perfect* form of **BE ABLE TO.**

HAD (NOT) BEEN ABLE TO + (base form verb)

Mark was upset at the end of class yesterday because he **hadn't been able to finish** the test.

2. To talk about **necessity** before a past time, use the *past perfect* form of **HAVE TO.**

HAD (NOT) HAD TO + (base form verb)

We **had never had to cook** for ourselves until we moved here.

PRACTICE 2–1 Using the Past Perfect Tense

*A.   You and your friend made plans to go to a movie last night. You agreed to pick him up at 8:30. When you got there, however, he wasn't ready. Use the following cues with the **past perfect tense** to explain why he wasn't ready.*

He wasn't ready because . . .

1. fall asleep
2. not set his alarm
3. [just] wake up
4. not take a shower yet
5. not eat dinner

B.   Use the following cues to ask questions about the friend who wasn't ready. A classmate should answer the questions.

EXAMPLE   eat dinner?

Student A: **Had** he **eaten** dinner when you got there?
Student B: No, he **hadn't.**

1. take a nap?
2. shave?
3. why / not take a shower yet?
4. forget about the plans to go to a movie?

FOCUS 3   Using Adverbs with the Past Perfect Tense

The same adverbs that occur with the present perfect tense also occur with the past perfect tense.

A. EVER, NEVER: Experiences before a specific past time

Janti: I was really nervous when I left my country to come here because I *had* **never** *traveled* to a foreign country before.

Yang: *Had* you **ever** *been* away from home before?

Janti: No, I *hadn't.* That was my first time. And I was a little homesick during my first few months here.

B. YET, STILL, ALREADY: Events completed before a specific past time

Bill lost his passport somewhere on campus last week. When I talked to him this morning, he **still** *hadn't found* it. I told him to check with the Lost and Found, but he'*d* **already** *checked* there. No one *had returned* it **yet.**

C. JUST: Events that happened a short time before a specific past time

The movie *had* **just** *started* when we took our seats.

I called you at the office yesterday, but you'*d* **just** *left.*

PRACTICE 3-1   Using Adverbs with the Past Perfect Tense

A.   *Use the cues with the **past perfect tense** to answer the following questions.*

EXAMPLE   Amelia: Why was Chen nervous when he got on the plane to come here?

         Charles: [never] fly

                 He'**d never flown** in a plane before.

1.   NORTON: Why was Ralph so upset when you saw him earlier this morning?

     ALICE: [just] fail a quiz

2.   LINEE: Why didn't you read the newspaper when you got up this morning?

     TONY: [yet] not arrive

3.   LEONARD: Why did Maria and Joe's landlord call them last week?

     SANDY: [still] not pay last month's rent

4.   OLLIE: Why didn't Sherry want to go to the movie with you on Friday?

     FRAN: [already] see it

5.   VLADIMIR: Was Alex still looking for a job when you talked to him last week?

     NIKITA: Yes. [still] not find [= *ability*] / a part-time job

6. ALLY: Why was Luis so excited about the snow last night?

    CHRIS: [never] see snow

7. BILLY: Why was Haile's cooking so awful during his first few
            months here?

    MANDY: [ever] not cook [= *necessity*]

B. *Latisha is a student assistant in the main office of an intensive English language
program. The following list shows what Latisha did yesterday:*

9:00 A.M.–11:00 A.M.	typed five letters
11:00 A.M.–1:00 P.M.	filed 100 student files
1:00 P.M.–2:00 P.M.	ate lunch
3:00 P.M.–4:00 P.M.	entered data for new students onto the computer
4:00 P.M.	took all the office mail to the campus post office
4:30 P.M.–5:00 P.M.	did some photocopying for the secretary

You dropped by the office at about 2:10 P.M. yesterday. Use the cues with the
adverbs **STILL, YET, ALREADY,** and **JUST** to talk about the things Latisha had
or hadn't done when you got there.

EXAMPLE   type letters
            When I got there, she **had already typed** five letters.

1. file student files
2. finish eating lunch
3. enter data for new students onto the computer
4. take the office mail to the campus post office
5. do the photocopying

C. *Answer the following questions with complete sentences. Use the* **past perfect
tense.**

1. What is something that you'd never eaten until you came here?
2. Is there anything that you'd never had to do before you came here?
3. When it was time for you to go to the airport to come here, was
    there anything that you hadn't been able to do?
4. While you were sitting on the plane to come here, did you think of
    anything that you had forgotten to bring with you? If so, what?
5. Had you ever studied English before you started studying here?

FOCUS 4   Time Clauses with **WHEN**

Match each sentence to the picture it describes (Figs. 11–3, 11–4, 11–5).

Everybody ate when Fred got home.
Everybody was eating when Fred got home.
Everybody had eaten when Fred got home.

FIGURE 11-3

FIGURE 11-4

FIGURE 11-5

A time clause gives the time focus of a sentence. When a sentence has a simple past time clause with **WHEN,** the verb of the main clause determines the relationship in time between the two actions.

Main Clause: Simple Past	+	Time Clause: When + Simple Past
Everybody **ate**		**when** Fred got home.

The action of the main clause immediately followed the action of the time clause.

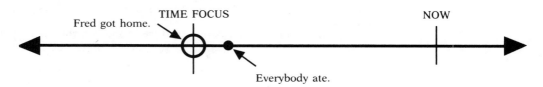

Main Clause: Past Progressive	+	Time Clause: When + Simple Past
Everybody **was eating**		**when** Fred got home.

The action of the main clause was already in progress when the action of the time clause occurred.

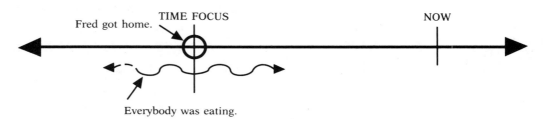

Main Clause: Past Perfect	+	Time Clause: When + Simple Past
Everybody **had eaten**		**when** Fred got home.

The action of the main clause finished before the action of the time clause.

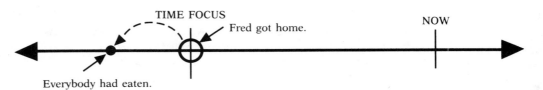

PRACTICE 4-1 Using Different Past Tenses

A. The sentences in each group all have the same past time focus. What is the specific time focus of each group? (HINT: Look at the time clause.) How do the sentences in each group differ in meaning?

1. a. John left the restaurant when we got there.
    b. John was leaving the restaurant when we got there.
    c. John had left the restaurant when we got there.

2. a. When I got to class, the teacher passed back the homework.
   b. When I got to class, the teacher had passed back the homework.
   c. When I got to class, the teacher was passing back the homework.

B.   *Use the cues to make sentences based on the following situations. Each sentence should contain a time clause using the simple past tense with* **WHEN**. *In the main clause, use the* **simple past, past progressive,** *or* **past perfect tense.**

EXAMPLE   I learned to drive in snow in this country. Last month, I had a car accident because of the snow.

a. *never drive in snow // come here*
   I **had** never **driven** in snow when I came here.

b. *learn to drive in snow // come here*
   I **learned** to drive in snow when I came here.

c. *drive in snow // have an accident*
   I **was driving** in snow when I had an accident.

1. I dropped a glass, and it broke. I cleaned it up before my roommate got home.

   a. unload the dishwasher // drop a glass
   b. drop it // it break
   c. clean up the mess // my roommate / get home

2. The phone rang and woke Angie up.

   a. sleep // the phone / ring
   b. the phone / ring // answer

3. Angie woke up. Then the phone rang.

   a. [just] wake up // the phone / ring
   b. not sleep // the phone / ring

PRACTICE 4-2   More Practice with Past Forms

Answer the following questions using the cues. Use one of these tenses in each response: **simple past, past progressive,** *or* **past perfect.**

EXAMPLE   Why wasn't Mary Beth able to answer the question when the teacher called on her?
   a. not pay attention
      She **wasn't paying** attention.
   b. not know the answer
      She **didn't know** the answer.
   c. not prepare the lesson
      She **hadn't prepared** the lesson.

1. When I saw my cousin last week, he was very worried. Why?

   a. [still] not receive money from his parents
   b. not have any money
   c. [yet] not pay his rent

2. Why was Sandra in such a good mood when we saw her yesterday morning?

    a. [just] receive a letter from her boyfriend

    b. expect good news from home

    c. [just] buy a new car

3. Why was Rudy embarrassed in class this morning when the professor asked for his homework?

    a. not have it

    b. forget it at home

    c. it / lie on his kitchen table

CLOSE-UP   Time Expressions with BY

1. Ms. Gibson left work a few minutes early so that she could get to the post office before it closed at 5:00 P.M. On the way to the post office, she had to stop at a railroad crossing for a very long train. She didn't get to the post office until 5:15. **By that time, the post office had closed.**

Was Ms. Gibson able to buy stamps?
What time does the expression BY THAT TIME refer to?

2. I had to work very late yesterday evening. **By the time I got home, my roommates had eaten,** so I went out for a hamburger.

When did my roommates eat dinner?

Past Time Focus with BY

Here are some time expressions with **BY** that occur with the past perfect tense. These time expressions focus on a past time. The action of the past perfect verb happened sometime before the time focus.

The time word **BY** can occur in a time phrase or a time clause.

Time Phrase or Clause	Example
BY + a specific time	Everyone had eaten **by** seven o'clock.
BY THEN	I got home at seven o'clock. Everyone had eaten **by then.**
BY THAT TIME	I got home at seven o'clock. **By that time,** everyone had eaten.
BY THE TIME (THAT) + (simple past clause)	**By the time** I got home, everyone had eaten.

Close-Up
PRACTICE   USING BY

A. *Read each situation and complete the sentence.*

1. I didn't get to the party last Friday until around midnight. By that

time, _____.

2.   Last week, Diane told me that she was engaged. Yesterday she told me that her engagement was a secret and that I shouldn't tell a soul. It was too late.

By then, _____.

3.   Karl got to the bus stop a few minutes late this morning.

Unfortunately, by that time, _____.

B.   *Bruce has always had trouble getting places on time. Yesterday, he had many things to do. As usual, he was late for everything. Use time clauses with **BY THE TIME** to talk about Bruce's problems. Fill in empty brackets with your own cues.*

EXAMPLE   He went to the bank.
                   (get to the bank // closed)
                   By the time he got to the bank, it had already closed.

1.   He went to a movie.
     (get to the ticket window // [   ])
2.   He had to go to a meeting.
     (find the right room // [   ])
3.   He went to the train station to catch a train home.
     (get there // [   ])
4.   It was past midnight when he got home.
     (get home // his wife / [   ])

FOCUS 5   The Past Perfect Progressive Tense

A.   Using the past perfect progressive tense

The *past perfect progressive* tense refers to activities in progress shortly *before a past time focus.*

When I saw Mary this morning, her eyes were all red because she **had been crying.**

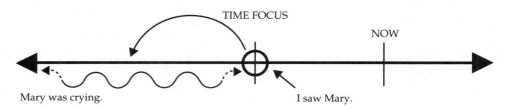

B.   Forming the past perfect progressive tense

Subject	+	HAD (NOT) "before the time focus"	+	BEEN + -ING Verb (in progress)
Mary		had		been crying.
I		hadn't		been crying.
The children		had		been crying.

C.   Questions and answers

To form a question, move the auxiliary **HAD** before the subject. Use **HAD** and **HADN'T** for short forms.

When you saw her, what **had** she **been doing?** <u>She**'d been crying.**</u>
Had she **been crying** when you saw her? <u>Yes, she **had.**</u>
She **hadn't been cutting** onions, **had** she? <u>No, she **hadn't.**</u>

PRACTICE 5-1 Past Perfect Progressive

*Use the cues to answer the question with the **past perfect progressive.***

EXAMPLE   Why was Brenda out of breath when she got to class this morning?
(run) She**'d been running.**

I visited Mark yesterday afternoon. He was tired, and he looked a mess. How
come?

1. clean the house
2. work on his car
3. paint the garden fence
4. take care of the kids

**GETTING
READY TO
FOCUS**   *Up to a Past Time*

The Royal Time Line

FIGURE 11-6

The following time line shows some important dates in the relationship between Princess Diana and Prince Charles of England.

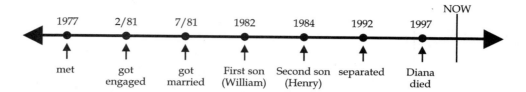

Use the information about the royal couple to complete the following sentences.

1. Charles and Diana first met _____ years ago.

2. They got engaged in _____.

3. They **had known** each other for _____ years when the got engaged.

4. They got in engaged in _____ of _____.

5. They got married in _____ of the same year.

6. They **had been** engaged for _____ months when they got married.

7. They had their first child in _____.

8. They **had been** married for _____ when they had their first child.

9. They **had been** married for _____ when their second son was born.

10. They **had been** married for _____ years when they announced their separation.

11. Diana died _____ years ago. She **has been** dead since _____.

FOCUS 6   Situations Continuing Up to a Past Time

Like the present perfect and present perfect progressive tenses, the *past perfect* and *past perfect progressive* tenses can occur with the time words **FOR** and **SINCE** to refer to a time period that continues from one point in time up to another point.

A.   Review of the present perfect and present perfect progressive tenses

Use the present perfect or present perfect progressive tense with **FOR, SINCE,** and **HOW LONG . . . ?** to refer to activities or situations that began in the past and continue or repeat **up to now.**

Charles and Diana **have known** each other since 1977.
They **have been living** apart since 1992.

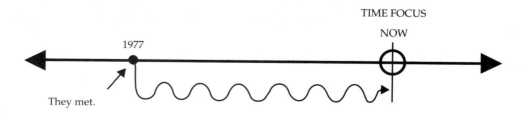

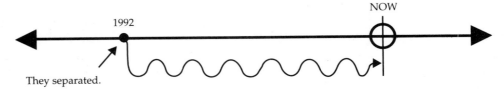

B. Past perfect and past perfect progressive with FOR, SINCE, HOW LONG . . . ?

Use the past perfect or past perfect progressive tense with the time words **FOR**, **SINCE**, and **HOW LONG . . . ?** to indicate an activity that began in the past and continued or repeated **up to the past time focus.**

> Charles and Diana **had been** married for one year when they had their first child. They **had been having** problems for quite a while when they announced their separation.

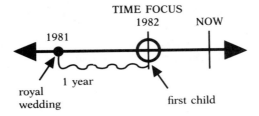

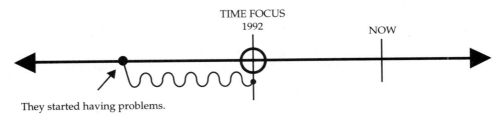

PRACTICE 6-1 Understanding Past Time Periods

Use the information from the article (Fig. 11–7) to answer the following questions.

Man remarries computer date

Associated Press

IZMIR, Turkey — A man who divorced his wife after a bitter court battle and turned to a computer service to find himself the "ideal" mate was surprised when — from 2,000 prospective brides — the machine selected his former wife.

"I decided to give a try by being more tolerant toward her," the Anatolia News Agency quoted Suleyman Guresci as saying before remarrying Nesrin Caglasa.

The couple, whose first marriage lasted 21 years, divorced nine months ago after living apart for six years, the news agency said.

FIGURE 11–7

Source: Akron Beacon Journal, Nov. 15, 1986; Associated Press.

1. How long had Suleyman and Nesrin been married when they got a divorce?
2. How long had they been living apart when their divorce became final?
3. How long had they been divorced when Suleyman got the computer match?
4. When Suleyman got the results of his computer match, who had the computer matched him up with?
5. Assuming that Suleyman and Nesrin are still married today, how long has their second marriage lasted?

PRACTICE 6-2 Mixed Verb Tenses

It is now midnight. Ed is studying for his physics test. He started studying at 5:00 P.M. Here is Ed's schedule for the evening.

5:00   Start studying physics

6:30   Finish looking over Chapters 1 and 2; take a break for dinner

7:00   Study some more

9:00   Call from girlfriend

9:30   Study some more

11:00   Finish looking over Chapters 3–6; have a cup of coffee; continue studying

12:00   **Now** (still studying)

1:30   Go to bed

Use the following cues to ask questions about Ed. Answer each question with a complete sentence based on the information in the schedule.

EXAMPLE   when / Ed / start studying / his test?

       When **did** Ed **start studying** for his test?
       He **started studying** at 5:00.

1. how long / Ed / study / his physics test?
2. what time / eat dinner?
3. how long / study // when / eat dinner?
4. how many chapters / finish studying // when / eat dinner?
5. what / do / after dinner?
6. what / do // when / girlfriend / call?
7. how long / study // when / girlfriend / call?
8. how long / talk to her?
9. what / do // after / talk to her?
10. how long / study // when / have a cup of coffee?
11. how many chapters / look over // when / take the coffee break?
12. how much longer / study?

Short Speech

Think about a famous person who had achieved many things by the time he or she died. You can choose a person from your country or from another country. You might need to go to the library to get information.

Prepare a short talk (two minutes) about this person's accomplishments. Try to use what you have learned about the different past tenses.

Writing Practice

Write a short composition about a person who accomplished great things in his or her lifetime. Choose someone who is no longer living. Your composition should describe some of this person's accomplishments. Try to use what you have learned about the different past tenses.

DEVELOPING YOUR SKILLS AND KNOWLEDGE

Chapter Exercises

EXERCISE I

Forming the Past Perfect Tense

Fill in each blank with the past perfect form of the verb indicated.

1. Before Clint Eastwood became an actor, he _____
   (hold)
   many different jobs.

2. For example, he _____ as a firefighter and as a gas
   (work)
   station attendant.

3. He _____ in the Army.
   ([also] serve)

4. But he _____ to become an actor.
   ([always] want)

5. At first, Clint Eastwood did not have much success in Hollywood.

   Finally, he went to Europe to star in some western movies. When he

   left Hollywood, he _____ much experience in movies.
   (not / have)

   He _____ some "walk-on" roles in low-budget films.
   ([only] have)

   However, when he returned to Hollywood in 1967, many filmmakers

   wanted him in their movies. His cowboy movies

   _____ him a star!
   (make)

EXERCISE 2 Using the Past Perfect Tense

Read each situation and complete the sentence that follows.

EXAMPLE When Angie walked into the kitchen, she saw Steve holding a broken bag. The groceries were all over the floor. She realized that the grocery bag had **broken.**

1. This morning, Angie got to work late and had trouble finding a parking place. She ended up parking next to a fire hydrant. When she came out after work, there was a piece of paper under her windshield wiper. "Oh no!" she thought.

    A police officer had _____ because she had _____.

2. The next day, Angie parked in the parking lot where she was supposed to. When she got in the car after work, it wouldn't start.

    The battery was dead because she had _____.

3. She called AAA to come recharge her battery. When the mechanic arrived, he asked to see her AAA membership card. When he looked at the date on the card, he said, "This card is not valid. It expired one week ago."

    Angie realized that she hadn't _____.

EXERCISE 3 Questions and Answers

*Use the information in each situation to write a question with **ever**. Then write an appropriate short answer.*

EXAMPLE The Romanian gymnast Nadia Comaneci received a perfect score of 10 in the 1976 Olympics.

Had she ever received a perfect score before?
No, she hadn't. In fact, it was the first time that any gymnast had ever gotten a perfect score.

1. Sir Edmund Hilary climbed to the peak of Mount Everest in 1953.

    Question: _____?

    Answer: _____. In fact, it was

    the first time that anyone had ever reached the top.

2. Steffi Graf won the Wimbledon women's singles tennis

    championship in 1993.

    Question: _____?

    Answer: _____. It was her fifth

    championship there.

3. The Argentines won the World Cup soccer championship in 1978.

    Question: _____?

    Answer: _____. That was their

    first time.

EXERCISE 4 Past Perfect with Adverbs

Use the cues to answer the following questions.

EXAMPLE   Meg: Why was Rehan so excited to see the snow last night?
  Blanche: [never] see snow
           She **had never seen** *snow.*

1.   TODD: Why didn't Chan want to go to the planetarium with his
            friends last weekend?
    GRACE: [already] go there

2.   MORTON: Why didn't the graduate school allow George to start his
             graduate studies last semester?
    MORELY: [yet] not pass the TOEFL

3.   DIANE: Why was Yong in such a good mood when he came to
            class today?
    KAREN: [just] receive a letter from home

4.   RICK: Why did John have to wear dirty jeans to the picnic
            yesterday?
    BERTHA: [still] not have time to do laundry

EXERCISE 5 Time Clauses with Past Tenses

*Fill in each blank with the appropriate form of the verb indicated. Use the **simple
past, past progressive,** or **past perfect** tense.*

Steve had a terrible day yesterday. He _____ the garbage
                                         (take out)
when he _____ and _____ on an icy step.
          (slip)   (fall)
When he _____, he _____ that his hand
          (stand up)   (see)
_____. He _____ that he
    (bleed)   (realize)
_____ himself. In addition, the garbage
    (cut)
_____ all over the sidewalk because he
    (lie)
_____ the bag. After he _____ up the mess,
    (drop)   (clean)
he _____ back inside. His hand _____ so
      (go)   ([still] bleed)
he _____ it with soap and water and _____
      (wash)   (put)
a bandage on it. After his hand was bandaged up, he

_____ blood on the white carpet. The blood
    (see)
_____ from his injured hand. He _____ to
    (drip)   (try)
clean the carpet when his wife _____ home. She asked
                                    (come)
him what he _____. She _____ sorry for
                (do)   (feel)
him when she _____ what _____.
                (hear)   (happen)

Fill in each blank with an appropriate form of the verb indicated.

1.   In 1983 Sally Ride was the first American woman to go into space.

No other American woman _____ in space before.
([ever] travel)

She _____ 32 years old when she
(be)

_____ in the space shuttle *Challenger*. Sally Ride
(fly)

_____ her husband, Steven Hawley, while she
(meet)

_____ for the *Challenger* flight. He
(train)

_____ to fly in space. They _____
([also] train)   (be)

married since 1982. They _____ married for only one
(be)

year when Sally _____ the first American woman to
(become)

go into space.

When Sally _____ to the astronaut training
(apply)

program, she _____ undergraduate degrees in English
([already] receive)

and astrophysics and a doctoral degree in astrophysics from Stanford

University. She _____ the space training program in
(enter)

1978. She _____ to become an astronaut for five
(train)

years when she finally _____ into space on June 18,
(go)

1983. When the space shuttle _____ back on earth,
(land)

Sally and the other astronauts _____ in space for six
(travel)

days. Sally told some reporters that she _____ so
([never] have)

much fun in her entire life!

2.   KIM: Hey, Ted! I _____ you for a long time! Where
(not / see)

_____ these days?
(you / live)

TED: Believe it or not, I _____ in the dormitory
(live)

now.

KIM: The dormitory? How long _____ there?
(you / live)

TED: For six weeks. I _____ into the dorm at the
(move)

end of last semester.

KIM: Why _____?
(you / move)

TED: Because our landlord _____ the house that we
(sell)

_____ at the end of last semester.
(rent)

KIM: Gee! How long _____ there when he sold it?
(you / live)

TED: Let's see. I think we _____ there for over two
(live)

years at that time.

KIM: Wow. That's rough.

TED: Yeah. And to make matters worse, we _____
([just] paint)

the living room and the kitchen when he told us that we

_____.
(move [= necessity])

KIM: Well, how _____ the dorm?
(you / like)

TED: It's actually not too bad. But it is a little noisy sometimes. For

example, last night I _____ to study when
(try)

somebody pulled the fire alarm. We all had to leave the

building for almost an hour. By the time I went back to my

room, I _____ everything! So, I
(forget)

_____ the same chapter all over again.
(read [= necessity])

KIM: That's terrible! How much longer _____ in the
(you / live)

dorm?

TED: Probably just until the end of this semester. Then, I

_____ an apartment.
(look for)

KIM: Well, I _____ into the dorm next semester, but
(move)

after talking to you, I might change my mind! I

_____ peace and quiet!
(like)

12 *Gerunds and Infinitives*

THE BIG PICTURE

Gerund Subjects and Objects
Anticipatory "It"
Infinitive Verbs
Causative Verbs

AT A GLANCE

Subjects and Objects

Look at the list below. What are some things in the list that you like or do not like?

to meet new people	black and white movies
cold showers	babysitting
English prepositions	cartoons
waiting in line	watching rock videos
dancing	trying new types of food
getting up early	to talk on the phone in English
hot, spicy food	

I like _____.   _____ is (are) fun.

I don't like _____.   _____ is (are) hard.

In this chapter, you will practice using GERUNDS and INFINITIVES as subjects and objects of verbs. You will see that some verbs can take a gerund object while other verbs can be followed by infinitive verbs.

FOCUS 1   Gerund Subjects

What is the subject of the highlighted verb in each of the following sentences?

Ping-Pong **is** a lot of fun.

Playing Ping-Pong **is** a lot of fun.

Watching an international Ping-Pong championship **is** a lot of fun too.

Violence on TV **upsets** me.

Seeing violent TV shows **upsets** me.

Seeing violence on TV and hearing violence in music **upset** me.

A.   **Introduction to gerund subjects**

    1.   The subject of a verb is a type of noun.

        It can be a *thing*: ping-pong, violence.

        It can also be an *activity*: playing ping-pong, seeing violence.

    2.   An activity or verb that acts as a *noun* in a sentence is called a **gerund.** All verbs can have a gerund form. A gerund has the same form as an -ING verb. Follow the spelling rules for -ING verbs in Appendix A. (Keep in mind, however, that a gerund does not function as a verb; it functions as a noun.)

        Swimming is fun. I enjoy **taking** long walks.

3. A gerund is a non-count noun. When a gerund is the subject, it takes a singular verb and can be replaced by the pronoun **IT**.

> **Watching** violent TV shows *upsets* me.
> **It** *isn't* healthy for children.

4. A gerund can be part of a *gerund phrase*. It can have the same objects and prepositions that a verb has.

> **Thinking *about* food** makes me hungry.
> **Buying presents *for* all my relatives** is expensive.
> **Buying all my relatives presents** is expensive.

5. To make a gerund negative, add **NOT** before the gerund.

> **Not *owning*** a car can be very inconvenient in this town.

B. Ability and necessity in gerunds

1. The gerund for "ability" is **(NOT) BEING ABLE TO** + **(base form verb)**

> **Being able to *speak*** English well will help me in my career.

2. The gerund for "necessity" is **(NOT) HAVING TO** + **(base form verb)**

> **Having to *take care of*** an apartment is a new experience for us.

PRACTICE 1-1   Gerund Subjects

A.   In each of the following sentences, change the subject to a subject that includes a gerund.

EXAMPLE   Violence on TV bothers me.
Watching violence on TV bothers me.

1. English is difficult.
2. A car can be expensive.
3. Letters take a long time.
4. Letters are fun.
5. Homework helps students practice their English.

B.   Complete each sentence with a gerund or gerund phrase subject.

EXAMPLE   _____ makes me nervous.

> **Taking tests** makes me nervous.
> **Driving in bad weather** makes me nervous.
> **Not being able to understand everything** makes me nervous.

1. _____ gives me a headache.
2. _____ is a good way to practice English.

3. _____ is dangerous.

4. _____ makes me tired.

5. _____ was a lot of fun.

FOCUS 2   Anticipatory **IT** as Subject

Going camping is fun. [*What is fun?*]

It is fun **to go camping.** [*What is fun?*]

It is possible to use **IT** instead of a gerund subject. Use the subject **IT** to "signal" that more information is coming.

It is fun **to go** camping. [*What is fun?*→*To go camping.*]

A.   Introduction to infinitive verbs

An infinitive verb consists of **TO** + (base form verb). Some examples of infinitive verbs are:

TO BE   **TO GO**   **TO HAVE**   **TO DO**

B.   Forming sentences with anticipatory IT

Use an infinitive verb after expressions with **IT**. The preposition **FOR** can indicate the noun that is performing the action of the infinitive.

It + BE* +	Adjective +	(FOR somebody) (optional) +	TO + Base Form Verb (infinitive verb) +	Rest of Sentence
It is	dangerous	(for anybody)	**to go**	jogging at night.
It is	difficult	(for some people)	**to learn**	English.
It will be	impossible	(for us)	**to finish**	the homework tonight.
It was	crazy	(for you)	**to walk**	home in the rain.

It *upsets* me **to see** violence on TV.

It *bothers* Mr. Jones **to be** around cigarette smoke.

It *will hurt* you **to miss** a lot of classes.

PRACTICE 2-1   Gerund Subjects and **IT**

A.   Complete each of the following sentences with your own opinion. Your classmate should rephrase your idea with a gerund subject.

EXAMPLE   It is difficult to _____.

        Student A: It is difficult to **learn English.**

        Student B: My classmate thinks that **learning English is difficult.**

1. It isn't easy to _____.

2. It is rude for people to _____.

---

*You will also see the subject **IT** used with other verbs as a "signal" for an infinitive.

3. It takes a long time to _____.

4. It is very expensive to _____.

5. It might be interesting to _____.

B. *Rephrase each of the following statements. Use the subject **IT** with **an infinitive**. Fill in empty brackets with your own cues.*

EXAMPLE   John: Learning English is difficult.

Paula: John thinks that **it is difficult to learn English.**

1. JIM: Living alone can be lonely.
2. MRS. QUINN: Living in a foreign culture takes a lot of patience.
3. ALI: Going through culture shock is normal for foreign students.
4. TOMAS: Knowing English will be useful for me.
5. NOOR: Having to think in English all the time is exhausting!
6. YOU: [   ] is a lot of fun.

FOCUS 3   Gerund Objects

A.   Different objects

Certain verbs need objects. Can you think of some different ways to complete the following sentences?

I enjoy _____ in the summer.

Let's discuss _____.

1. An object can be a *noun:*

   I enjoy **tennis** in the summer.
   Let's discuss **the classroom.**

2. An object can be a *gerund:*

   I enjoy **playing tennis** in the summer.
   Let's discuss **changing the classroom.**

B.   Verbs that are followed by gerunds

Some verbs can have gerund objects and others cannot. Here are some common verbs that can be followed by gerund objects.

appreciate	Raul *appreciates* **having** his family here.
avoid	Karl *avoids* **driving** in snow whenever possible.
can't help	I *can't help* **sneezing** when there's a cat in the room.
consider	I'm *considering* **pursuing** a master's degree here.
discuss	The students *discussed* **taking** a trip to Niagara Falls.
enjoy	Henry's family *enjoys* **playing** cards together.
finish	We *have to finish* **painting** our house by next week.
go	Let's *go* **fishing / shopping / camping.**
keep	This calculator *keeps* **giving** me the wrong calculations.
mind	*Do you mind* **waiting** for me?
postpone	The instructor *postponed* **giving** the quiz.

practice	Alice is trying *to practice* **using** gerunds in her essay.
quit	Mary *quit* **biting** her fingernails last year.
recall	I *don't recall* **meeting** your sister.
regret	I *regret* not **bringing** photographs of my family.
stop*	Please *stop* **being** so noisy.

PRACTICE 3-1   Using Gerund Objects

Use each of the following cues to ask a classmate a question. Your classmate should respond with a complete sentence and then return the question. Respond to your classmate's question.

EXAMPLE   what / you / enjoy / do / rainy days?

Student A: What do you enjoy doing on rainy days?
Student B: I enjoy reading a good novel. What about you?
Student A: I enjoy listening to music.

1. what kind of movies / you / enjoy / see?
2. what time / you / finish / study / last night?
3. where / you / [usually] go / shop / for food?
4. what / you / regret / not / bring with you to this country?
5. how many times / you and your friends / go / dance // since / you / get here?
6. what / you / [often] avoid / do?
7. what / you / enjoy / not / do [= *necessity*] / weekends?
8. what / you / appreciate / do [= *ability*] / here?

FOCUS 4   Gerunds as Objects of Prepositions

A. **A *gerund* or *gerund phrase* can also function as the *object of a preposition*. An infinitive verb *cannot* follow a preposition.**

Michelle never hands in a test *without* **checking** it over first.
Pablo got the TV to work *by* **adjusting** the antenna.
We decided to lease a car *instead of* **buying** one.

---

*Use a gerund after the verb STOP to indicate that an activity no longer continues.

EXAMPLE   Bill stopped **smoking** last year. *[He doesn't smoke any more.]*
Please stop **making** noise! *[Don't continue this activity.]*

Use an infinitive after the verb STOP to indicate that an activity stops **in order to** begin another activity.

EXAMPLE   I studied all day yesterday. At 5:00, I stopped **to eat.** *[I stopped studying in order to eat.]*
On my way home from work, I stopped **to pick up** some milk. *[I stopped driving in order to get milk.]*

B. Multiple-word verbs and verbs or adjectives that occur with prepositions are followed by a gerund object or a gerund phrase object.

    1. Verbs with prepositions:

        Are you *thinking* **about going** anywhere for vacation?

        Some of my friends have been *talking* **about taking** a trip.

        I'm *looking forward* **to not studying!**

        I might have to *put* **off making** plans for the break.

    2. Adjectives with prepositions:

        I sometimes get *tired* **of having to speak** English.

        Lanh is *proud* **of being** an American citizen.

        Miriam is *interested* **in learning** more about our customs.

        Some students can't get *used* **to eating** American food.

        Are you *used* **to going** to class every day?

PRACTICE 4-1   Prepositions and Gerund Objects

Use the information from the following conversation to complete each of the sentences that follow with an appropriate preposition and gerund phrase.

JIM: What are you planning to do this weekend?

SUE: My cousins have invited me over, so I might go there. I can't decide. I have a composition that I really should write this weekend. I'd really like to finish it.

JIM: You've certainly had to write a lot of papers this term.

SUE: I know. I can't wait until the end of the semester! No more papers to write! I will certainly be glad to be on vacation!

JIM: Do you have many final exams?

SUE: Only one . . . with Dr. Lyons. I'm nervous because I've heard his exams are tough! I'll be so upset if I get a bad grade. Do you have any special plans for the weekend?

JIM: Not really. I would really like to learn more about photography, and there's a new photography exhibit at the modern art museum. The photographer will be there to answer questions. I might drop in and take a look.

SUE: Sounds fascinating.

EXAMPLE   What are Sue's plans for the weekend?

    She's thinking _____.

    She's thinking **about visiting her cousins.**

    1. If she decides not to go, what will her reason be?

        She doesn't think it's a good idea to put _____.

        She might stay here and work on the composition instead

        _____.

    2. Why can't Sue wait until the end of the semester?

        She is looking forward _____.

        She is tired _____.

3. What is she worried about?

She is nervous _____.

She is afraid _____.

4. What are Jim's plans for the weekend?

He is talking _____.

5. Why does he want to go there?

He is very interested _____.

PRACTICE 4-2   More Practice with Gerunds

Use each of the following cues to ask a classmate a question. Add necessary prepositions. Your classmate should respond with a complete sentence.

EXAMPLE   what / you / think / do / this coming weekend?

Student A: What are you thinking about doing this coming weekend?

Student B: I'm thinking about having a party.

1. what / you / [sometimes] put off / do?
2. what / you / afraid / do?
3. what places / you / interested / visit / here?
4. what / you / look forward / do / at the end of this term?
5. what / you / look forward / not / do [= *necessity*] / at the end of this term?
6. what / you / tired / do?

CLOSE-UP   **More Polite Requests**

You have already practiced some different ways to make polite requests. Notice how Sarah makes a polite request in the following conversation. Also notice how Mike responds.

Sarah and Mike have just gotten out of class.
Mike: Let's go get a bite to eat.
Sarah: Sounds great. I'm starving. But I have to ask the teacher a question. **Would you mind waiting for me?** It shouldn't take long.
Mike: **Of course not.** Take your time.

A question with **WOULD YOU MIND** . . . is a request that means: "Would it inconvenience you or cause a problem for you to do this?" Responding to this type of question can be confusing, even to English speakers. A negative response means: "No, it is not a problem. I can carry out your request." An affirmative response with "yes" is not very common because it is not polite. However, you might hear responses such as "Sure" or "OK."

WOULD YOU MIND	+	(NOT) Gerund Phrase	Response
Would you mind		**closing** the door?	Not at all.
Would you mind		**not making** so much noise?	OK. Sorry.
Would you mind		**being** a little more quiet?	OK.
Would you mind		**carrying** this for me?	No problem.
Would you mind		**sharing** your book with me?	Of course not.
Would you mind		**waiting** for me?	Sorry, I can't.
Would you mind		**not discussing** that here?	Sure.

Close-Up

PRACTICE   **POLITE REQUESTS**

Imagine that you are sitting on an airplane in the middle of the row. What would you say to the people sitting next to you? Change each of the following commands to a polite request with **WOULD YOU MIND . . . ?** *Your classmate should take the role of another passenger and respond to your request.*

EXAMPLE   Please move your bag.

Passenger A: Excuse me. Would you mind moving your bag?
Passenger B: Oh sure! Sorry about that!

1. This is the nonsmoking section. Please don't smoke.
2. Let me get out.
3. Get me a blanket from the overhead compartment.
4. Ask the flight attendant to come here.
5. Pass me that magazine.

FOCUS 5   Using Infinitives

A.   Verbs that require infinitives

Not all verbs can have gerund objects. Some verbs are followed by *infinitive verbs* (**TO + base form verb**). Here are some verbs that are followed by *infinitives:*

ask	The student *asked* **to leave** class early.
can afford	I *can't afford* **to buy** a car right now.
decide	We *decided* **to take** a trip last weekend.
expect	John *expects* **to begin** his graduate studies next semester.
forget	Oh no! I *forgot* **to turn** the stove off!
hope	Everybody *hopes* **to pass** the exam.
learn	Where did you *learn* **to speak** such good English?
manage	The thief *managed* **to get** in the house by picking the lock.
need	I *need* **to pick up** something at the store on the way home.
offer	Barbara *offered* **to give** me a ride to the picnic.
plan	I'm *planning* **to go** shopping this weekend.
promise	Frank *promised* not **to be** impatient with the children.
refuse	Why *did you refuse* **to give** him an answer?
seem	The students *seem* **to be** in a good mood today.

try*	Have you ever *tried* **to do** a jigsaw puzzle?
wait	I can't *wait* **to see** my family!
want	I *want* **to bring** my family some souvenirs.
would like	Where *would you like* **to go** for lunch?

B. Negative infinitives

To form a negative infinitive, add **NOT** before **TO** + (**base form verb**):

> We decided *not* **to see** that movie.
>
> Please promise *not* **to tell** anybody what I just told you.
>
> Children need to learn *not* **to play** with matches.

C. Verbs that can be followed by gerunds or infinitives

Some verbs can have either **gerund** or **infinitive objects** with no difference in meaning:

Subject	+	Verb	+	Infinitive or Gerund
She		**began**		to sing / singing.
They		**started**		to eat / eating.
He		**continued**		to speak / speaking.
I		**like**		to read / reading.
They		**love**		to dance / dancing.
I		**hate**		to diet / dieting.
You		**can't stand**		to argue / arguing.

PRACTICE 5-1   Infinitives

Complete each sentence with an infinitive or infinitive phrase.

1. I need _____ before next week.

2. I would like _____ before I go back to my country.

3. Before I left my country, I promised not _____.

4. I want _____, but I can't.

5. I often forget _____.

6. Last week I decided _____.

7. My friend offered _____.

8. The student in the office is waiting _____.

9. When I feel depressed, I try not _____.

10. Someday, I hope _____.

PRACTICE 5-2   Gerunds or Infinitives

Use the following cues to form questions. Add any necessary prepositions. Your classmate should respond to each question with a complete sentence and return the question to you. Respond to your classmate's question.

---

*Try = make an effort.

what / like / do / evening?

        Student A: What do you like to do in the evening?
                         (What do you like doing . . .)
        Student B: I like to watch TV. What about you?
        Student A: I like to read.

1. what kind of music / enjoy / listen?
2. what / hate / do / winter?
3. what / would like / learn / do?
4. what / try / avoid / talk?
5. what / would like / see / this country?
6. what kind of books / interested / read?
7. what time / you / [usually] start / do your homework?

FOCUS 6   Verbs of Influence

A.   Introduction to verbs of influence

Some verbs indicate that one person is influencing another person to do something.

> Toshio **asked to leave** class early. [*Who asked to leave? Who left?*]

> Ivan **asked** the teacher **to explain** the meaning of a word. [*Who asked about the meaning of the word? Who explained it?*]

> Marta didn't want to go to the disco, but her friends **persuaded** her **to go** with them. [*Did Marta want to go to the disco? Did she go? Why?*]

> Our teacher **makes** us **speak** only English in class. [*Who has to speak English in class? How come?*]

B.   Verbs of influence: Objects followed by infinitives

Some verbs of influence need an object before an infinitive verb. This type of influencing verb includes:

advise	encourage	*need	tell
allow	*expect	order	urge
*ask	get	persuade	*want
cause	†help	remind	*would like
convince	invite	require	

---

*These verbs can occur with or without an object. When these verbs occur with an object, they are functioning as verbs of influence.

> We **would like** to go out tonight. Toshio **has asked** to come with us. [*no object*]
> We **would like** Toshio to join us. We **will ask** *him* to go out with us. [*with object*]

†*Help* can be followed by a base form as well as an infinitive.

> I **helped** John *move.*
> I **helped** John *to move.*

Subject	+	Influencing Verb	+	Object	+	(NOT) Infinitive	+	Rest of Sentence
Your parents		will allow		**you**		**to study**		the cello.
My aunt		is encouraging		**my cousin**		**to audition**		for the school play.
My faculty adviser		expects		**me**		**to take**		English composition.
My father		would like		**my sister**		**to apply**		to colleges in Massachusetts.
The biology teacher		advised		**Sally**		**to review**		her final exam.
I		told		**my mom**		**not to worry**		about my grades.
Jim's parents		remind		**him**		**not to party**		all the time.
We		have persuaded		**the dean**		**not to cancel**		the homecoming weekend.
He		warned		**us**		**not to break**		the rules he has set.

C. Causative verbs: Objects followed by base form verbs

The following three influencing or "causative" verbs need objects. However, the object is followed by a base form verb.

LET (to allow)
HAVE (to cause, hire, or ask)
MAKE (to force or require)

Subject	+	Causative Verb	+	Object	+	Base Form Verb	+	Rest of Sentence
Jim's dad		**lets**		**him**		**drive**		the family car.
Fred		**has**		**a tailor**		**make**		his suits.
The teacher		**made**		**me**		**rewrite**		my essay.

Do *not* use an infinitive after **LET, HAVE,** or **MAKE.**

[MISTAKE: Don's parents won't let him ~~to~~ travel alone.

I had my sister ~~to~~ cut my hair.

Karen makes her children ~~to~~ go to bed early.]

PRACTICE 6–1   Verbs of Influence

A.   *Give examples of things that . . .*

1. you can have a mechanic at a garage do.
2. you will never let (or have never let) your children do.
3. your teachers make you do.
4. you expect a good friend to do.
5. your family warned you not to do here.

B.   *Read each situation and complete the sentences that follow.*

1. Mr. and Mrs. Smith are very strict parents.

   a. They never let their children _____.

   b. They make their children _____.

2. Mr. and Mrs. Jones, on the other hand, are very lenient (not strict) parents.

   a. They often let their kids _____.

   b. They rarely make them _____.

3. The Parkers have just hired some neighborhood teenagers to help them with their spring cleaning.

   a. The Parkers are going to have the teenagers _____.

   b. However, they aren't planning to ask them _____.

   c. If there is enough time, they would also like to have them _____.

FOCUS 7 Short Forms for Infinitives

Look at the following sentences. What does the word **TO** *refer to in each sentence?*

> Wilhelm doesn't diet now, but **he used to.**
> I know I don't have to wait for you, but **I want to.**
> Sherry never walks alone at night because **her family warned her not to.**

It is not always necessary to repeat the information of the infinitive verb. The short form for an infinitive phrase is **TO.**

Long form:
I know I don't have to wait for you, but **I want to wait for you.**

Short form:
I know I don't have to wait for you, but **I want to.**

Do not use auxiliaries or other verbs in short forms for infinitives.

> [MISTAKE: I know I don't have to wait for you, but I want to ~~do~~.]

PRACTICE 7–1 Short Forms for Infinitives

Complete the responses to the questions with short form infinitives. Add objects if necessary. Do not repeat any unnecessary information.

EXAMPLE   Tom: Why are you waiting for Jim? (want)
          Mary: Because I want to. (Because he wants me to.)

1. HENRY: Why don't you buy a car?

   SID: Because I _____.
                              (not / afford [= *ability*])

2. JIM: Did you cry during the movie?

   TAMMY: Yes, I did. I _____, but I couldn't
                                (try / not)
   help myself.

3. BEVERLY: Does your teacher make all of you read the newspaper

   every day?

   LIZA: No, but he _____.
                              (encourage)

4. CHRIS: Why aren't you taking the freeway home?

   TARA: My brother _____. There's a lot of
                                (warn / not)
   construction there.

5. NED: Why are you babysitting for those children?

   RUFUS: My friend _____.
   (ask)

A WIDER ANGLE

Impromptu Speeches

An impromptu speech is a speech given without preparation. Your teacher will give you a topic and ask you to talk for one minute on that subject. When you finish, your classmates might want to ask you some questions.

Writing Practice: Raising Children

If you have children, write a short composition on Topic 1. If you do not have children, write a short composition on Topic 2.

TOPIC 1: Describe your philosophy of raising children. How have you raised or been raising your children? What is your definition of a "good" parent? What advice can you give to couples who are thinking about having children someday?

TOPIC 2: Describe your philosophy of raising children. Would you like to have children someday? Why or why not? What kind of parent will you try to be? What are some of the things that you will or will not do as a parent?

DEVELOPING YOUR SKILLS AND KNOWLEDGE

Chapter Exercises

EXERCISE 1 Gerund Subjects

Complete each of the following sentences with a gerund subject.

EXAMPLE   <u>Interrupting someone</u> is rude.

1. _____ makes me depressed.

2. _____ is very frustrating.

3. _____ puts me in a good mood.

4. _____ is a good way to relax.

5. _____ can make you sick.

EXERCISE 2 The Subject IT

A. *Complete these sentences with your own ideas.*

1. It is very expensive _____.

2. It didn't use to be possible for people _____.

3. It is difficult for me _____.

4. It has been interesting for us _____.

B. *Rewrite each of the following sentences by changing the gerund subject to the subject* **IT**. *Your new sentence should have the same meaning as the one that is given.*

EXAMPLE   Getting letters from home is wonderful.
It is wonderful **to get** letters from home.

1. Driving in snow can be scary.
2. Having a party might be fun.
3. Getting a visa to come here was difficult for Charlie.
4. Living in a foreign country is quite challenging.
5. Receiving bills depresses me.
6. Finding time to write letters has been impossible for me.

EXERCISE 3   Gerund Objects

Use the information given to answer each question with a complete sentence. Your answer should contain a gerund phrase.

EXAMPLE   Doreen plays tennis. Doreen enjoys this.
What does Doreen enjoy?
She enjoys **playing tennis.**

1. Melina can't drive. Melina hates *this.*
What does Melina hate?
2. Paolo doesn't have a phone. Paolo is tired of *this.*
What is Paolo tired of?
3. Carol and Jack have scholarships. They appreciate *this.*
What do Carol and Jack appreciate?
4. I'm going to Hawaii next month. I'm looking forward to *this.*
What are you looking forward to?
5. Gary isn't an athlete. He regrets *this.*
What does Gary regret?

EXERCISE 4   Prepositions

Fill in each blank with an appropriate preposition.

1. We are interested _____ learning more about the American election system.

2. Is the landlord responsible _____ shoveling the snow from the sidewalks?

3. Chang is nervous _____ starting his graduate studies.

4. David should have thought _____ buying medical insurance before his accident.

5. Are you looking forward _____ finishing this term?

EXERCISE 5   Requests

Complete each of the following exchanges with an appropriate question or response.

1. MARISA: _____?

   CARL: Of course not. I'll be happy to show you. First you push this button, and then you turn these knobs. Now you're ready to use it.

   MARISA: Thanks. I appreciate it.

2. TEDDY: Would you mind lending me your pencil sharpener?

   NORA: _____. Here you go.

   TEDDY: Thanks a lot.

3. MERV: Would you mind letting me borrow your car?

   SONJA: _____.

   MERV: That's OK. Maybe I can borrow my roommate's car.

4. LUCY: _____?

   CHUCK: Sorry. I'll turn it down right away.

5. WYNTON: _____?

   LISA: Yes, of course. I'll be happy to!

EXERCISE 6   Gerunds and Infinitives

Fill in the blanks with the appropriate forms of the verbs indicated. Think about verb tenses.

SPIRO: When you called last night, I _____
(try / figure out)
some problems for my accounting class. After I got off the

phone, I _____ them for several
(continue / work on)
more hours. Finally, I _____ all of
(manage / answer)
the problems.

RICHARD: What time _____ them?
(you / finish / work on)

SPIRO: At around midnight.

RICHARD: I'm never going to take accounting. It has always been difficult

for me _____ calculations without
(do)
_____ a calculator.
(use)

SPIRO: Really? _____ with numbers has
(work)
always been easy for me. That's why I

_____ finance instead of
(decide / major in)
_____ history.
(study)

EXERCISE 7 Verbs of Influence

Use the information from the following conversation to complete the sentences that follow.

SUSAN: OK. Everybody listen up! I'm going to have a dinner party, and all of you are going to help! Lisa, would you mind buying the drinks?

LISA: No problem. I'll be happy to.

SUSAN: Carrie, I'd like you to help me write the invitations.

CARRIE: OK.

SUSAN: And Carrie, you have to promise to clean up your room before the party.

CARRIE: Okay, if you insist.

SUSAN: Tina, you'll be in charge of making the dessert.

TINA: Great! Can I also make a salad?

SUSAN: Well . . . I was planning to make my special Greek salad, but if you really want to, go ahead.

1. Susan wants all of her roommates _____.

2. She's asked Lisa _____.

3. She's going to have Carrie _____.

4. She's also going to make Carrie _____, even though Carrie doesn't really want to.

5. She's having Tina _____.

6. She also agreed to let Tina _____.

13 *Passive Constructions*

```
┌─────────────────────────────────────────────────┐
│  ┌──────────────────────────────────┐           │
│  │   THE BIG PICTURE                │           │
│  └──────────────────────────────────┘           │
│   Passive Forms and Uses                         │
│   Causative Passive Verbs                        │
│   Participial Adjectives                         │
│                                                  │
└─────────────────────────────────────────────────┘
```

AT A GLANCE

The Statue of Liberty

FIGURE 13–1

Are you familiar with the statue in Fig. 13–1? Where is it located? What does the statue symbolize? What is the statue doing? What is happening to the statue in this photograph?

The Statue of Liberty, a gift from France, was officially unveiled in 1886. From that time on, "Miss Liberty" has been a symbol of freedom, especially for the millions of immigrants who came to the United States to escape from persecution, poverty, and war. From 1892 to 1954, over 12 million immigrants were processed at the immigration center on Ellis Island behind the Statue of Liberty.

To celebrate the statue's hundredth birthday, massive renovations of the statue were undertaken, and plans for a four-day centennial celebration were made for July 1986. Today, Liberty Island and Ellis Island receive thousands of tourists daily.

FOCUS I Understanding Passive Constructions

A. Active constructions

In active constructions, the subject of the verb is the "doer" or "performer" of the action. In other words, the subject is responsible for the action of the verb. We can say that there is an **active** relationship between the subject and the verb.

> Sentence 1:
>
> **France gave** the Statue of Liberty to the United States in 1886.
>
> *What is the subject of the verb GAVE?*
>
> *What is the object of the verb GAVE?*
>
> *Who performed this action (GAVE): France or the Statue of Liberty?*

Sentence 1 gives an example of an active construction. The subject (**FRANCE**) is also the "performer" of the action (**GAVE**).

B. Passive constructions

In passive constructions, the subject of the verb does **not** perform the action. Instead, the subject "receives" the action. In other words, something **happens to the subject.** Something or someone else is responsible for performing the action. In this case, we can say there is a **passive** relationship between the subject and the verb.

> Sentence 2:
>
> **The Statue of Liberty was given** to the United States by France.
>
> *What is the subject of the verb WAS GIVEN?*
>
> *Who performed this action: France or the Statue of Liberty?*
>
> *What happened to the Statue of Liberty in this sentence?*

Sentence 2 gives an example of a passive construction. The subject (**the Statue of Liberty**) is *not* the "performer" of the action.

C. Using passive constructions

As you have just seen, a passive construction indicates that something or someone other than the subject is responsible for the action of the verb. The passive is used to focus on the fact **that something happened to the subject.** There may or may not be any mention of the person or thing responsible for the action.

The passive is often used when the person or thing responsible for the action is:

  1. not important or relevant in a particular situation

    Many new immigrants **were processed** on Ellis Island.
    The flame on the statue's torch **has been replaced.**

  2. not known

    My books **were stolen** yesterday.
    These keys **were left** in the classroom this morning.

3. obvious

> Reading **is taught** in the first grade. *[By teachers, of course.]*
> My car **is being fixed** today. *[By a mechanic, most likely.]*

In all of these situations, the passive construction focuses on the "receiver" of the action, not the "doer."

D.   Using phrases with BY

In some passive sentences, although the main focus is on what happened to the subject, it is also important to mention who or what is responsible for the action Use a phrase with **BY** to indicate who or what performed the action.

> The Statue of Liberty was designed **by Frederic Auguste Bartholdi.**
> *Romeo and Juliet* was written **by Shakespeare.**

PRACTICE 1-1   Understanding Active and Passive

*A.   Are the verbs in the following sentences **active** or **passive**?*

1. "Miss Liberty" **is holding** a torch in one hand and a tablet in the other.
2. The date of American Independence, July 4, 1776, **is inscribed** on the tablet.
3. The broken chains at her feet **symbolize** freedom.
4. The dent in her right arm **has been made** by one of the spikes in her crown.

*B.   In the following sentences, the verb forms have not been given. For each sentence, decide whether the relationship between the subject and the verb is **active** or **passive**. Do not try to give the appropriate verb form. Just decide if the verb should be active or passive.*

1. The original flame (**remove**) in 1983 because it (**damage**) by water.
2. The restoration committee (**hire**) a team of French metalworkers to build a new flame.
3. The committee (**decide**) that the new flame should (**build**) according to Bartholdi's original design.
4. The new flame (**cover**) with 24-karat gold leaf.
5. Lights (**place**) on the balcony around the flame. These lights (**illuminate**) the flame at night.

PRACTICE 1-2   Using Phrases with **BY**

*All of the following passive sentences include a phrase with **BY**. For each sentence, decide if the BY phrase is (or could be) necessary or important. Discuss your opinions with your classmates.*

1. This song was written by Michael Jackson.
2. This song was written by someone in 1934.
3. Coffee is grown in parts of Hawaii by coffee farmers.
4. This coffee was given to me by an old and dear friend.
5. The cost of my surgery will be paid for by my insurance company.
6. The TOEFL test is going to be given on Monday by the teachers.
7. The TOEFL tests will be corrected by the teachers.

8.   A new president was elected by the people last year.

9.   This committee was chosen by the president.

10.   The town was destroyed by a tornado earlier this month.

FOCUS 2   Introduction to Passive Verb Forms

A.   Verb tenses in the passive

Like active verbs, passive verbs can occur in different verb tenses. The rules and meanings of the verb tenses are the same for both passive and active verbs. All passive verbs have the auxiliary **BE** and end with a past participle. The form of the auxiliary **BE** indicates the time focus and verb tense.

Subject +	BE (verb tense) +	Past Participle +	Rest of Sentence
Tours of the island	**are**	given	almost daily.
A tour	**was**	given	to President Reagan in 1986.
Many tours	**have been**	given	since the renovation.
"Miss Liberty"	**had been**	visited	by many people before the renovation.
The statue	**is being**	visited	by some Japanese tourists today.
It	**was being**	visited	by some schoolchildren when I was there.
It	**will be**	visited	by our grandchildren in years to come.

B.   Negative passive constructions

To make a passive construction negative, add **NOT (-N'T)** after the *first* auxiliary.

> The green color of the copper *won't be cleaned off.*
>
> The dent in the statue's right arm *hasn't been fixed.*

C.   Questions and short forms

To form a question, move the first auxiliary before the subject. Use the first auxiliary for short forms.

> **Was** the statue's hundredth birthday **celebrated** in 1986? Yes, it **was.**
>
> **Has** the taxpayers' money **been used** for the renovation? No, it **hasn't.**
>
> Government money **won't be spent** for repairs, **will** it? No, it **won't.**
>
> How **were** the renovations **financed?** By private donations.
>
> What **has been placed** in the museum? The old torch **has.**
>
> Who **was invited** to the 1986 celebration of the statue? Many celebrities **were.**
>
> The statue's hundredth birthday celebration **was planned** by David Wolper, and so **were** the 1984 Summer Olympics festivities.
>
> The interior of the statue **has been renovated,** and so **has** the exterior.

FOCUS 3   Passive Forms of Simple Present and Simple Past Verbs

Passive constructions that refer to general facts or states use the present form of the auxiliary **BE (IS, AM, ARE)**. Use the past form of the auxiliary **BE (WAS, WERE)** to make a simple past passive verb.

Some students have organized a trip to see the Statue of Liberty.

Simple Present Passive				Simple Past Passive			
Subject +	BE "passive" +	Past Participle		Subject +	BE "passive" +	Past Participle	
I	am	**included** in the group.		I	was	**asked** yesterday.
Trips	are	often **organized** by students.		You	were	**called** last night.
Jim	isn't	**expected** to come.		Jim	wasn't	**told** at all.

PRACTICE 3–1   Simple Present Passive

Use the cues to ask questions about the following goods and products. Your classmate should answer each question with a complete sentence or short answer. Fill in empty brackets with your own cues.

EXAMPLE   oil / produce / Saudi Arabia? (yes)

Student A: Is oil produced in Saudi Arabia?
Student B: Yes, it is.

1. cars / manufacture / Japan? (yes)
2. silk / make / Thailand? (yes)
3. nuclear energy / use / for electricity / your country? [   ]
4. [   ] / manufacture / your country? [   ]
5. what natural resources / find / in your country? [   ]

PRACTICE 3–2   Simple Past Passive

*Here is a list of important dates in the history of the United States. Use this information to complete the following sentences with the **simple past passive**.*

1492:   Columbus discovers America
1776:   Representatives of the American colonies sign the Declaration of Independence
1783:   England recognizes the independence of the United States
1787:   Delegates in Philadelphia write the Constitution of the United States
1789:   Americans elect George Washington as the first president of the United States
1865:   An amendment to the Constitution sets all slaves free
1920:   A constitutional amendment gives women the right to vote

1. In 1492, America . . .

2. In 1776, the Declaration of Independence . . .

3. In 1783, the independence of the United States from England . . .

4. In 1787, the Constitution of the United States . . .

5. In 1789, George Washington . . .

6. In 1865, all slaves . . .

7. Women . . . until 1920.

Passive Forms of Perfect Verbs

To form a **present perfect passive** verb, use **HAS** or **HAVE** with **BEEN** and a past participle. Use **HAD** with **BEEN** and a past participle to form the **past perfect passive**.

Workers have repaired and modernized many things in the statue.

Present Perfect Passive						
Subject	+	HAS/HAVE "before now"	+	BEEN "passive"	+	Past Participle
The flame		has		been		replaced.
Many iron beams		have		been		replaced.
The copper skin		hasn't		been		replaced.

Past Perfect Passive						
	Subject	+	HAD "before a past time"	+	BEEN "passive"	+	Past Participle
They replaced the flame because	it		had		been		damaged by corrosion.
They replaced the beams because	they		had		been		damaged by corrosion.
The skin wasn't replaced because	it		hadn't		been		damaged by corrosion.

PRACTICE 4–1 Present Perfect Passive

Mail-order catalogs are a popular way for Americans to shop. By ordering from a catalog, they avoid driving, parking, and dealing with crowds.

Ted is the manager of a mail-order catalog company. A few days ago, Ted made a list of things that needed to be done. A check mark (√) indicates things that have already been taken care of.

1. Hire three new models for photographs.√
2. Publish the new catalog.
3. Take pictures for the holiday catalog.
4. Mail boxes of catalogs to New York.
5. Pay the electric bill.√
6. Send bills to customers who still owe money.
7. Deliver MacNeil and Company's order.
8. Order a hundred pairs of boots from Joe's Shoes.
9. Contact Marie Simmons about sweaters.
10. Place an advertisement in *The New York Times*.√

*Use the following subject cues to ask questions with **YET**. Your classmate should respond to each question with a complete sentence using **STILL** or **ALREADY**. All questions and answers should be passive.*

EXAMPLE   the models?
             Student A: **Have** the new models **been hired yet?**
             Student B: Yes, they **have already been hired.**

the new catalog?

Student A: **Has** the new catalog **been published yet?**

Student B: No, it **still hasn't been published.**

1. pictures for the holiday catalog?
2. boxes of catalogs?
3. electric bill?
4. bills to customers?
5. MacNeil and Company's order?
6. boots?
7. Marie Simmons?
8. advertisement?

PRACTICE 4-2 Past Perfect Passive

The city council voted to tear down several old buildings downtown in order to build a parking lot and several other new buildings. They went ahead with their plans without consulting the Historical Society.

Use the cues to complete the sentence with the past perfect passive.

The Historical Society members were very upset when they found out that . . .

1. a historical house / tear down
2. a parking lot / build in its place
3. the old town hall / not / preserve
4. several old oak trees / take out
5. the Historical Society / not / consult beforehand

FOCUS 5 Passive Forms of Future Verbs

Use **BE GOING TO** or **WILL** with **BE** and a past participle to form future passive verbs.

When is the next celebration for the Statue of Liberty?

		Future Passive			
Subject	+	**BE GOING TO / WILL** "future"	+	**BE** "passive"	+ **Past Participle**
Her two-hundredth birthday		**is going to**		**be**	**celebrated** in 2086.
The occasion		**will**		**be**	**celebrated** in 2086.

PRACTICE 5-1 Future Passive

Mr. and Mrs. MacNaught have hired a cleaning service to do their spring cleaning tomorrow. Here is a list of things that they will ask the cleaning people to do.

1. Wash windows
2. Vacuum and shampoo carpets
3. Sweep kitchen floor

4. Scrub bathtub
5. Mop bathroom floor
6. Dust bookshelves

Now complete the following sentences about what is going to happen tomorrow when the cleaning service comes.

1.   Will they clean the bathroom?

   Yes. The bathtub _____, and the floor

   _____.

2.   What about the carpets in the house?

   The carpets _____.

3.   Is the kitchen floor going to be waxed?

   No, but it _____.

4.   Is anything else going to be done tomorrow?

   Yes. The windows _____, and the

   bookshelves _____.

FOCUS 6   Passive Forms of Progressive Verbs

The only progressive tenses that normally occur in the passive are present progressive and past progressive. To form a progressive passive, use a form of **BE**, (**IS, AM, ARE, WAS, WERE**) with **BEING** and a past participle.

A.   Present progressive passive

Some students are organizing a trip to the Statue of Liberty.

Subject +	BE "now in progress" +	BEING "passive" +	Past Participle
A trip to the statue	is	being	**discussed.**
Plans for the trip	are	being	**organized** by some students.
A birthday party	isn't	being	**planned** right now.

B.   Past progressive passive

When David and his family went to New York in the summer of 1985, there was a giant scaffold around the Statue of Liberty, and Liberty Island was closed to tourists.

	Subject +	BE "in progress in the past" +	BEING "passive" +	Past Participle
At that time,	parts of the internal structure	were	being	**repaired.**
At that time,	the exterior of the statue	was	being	**cleaned.**
At that time,	tourists	weren't	being	**allowed** in.

Progressive Passive

A. *Use the cues to answer the questions about things that are happening right now.*

EXAMPLE   Why is there scaffolding around the statue?
                   (it / renovate)
                   It's being renovated.

1. Why is your car at the mechanic?
   (the brakes / fix)
2. Why is that first-grade boy staying after school?
   (he / punish for something)
3. What's happening to those demonstrators over there?
   (they / arrest)
4. What's happening to that old oak tree over there?
   (it / cut down)
5. Why don't you have your computer?
   (my computer / repair)

B. *A reporter arrived at the scene of a large fire at an apartment building. When she got there, the firefighters had already arrived. Use the following cues to describe what was happening when the reporter arrived.*

EXAMPLE   a woman / carry / out of the building
                   A woman was being carried out of the building.

1. the residents of the building / evacuate by the firefighters
2. a man / treat for smoke inhalation
3. a child / put in an ambulance
4. the streets around the building / block off by the police
5. the residents / take to nearby hotels for the night

Passive with Different Tenses

Read the situation. Use the cues with a passive construction to answer the question about the situation. Think about the time focus of the action.

EXAMPLE   Somebody took my calculator yesterday.

       Question: What happened to your calculator?
         Answer: (it / steal) It **was stolen** yesterday.

1. These shoes are from Italy.
   Q: Are your shoes from Spain?
   A: No. (they / make . . .)
2. They are going to show Ron Howard's newest film on TV tomorrow night.
   Q: Have they shown Ron Howard's newest movie yet?
   A: No. (it / show . . .)
3. I took my car to the mechanic's this morning. I'll pick it up tomorrow.
   Q: Where's your car?
   A: (it / the garage / fix)

Q: Will it be ready this afternoon?

A: No. (it / [probably] not / fix / until tomorrow)

4. There was an audience when they filmed this TV show.

Q: Were there any people in the audience when they made this show?

A: Yes. (this show / record / in front of a live audience)

5. Nigeria exports a great deal of its oil.

Q: Do Nigerians consume most of the oil that the country produces?

A: No. (a great deal of its oil / export / other countries)

6. Beth Archer is running for president of the student body.

Q: Do you think Beth Archer is going to lose the election?

A: No. (I / think // she / [probably] elect)

7. The instructions for assembling this bicycle are on that paper.

Q: Where can I find out how to put this bike together?

A: (the procedures / explain . . .)

8. Someone broke into the Wilsons' house while they were on vacation.

Q: Why were the Wilsons upset when they arrived home?

A: (their house / break into // and / many things / take)

9. When Bill got to the meeting last night, everyone was discussing ideas for raising money for a new project.

Q: Had they made any decisions by the time Bill arrived?

A: No. (different plans / [still] discuss.   nothing / decide [yet])

FOCUS 7   Choosing Active or Passive

Not all verbs can occur in passive form. If you consider meaning instead of grammar, the subject of a passive construction is actually the object of the action. Something happens to the passive subject. Therefore, a verb that cannot have an object cannot be passive.

	Subject	+	Verb	+	Object
active:	Bartholdi		designed		the statue.
	Subject		Verb		Rest of Sentence
passive:	The statue		was designed		by Bartholdi.
	Subject	+	Verb	+	Rest of Sentence
active:	Bartholdi		came		to the United States in 1871.

The verb **COME** is followed by an adverb of place, not by an object. Therefore, it can never be passive. Examples of verbs that do not normally occur with passive constructions include **HAPPEN, OCCUR, TAKE PLACE, GO, COME, ARRIVE, DEPART, FALL,** and **SLEEP.**

PRACTICE 7-1   Choosing Active or Passive

*The following sentences all contain active constructions. Decide whether or not the verb in each sentence can be changed to passive. If it is possible, change the sentence using a passive construction. Include a phrase beginning with **BY** if it is appropriate.*

Bartholdi *designed* the Statue of Liberty.

The Statue of Liberty **was designed** by Bartholdi.

The statue *stands* on a small island.

[*No passive sentence is possible.*]

1. Melina *went* back to her country last month.
2. Many changes *had occurred* while she was away.
3. When she *got* home, the changes *surprised* her.
4. The government *had paved* the road by her house.
5. Construction workers *were building* new apartments everywhere.
6. The city *had planted* a lot of new trees.
7. The city *was going to build* a park in the center of town.
8. A lot of tourists *had started coming* to her hometown.
9. Melina *felt* happy about the great things that *were happening* in her town.

PRACTICE 7-2   More Active and Passive

Use the cues to make sentences about immigrants who came to the United States through Ellis Island. Some of the sentences will be active; others will be passive.

1. Ellis Island / locate / behind the Statue of Liberty
2. 17 million immigrants / land in the United States at Ellis Island earlier this century
3. 80 percent of the immigrants / allow to stay here
4. some of them / stay on Ellis Island for several days // while / their documents / process by immigration officials
5. 300,000 of them / deport back to their countries

FOCUS 8   Passive Modal Auxiliaries and Expressions

Modal expressions can also occur in passive constructions.

This building is old and abandoned. It is a dangerous firetrap.

Subject	+	Modal Expression "advice, possibility, necessity"	+	BE "passive" (base form)	+	Past Participle	+	Rest of Sentence
It		can		be		boarded		up.
It		should		be		condemned.		
It		ought to		be		shut		up soon.
It		has to		be		torn		down.
It		must		be		done		by next year.
It		had better		be		gone		before that.
It		is supposed to		be		razed		by next month.
It		might		be		destroyed		before that.

Advice Given Too Late

The abandoned building burned down last night.

Subject	+	SHOULD "opinion"	+	HAVE "past"	+	BEEN "passive"	+	Past Participle	+	Rest of Sentence
That building		should		have		been		torn down		ages ago.

PRACTICE 8-1   Modal Expressions with Passive Verbs

Use the cues to make sentences. Supply the appropriate modal expressions. Fill in empty brackets with your own cues.

EXAMPLE   This building is so old that it is dangerous.

(it / tear down [= *advice*])
It **should be torn** down.

1.   Don't forget to sign your name at the bottom of the page.
(this document / sign [= *necessity*] / by you)

2.   I'd like to send this package by first-class mail.
(when / it / deliver [= *future*]?)
(it / deliver [= *expectation*] / on Monday // but / it / not deliver [= *possibility*] / until Tuesday)

3.   Some medicine bottles are "childproof."
(they / not open [= *ability*] / easily / by children)

4.   Bill broke his ankle during basketball practice yesterday.
(he / take [= *necessity*] / the hospital)

5.   This milk smells sour.
(it / [   ] / drink)
(it / [   ] / throw away / a long time ago)

FOCUS 9   Causative Passive

A.   Using causative HAVE

The verb **HAVE** sometimes has a **causative** meaning. It means to request, require, or hire someone to do something. Causative **HAVE** can be followed by an object and an active base form verb.

> The restoration committee **had** a team of Frenchmen **make** a new flame for the torch.

> Did the committee make the new flame?
> Who made it?
> Why did they do it?

Causative **HAVE*** can also occur with a passive object and verb.

> The restoration committee **had** a new flame **made** (by a team of Frenchmen).

> What was made?
> Why was it made?
> Who made it?

---

*In conversation, **get** is sometimes used instead of causative passive **have**:
I'm going to **have** my picture taken.
I'm going to **get** my picture taken.

B. Forming sentences with causative HAVE

When the resulting action is passive, use a past participle. To indicate the person or thing responsible for the action, a phrase beginning with **BY** may be used. Once again, the causative passive form focuses on what was done.

Subject	+	HAVE "causative"	+	Object	+	Past Participle "passive"	+	Rest of Sentence
They		have had		the exterior of the statue		cleaned.		
They		had		part of the statue's nose		repaired.		
They		had		a new elevator		installed.		
They		will have		more gold		put on		the flame later.
I		want to have		my picture		taken		next to the statue.

PRACTICE 9-1   Causative Passive

Bob has just bought a house. He got the house for a good price because it is old and not in very good condition. He plans to hire people to remodel the house. Following is a list of the things he wants to have done.

Change these causative sentences to the passive form to focus on what is going to happen, instead of who will carry out the action.

EXAMPLE   Bob wants to have some painters paint his house.
He wants to **have** his house **painted.**

1. He wants to have some plumbers put in new plumbing.
2. He's planning to have some workers remodel the kitchen.
3. He would also like to have some workers carpet all the floors.
4. He will probably have a plumber install a new bathtub in the bathroom.
5. He needs to have an electrician rewire the house.

PRACTICE 9-2   More Causative Passive

Marie had been having many problems with her car until she finally decided to take it to the mechanic last week.

Use the cues to form sentences explaining what Marie had done to her car. Fill in the empty brackets with your own cues.

EXAMPLE   the brakes / check
She **had** the brakes **checked.**

1. the oil / change
2. the tires / rotate
3. the spark plugs / replace
4. the heater / fix
5. the engine / tune up
6. [   ]

Adjectives from Participles and Their Prepositions

A. Past participles as adjectives

Many adjectives in English come from *past participles.* Like other adjectives, these past participles are used with the verb **BE** and other linking verbs to describe the situation of someone or something.

Here are some examples of adjectives from past participles:

> The window is **broken / closed / shut.**
>
> My puppy is **gone / hurt / lost.**
>
> John feels **depressed / tired / worried / excited.**

B. Adjectives with prepositions

Many past participle adjectives can occur with certain prepositions other than **BY.** Here are some common adjective and preposition combinations. You can find other examples in Appendix C.

be engaged **to**
be married **to**
be divorced **from**   ⎤
be disappointed **in**   ⎦ someone

be bored **with**
be involved **in**
be pleased **about**
be upset **over**
be disappointed **about/at**   ⎤ something
be excited **about**
be exhausted **from**
be made **of**
be composed **of**

be interested **in**
be bored **with**
be involved **with**
be satisfied **with**
be pleased **with**
be upset **with**
be disappointed **with**
be excited **about**
be tired **of**
be exhausted **from**
be frightened **of**   someone or something
be scared **of**
be terrified **of**
be worried **about**
be finished **with**
be done **with**
be related **to**
be acquainted **with**
be used **to**
be accustomed **to**

PRACTICE   **ADJECTIVES AND PREPOSITIONS**

Use the following cues to form questions with adjectives from past participles. Add any necessary articles or prepositions. Your classmate should use the cues in parentheses to respond to each question with a complete sentence. Fill in the empty brackets with your own cues.

EXAMPLE   who / Cathy / engaged? (Dan)

Student A: Who is Cathy engaged to?
Student B: She's engaged to Dan.

1.   who / Chris / married? (Elizabeth)
2.   what / this shirt / made? (cotton)
3.   what animals / dolphins / related? (whales)
4.   what / water / composed? (hydrogen and oxygen)
5.   what / you / scared? [   ]
6.   what / you / get / excited? [   ]

FOCUS 10   Active and Passive Participial Adjectives

Because participial adjectives come from verbs, they can be active or passive.

A.   Active adjectives—present participles

An *"active" adjective* comes from a present participle (-ING verb). The noun that it describes is responsible for the "action" of the adjective.

History class **bores** me.

History class is **boring**. It is a **boring** class.

B.   Passive adjectives—past participles

A *"passive" adjective* is a past participle. The noun that it describes is *not* responsible for the "action" of the adjective. A passive adjective describes how the noun is affected by an action that was caused by something else.

History class **bores** me.

I am **bored** in history class. There are a lot of **bored** students in that class.

PRACTICE 10-1   Active and Passive Adjectives

A.   Form participial adjectives from each verb cue to complete the sentences that follow.

1.   *Confuse:* The passive voice **confuses** the students.

a. It is a _____ grammar point.

b. The students feel _____.

c. I would like to study something that isn't so

_____.

      d. The _____ students stayed after class to ask the
         teacher to explain the passive voice again.

  2. *Interest:* The customs and culture here **interest** me.

      a. I am very _____ in the culture here.

      b. I have come across some unusual and _____
         customs.

      c. Some of my classmates are _____ in learning
         more about life here.

      d. A group of _____ students attended an

         _____ lecture about the changing role of women.

B.   *Using participial adjectives from these verbs, answer the following questions with complete sentences.*

frighten	exhaust	interest	disappoint	relieve
surprise	frustrate	bore	excite	depress

  1. How do students usually feel when they get a low score on a test?

  2. How do you feel when you have something important to say, but you can't find the words in English to express yourself?

  3. Think about the last movie that you saw. How would you describe it? How did you feel as you were watching it?

A WIDER ANGLE

Group Discussion

Talk about the physical changes that have taken place in your hometown, country, or capital city over the past ten or twenty years. Talk about the future too. What other changes will probably be made? What else should or could be done?

Writing Practice: Famous Monuments

Write about a famous monument, building, or tourist site in your country. Include a physical description, a description of its location, any background information that you have, and an explanation of its purpose.

DEVELOPING YOUR SKILLS AND KNOWLEDGE   *Chapter Exercises*

EXERCISE I   Forming the Passive

Change the following sentences from active to passive.

EXAMPLE   The post office sends almost all mail by airplane.
              Almost all mail <u>is sent</u> by airplane.

1. At the post office, postal workers weigh the letters before they put postage on them.

   At the post office, letters _____ before postage

   _____.

2. They lost my letter to my embassy last month.

   My letter to my embassy _____ last month.

3. I mailed it a month ago, but they still haven't delivered it.

   It _____ a month ago, but it still

   _____.

4. Maybe it fell out of the letter carrier's bag while she was delivering it.

   Maybe it fell out of the letter carrier's bag while it

   _____.

5. I called the post office last Monday, but they still hadn't found it.

   I called the post office last Monday, but my letter still

   _____.

6. Maybe someone will find it years from now in the corner of a mailroom.

   Maybe it _____ years from now in the corner of a mailroom.

EXERCISE 2 More Passive

Fill in each blank with a passive form of the verb indicated. Be sure to choose an appropriate verb tense.

MARLO: This is an interesting photograph of the Statue of Liberty. Look

at all that scaffolding!

BRIAN: The picture _____ while the statue
                              (take)

_____.
        (renovate)

MARLO: Why _____ from the torch?
             (the flame / remove)

BRIAN: It _____ because it _____ by
           (remove)   (damage)
        corrosion.

MARLO: Were you able to visit the monument during your trip to New

York?

BRIAN: No. Tourists _____ to go to Liberty Island at that
                     (not / allow)
        time. Many things _____. The internal
                          ([still] repair)
        structures _____ yet.
                   (not / fix)

EXERCISE 3   Active or Passive

Use an appropriate form of the verb indicated to complete the sentences that follow. Some of the sentences need active verbs; others need passive verbs.

EXAMPLE   **(fix)**

a. The mechanic <u>is going to fix</u> the brakes in my car later today.

b. The brakes <u>are going to be fixed</u> later today.

1. **(take)**

   a. A tow truck _____ my car from the highway to a garage this morning.

   b. My car _____ to a garage by a tow truck this morning.

   c. While the mechanic _____ my car to the garage, the tow truck stalled.

   d. While my car _____ to the garage, the tow truck stalled.

2. **(check)**

   a. Right now, the mechanic _____ the car battery.

   b. Right now, the car battery _____.

   c. After he _____ the battery, he _____ the electrical system.

   d. After the battery _____, the electrical system _____.

   e. The mechanic _____ the brakes yet.

   f. The brakes _____ yet.

EXERCISE 4   Passives with Modal Verbs

Rewrite the following sentences, changing these active sentences to passive ones. Include a phrase beginning with BY if you think it is important. Make any other necessary changes.

EXAMPLE   They should tear down this building.
               This building **should be torn** down.

1. We must clean up the pollution in our rivers.
2. Your adviser has to sign this form before they will allow you to take this class.
3. Somebody from the company is supposed to meet John at the airport.
4. They should have installed a traffic light at that intersection years ago.
5. They might hold the graduation ceremony outside.
6. We mustn't tell Martha about our surprise.

EXERCISE 5   More Active and Passive

Fill in each blank with the correct form of the verb indicated. Decide if the verb should be active or passive, and choose an appropriate verb tense.

Starting on July 3, 1986, a four-day celebration _____ for
(hold)
the "new" Statue of Liberty. President Reagan _____ the
(push)
button that _____ the lights for the statue. The planners
(turn on)
were afraid that something _____ wrong, so a back-up
(go [= *possibility*])
lighting system _____. Many important guests
(install [= *necessity*])
_____ to attend the lighting of the statue. On July 4, ships
(invite)
from all over the world _____ New York Harbor for the
(enter)
celebration. That night, the largest fireworks display in the history of
America _____. Three different fireworks companies
(set off)
_____ to provide fireworks for the celebration. While the
(hire)
fireworks _____ on TV by people all over the country,
(watch)
synchronized music _____. Liberty Island
(hear [= *ability*])
_____ on Saturday, July 5, by the president's wife. Nancy
([officially] open)
Reagan _____ the first tour of the renovated statue. On
(take)
Sunday night, many famous performers _____ in an
(participate)
extravagant stage show. The celebration _____ for many
(remember)
years to come by the people who saw it. Who knows? Perhaps our
grandchildren _____ the next birthday celebration for the
(attend)
statue!

EXERCISE 6   Causative Passive

The cleaning service is coming to the MacNaughts' this afternoon. Here is a list of things that Mr. and Mrs. MacNaught want to have done.

wash living room windows	wax dining room floor
clean out fireplace	dust bookshelves
shampoo carpets	mop kitchen floor

Complete each of the following sentences with an appropriate verb.

EXAMPLES   They're going to have the bookshelves **dusted.**
They're planning to have the cleaning service **wax** the dining room floor.

1. They're planning to have the dining room floor
   _____.

2. They will also have the carpets _____.

3. They are going to have the cleaning service _____ the living room windows.

4. They aren't planning to have the kitchen windows
   _____.

5. They are going to ask them _____ the fireplace.

6. They would like to have the kitchen floor _____.

EXERCISE 7 Active and Passive Adjectives

Complete the following sentences with participial adjectives from the verbs indicated.

EXAMPLE   **Fascinate:** Art fascinates me.

a. I am <u>fascinated</u> by art.

b. I think art is <u>fascinating.</u>

1. **Depress:** The evening news depressed me last night.

   a. The news last night was _____.

   b. I felt _____ as I watched the news.

   c. Don't you get _____ when you hear the news about murders and fires?

   d. Why do they always put such _____ news items on TV?

2. **Exhaust:** Taking care of her three small children exhausts Jane.

   a. Jane is usually _____ by the end of the day.

   b. With three small children to take care of, she leads an

      _____ life.

   c. The children always seem full of energy while she feels

      _____.

   d. It is _____ to run around after children all day.

14 *Identifying and Specifying*

┌─────────────────────────────┐
│ **THE BIG PICTURE** │
└─────────────────────────────┘
Adjective Clauses

AT A GLANCE

Identification Cards

Do people in your country carry national identification cards? What kind of information is on these cards? What is the purpose of such a card?

What do people in this country use for identification? What do *you* use for identification here? What are some situations in which you need to show an ID card in this country?

Identifying Things

How can you identify the items in the following situations? What information can you give that will differentiate one item from all the others?

1. your suitcase at the baggage claim area of the airport
2. your jacket at a Lost and Found
3. your house or apartment building when giving directions to a visitor

Defining and Describing

In 1959, Dr. Meyer Friedman and Dr. Ray Rosenmann identified two types of personalities and discovered a relationship between these personalities and heart disease.

People with Type A personalities:

1. always walk, move, eat, and work quickly.
2. become impatient and angry when they have to wait for something.
3. feel guilty when they relax or vacation for several days.
4. often try to think about or do two or more things at one time.
5. often have nervous habits such as tapping their fingers or grinding their teeth.
6. are often very competitive, always trying to achieve more and to be more successful.

People with Type B personalities:

1. are not terribly worried about wasting time.
2. enjoy taking time to appreciate small things.
3. do not feel the need to be constantly achieving things.
4. have no trouble relaxing.
5. do not become impatient with situations that are not within their power to change.

Is your personality closer to Type A or Type B?

In this chapter, you will practice using structures for identifying and defining things. You will practice giving information that will distinguish one item from another.

Robert has just given his friends directions to his house. Here are some different ways he can identify which house is his.

Robert: When you get to Spring Drive, turn right.
1. Our house is the first house **on the right.** (prepositional phrase)
2. Ours is the **big blue** house. (adjective)
3. Our house is the one **that looks like a barn.** (adjective clause)

In sentence 3, Robert used an entire clause—an *adjective clause**—to identify his house.

A.   Understanding adjective clauses

An *adjective* is a word that describes a noun. Most adjectives in English come *before* the noun that they describe.

    a *big blue* house   the *first* house

An *adjective clause* is a type of dependent clause. Like an adjective, an adjective clause modifies or gives specific information about a noun.

B.   Important points about adjective clauses

There are three things to remember about adjective clauses:

    1.   An adjective clause comes *immediately after* the noun that it describes or identifies.

       I would like to see *the house* **that Robert built.**
       The house **that Robert built** looks like a barn.

    2.   Like all other clauses, an adjective clause must have a subject and a verb.

       The house **that <u>we</u> <u>are looking for</u>** is on Spring Drive.
                  subject   verb

Sometimes the subject of the adjective clause is the modified noun in the main clause. In this case, the verb must agree with the noun that it is describing.

       Robert lives in *a house* **that *looks* like a barn.**
       I haven't seen *many houses* **that *look* like barns.**

    3.   Like other dependent clauses, an adjective clause must be connected to a main clause. An adjective clause cannot stand alone. Many adjective clauses have connecting words** that connect them to the main clause. You will also see that some adjective clauses do not need a connecting word.

       <u>Robert lives in a house</u> **<u>that looks like a barn.</u>**
           main clause   adjective clause
       <u>The house</u> **<u>we are looking for</u>** <u>is on Spring Drive</u>
                  adjective clause
                main clause

---

*Another name for **adjective clause** is **relative clause.**
Another name for **connecting word in adjective clauses is **relative pronoun.**

In this chapter, you will see five different types of adjective clauses. The relationship between the modified noun and the adjective clause is different in each type. Furthermore, you will see that different types of adjective clauses require different connecting words.

Understanding Adjective Clauses

*A.   What does the adjective clause in each of the following sentences describe? Identify the **modified noun**—the noun that each adjective clause describes.*

1.   The architect **whose design we're going to use for our house** is very creative.
2.   I would like you to see the house **that he's designed for us.**
3.   The house **we're living in now** is much too small for our growing family.
4.   I would like to have a house **that has a lot of windows.**

B.   In each sentence, find the adjective clause that modifies the highlighted noun or noun phrase. Then find the main clause.

1.   Solar heating is **a type of heating** that uses the sun as its energy source.
2.   **Homes** that have solar heating use solar panels to collect the sun's energy.
3.   **One solar-heated home** I read about is built into the side of a mountain.
4.   We are hoping to find **an architect** who knows something about solar power in houses.

C.   Some, but not all, of the following sentences contain adjective clauses. For each sentence, decide if there is an adjective clause or not. If there is an adjective clause, identify it.

EXAMPLES   I bought a car from a car dealer north of town. [*no adjective clause*]
The car I bought there is in excellent condition. [*adjective clause: "I bought there"*]

1.   Sam would like to build a house in the country.
2.   He wants to live in a place where he can have peace and quiet.
3.   The type of house he's thinking about building will have a large fireplace.
4.   He is hoping to find a place with a lot of land and woods around it.

FOCUS 2   Type I Adjective Clauses: Modified Noun as Subject

Look at these examples of adjective clauses. Then answer the questions that follow.

1.   Stress is one of the factors **that can contribute to heart disease.**
2.   A person **who has a Type A personality** is a likely candidate for heart disease.

Which noun is the adjective clause describing?
What is the verb in the adjective clause?

What is the subject of the adjective clause?

What is the connecting word for the adjective clause?

A. Type I adjective clauses: Connecting words

This type of adjective clause must have the connecting word **WHO, WHICH,** or **THAT.** The connecting word refers to the noun that immediately precedes it. Although all of these connecting words may be used with adjective clauses that define or identify a noun, one may be preferred in a given situation:

1. **WHO:** modifies a noun that refers to **a person.**

WHO is appropriate in all situations, for informal as well as formal writing and conversation.

I have *a friend* **who has** a Type A personality.

2. **WHICH:** modifies a noun that refers to **a thing.**

The connecting word **WHICH** is usually used to define or identify a noun *only* in very formal written and spoken English. You may also hear **WHICH** more often in British English than in American English.

Stress is *a factor* **which contributes to heart trouble.**

3. **THAT:** modifies a noun that refers to a person or a thing.

The connecting word **THAT** usually refers to *a person* only in very informal conversation. In conversational and written English, the connecting word **THAT** is used much more frequently than **WHICH** to identify a noun that refers *to a thing.*

I have *a friend* **who *is* very impatient.**

People **who are impatient** may have Type A personalities.

B. Role of the modified noun

In this type of adjective clause, the connecting word refers to the modified noun and acts as the *subject* of the adjective clause. The verb in the adjective clause must agree with the modified noun.

PRACTICE 2-1 Type I Adjective Clauses

A.   Use the information from the situation to complete the following sentences. Use the connecting word WHO or THAT with an adjective clause.

EXAMPLE   My uncle had a heart attack last year.

I have an uncle <u>who had a heart attack last year.</u>

1. An accident occurred on Main Street last night.

    a. The police would like to get some information about the accident

    _____.

    b. The accident _____ was caused by icy conditions.

2. Some people saw the accident.

    a. The police want to talk to any witnesses _____.

    b. Some of the people _____ disagree about the details.

3. One man was taken to the hospital, but fortunately, the others were not hurt.

   a. The man _____ is in critical condition.

   b. The people _____ were very lucky.

PRACTICE 2-2 Using Type I Adjective Clauses

Use the information from each situation to respond to the questions that follow. Each response must contain an adjective clause.

EXAMPLE   Some people set unrealistic goals for themselves. These people have Type A personalities.

   Question: Which people have Type A personalities?
   Answer: **People who set unrealistic goals for themselves** have Type A personalities.

1. Calcium is an important mineral, but some people don't get enough calcium in their diets. These people should take calcium supplements. Calcium is important because it helps keep bones strong.

   a. What is calcium?
   b. Who should take calcium supplements?

2. Sir Alexander Fleming discovered penicillin in 1928. Penicillin is an antibiotic drug. It is used to fight infections.

   a. Who was Alexander Fleming?
   b. What kind of drug is penicillin?

3. There is usually a coin toss before a soccer game to see which team gets the ball first. The winner of the coin toss gets the ball. The object in soccer is to score more goals than the other team.

   a. Which team gets the ball first at the beginning of a soccer match?
   b. Which team is the winner of the match?

FOCUS 3   Type II Adjective Clauses: Modified Noun as Object

Look at these examples of adjective clauses. Then answer the following questions.

The doctor **whom I saw last week** told me to cut down on salt and fat in my diet.

Which doctor told you to cut down on salt and fat?
What is the subject of the adjective clause?
What is the verb in the adjective clause?
What is the object of the verb?

I'm going to follow the advice **that the doctor gave to me.**

Which advice are you going to follow?
What is the direct object of the verb **GAVE?**

A. Type II adjective clauses: Connecting words

This type of adjective clause uses the connecting words **WHO(M)*** *(person)*, **WHICH*** *(thing)*, and **THAT** *(person or thing)*. This type of adjective clause can also occur *without any connecting word.***

B. Role of the modified noun

In this type of adjective clause, the modified noun from the main clause is the *object* of the verb in the adjective clause.

The doctor *gave* **some advice** to me. I'm going to follow this advice.
object

Question: What advice are you going to follow?

Answer: I'm going to follow *the advice* **that my doctor gave to me.**

I'm going to follow *the advice* **which my doctor gave to me.**

I'm going to follow *the advice* **my doctor gave to me.**

I *saw* **a doctor** last week. He told me to change my diet.
object

Question: Which doctor told you to change your diet?

Answer: *The doctor* **who(m) I** *saw* **last week** told me to change my diet.

The doctor **that I** *saw* **last week** told me to change my diet.

The doctor **I** *saw* **last week** told me to change my diet.

Remember that the object of the verb in the adjective clause is a noun in the main clause. Do not repeat the object in the adjective clause.

[MISTAKE: The doctor whom I saw ~~him~~ last week gave me some advice.

I'm going to follow the advice that the doctor gave ~~it~~ to me.]

PRACTICE 3-1   Objects in Adjective Clauses

Answer the following questions for each sentence.

What is the adjective clause?
What noun does the adjective clause modify?
What is the verb in the adjective clause?
What is the object of the verb in the adjective clause?

1.   The diet that I started last week is very difficult to stick to.
2.   Nowadays, people are becoming more and more conscious of the things they eat.

---

*Use **WHOM** in formal written English. Use **WHO** or **WHOM** in conversational English. [When referring to things, **THAT** is used to define or identify a noun more often than **WHICH**. **WHICH** is used to define or identify a noun in very formal written and spoken English.] This type of adjective clause can occur *without* a connecting word in formal and informal spoken and written English.

3. One thing that you can do to prevent heart disease is to watch your diet.

4. Some of the things I have given up in my diet include salt, red meat, and sweets.

CLOSE-UP Prepositions in Adjective Clauses

In some adjective clauses, the noun being described may be the object of a preposition. The position of the preposition in the adjective clause depends on two things: the connecting word and the level of formality.

A. Common position for prepositions

In conversation and in a great deal of written English, the preposition remains inside the adjective clause, after the verb.

In other words, it keeps its regular position in the sentence. Prepositions can occur in this position with all connecting words.

I got this advice **from** a doctor. He is my neighbor.

Question: Which doctor is your neighbor?

Response: The doctor **who(m)** I got this advice **from** is my neighbor.

The doctor **that** I got this advice **from** is my neighbor.

The doctor I got this advice from is my neighbor. [*no connecting word*]

I'm talking **about** a diet. It is a low-sodium, low-fat diet.

Question: Which diet is a low-sodium, low-fat diet?

Response: The diet **that I am talking about** is a low-sodium, low-fat diet.

The diet **I am talking about** is a low-sodium, low-fat diet. [*no connecting word*]

B. Formal position for prepositions

Another position for the preposition is before the connecting word. This word order is considered very formal and can occur *only* with the connecting words **WHOM** and **WHICH**.

The doctor *from whom I got some advice* is my neighbor.

The diet *about which I am speaking* is a low-sodium, low-fat diet.

Close-Up
PRACTICE CONNECTING WORDS

Which of these connecting words can complete each adjective clause? Read the sentences aloud with all of the possibilities.

WHICH   **THAT**   **WHO**   **WHOM**   [*no connecting word*]

1. The man _____ I'm going to buy my car from is a retired dentist.

2. The man from _____ I'm going to buy my car is a retired dentist.

3. The man _____ is going to sell me his car is a retired dentist.

4. The car to _____ I am referring is a 1987 Ford.

5. The car _____ I am referring to is a 1987 Ford.

6. I'll be glad to have a car _____ is in such good condition.

PRACTICE 3-2   Type II Adjective Clauses

Use the information from each situation to complete the adjective clauses in the sentences that follow.

EXAMPLE   We went to see the movie *Dune* last night. It was terrible. We should have gone to see *Casablanca* instead.

a. The movie that <u>we went to last night</u> was terrible.

b. The movie that <u>we should have gone to</u> was *Casablanca*.

1. Last night Jill went to a movie. She'd already seen that movie three times.

   a. Last night, Jill went to a movie that

   _____ .

   b. Jill had already seen the movie that

   _____ three times.

2. Amy doesn't like to see violence in movies. Last week, Amy went to a movie with some friends. She walked out in the middle because she thought the movie was too violent.

   a. Violence in movies is something Amy

   _____ .

   b. The movie that _____ was too violent for her, so she left in the middle.

3. Joe read about a new film in the paper. He would like to see it this weekend. It was directed by Woody Allen.

   a. Joe would like to see the new film he

   _____ .

   b. The movie that _____ this weekend was directed by Woody Allen.

4. Clint Eastwood acted in some unsuccessful, low-budget films at the beginning of his acting career. Nobody had heard of him. Later, he achieved fame through his westerns. He made these westerns in Italy.

   a. The first films that _____ were not very successful.

   b. Before he made the westerns, Clint Eastwood was an actor

   who(m) nobody _____ .

c. His acting career finally got off to a good start through the westerns he _____.

PRACTICE 3-3 Using Adjective Clauses

Use the information from each situation to answer the question with a sentence containing an adjective clause. Use an appropriate connecting word. You can also choose to omit the connecting word in some of the sentences.

EXAMPLE   Dave's friend lent him his notebook. Dave accidentally threw it away.

What did Dave accidentally throw away?
He accidentally threw away the notebook (that) his friend had lent to him.

1. The teacher has just finished explaining a grammar point. Tomas is confused.
    What is Tomas confused about?

2. Luigi has been staying with an American family. He likes them a lot.
    Which family does Luigi like?

3. I finally received some money from the government. The government had owed me this money for a long time.
    What money did you receive?

4. Researchers have recently developed a new artificial sweetener. Sally uses this sweetener all the time.
    Which sweetener does Sally use?

5. Frederic bought some jeans last week, but he decided he didn't like them. He took them back and bought another pair of jeans yesterday. He plans to keep this pair.
    Which jeans did he take back?
    Which jeans is he planning to keep?

FOCUS 4   Type III Adjective Clauses: Connecting Word Indicates Possession

Look at these examples of adjective clauses. Then answer the following questions.

A man **whose heart didn't function properly** got a heart transplant.

What didn't function properly?
Which man got a heart transplant?
What is the subject of the adjective clause?
Who does this heart belong to?
What is the connecting word for the adjective clause?

The woman **whose heart he has now** died in a car accident.

What are the subject and verb of the adjective clause?
What is the object of the verb in the adjective clause?
To whom did the man's new heart originally belong?
Who died in a car crash?

A. Type III adjective clauses: Connecting words

Use **WHOSE + (noun)** to connect this type of adjective clause. The connecting expression can serve as the subject or object of the verb in the adjective clause.

B. The role of the modified noun

The connecting phrase **WHOSE + (noun)** indicates that the noun in the connecting word *belongs to* the modified noun of the main clause.

A man's heart didn't function well. He got a heart transplant.

Question: Who got a heart transplant?

Answer: *A man* **whose heart** didn't function well got a heart transplant.
⌐— belongs to —⌐

A woman died in a car crash. The man has *that woman's* heart now.

Question: Who died in a car crash?

Answer: *The woman* **whose heart** he has now died in a car crash.
⌐— belongs to —⌐

PRACTICE 4-1   Connecting Words

A.   *Fill in each blank with an appropriate noun.*

1. I have a friend whose _____ is a doctor.

2. I need to find someone whose _____ I can borrow.

3. Jim complained to the neighbors whose _____ constantly bothers him.

4. Would the person whose _____ is parked out front please move it immediately?

B.   *Fill in each blank with one of the following connecting words:*

WHO   WHOM   WHICH   WHOSE   THAT

1. I know a student _____ refused to buy health insurance in this country.

2. The student about _____ I am speaking didn't realize how expensive health care is in this country.

3. I told him about a woman _____ had appendicitis and had to go to the hospital for an emergency appendectomy.

4. The woman _____ the doctors operated on did not have insurance either.

5. The student was surprised to hear about someone _____ medical bills were more than $7,000.

6. The student comes from a country _____ government pays for all medical expenses.

7. I also told him about another student _____ unexpected medical expenses cost him $5,000.

8. These medical costs were the result of a car accident _____ he was involved in.

Type III Adjective Clauses

Use any of the following cues to complete the sentences. Add any necessary words.

EXAMPLE   room / (always) neat
                 I have a roommate whose room is always neat.

family / call frequently	family / visit all the time
study habits / similar to mine	study habits / very different from mine
grades / pretty good	grades / not very good
opinions / I / agree	opinions / different from mine
taste in music / the same as mine	taste in music / I / not like

1. I wouldn't mind having a roommate whose _____.

2. I would like to live with someone whose _____.

3. I would rather not live with a person whose _____.

4. It might be difficult to live with people whose _____.

5. I have never lived with anyone whose _____.

Using Type III Adjective Clauses

*Use the information in the situations to answer the questions. Include an adjective clause with **WHOSE** in each answer.*

EXAMPLE   Somebody's dog keeps barking. I feel like complaining to that person.

             Who do you feel like complaining to?
             I feel like complaining to the person **whose dog keeps barking!**

1. I'm going to call my friend. Her mother is in the hospital.
   Which friend are you going to call?

2. My neighbors' children broke my window. They are going to pay for it.
   Which neighbors are going to pay for your window?

3. The man is my lawyer. We just drove by his office.
   Who is your lawyer?

4. Some children's parents read out loud to them. These children learn to read quickly.
   Which children learn to read quickly?

5. If a person's blood pressure is high, he or she is at risk for heart disease and other medical problems.
   What kind of person is at risk for heart disease and other medical problems?

Mixed Adjective Clauses: Types I, II, and III

Use the information in each situation to answer the questions. Your answers should contain adjective clauses.

1. This soap is on sale. If a person's skin is very sensitive, he or she shouldn't use this soap.

    a. Which people should avoid this soap?
    b. Which soap should people with sensitive skin avoid?

2. I mailed a lot of letters yesterday. I sent one of the letters by Express Mail. That letter contained my income tax form.

    a. Which letter contained your income tax form?
    b. Which letter did you send by Express Mail?

3. Jim had lunch with a woman yesterday. She had sold him her car.

    a. Who(m) did Jim buy his car from?
    b. Who(m) did Jim have lunch with yesterday?

4. Some of my flowers are dying. I'm going to transplant them. My sister gave me some new flowerpots. I'm going to use those pots.

    a. Which flowers are you going to transplant?
    b. What are you going to put the plants in?

5. The signatures of some of the employees were on the letter. The letter complained about working conditions in the factory. The supervisor called those employees into his office.

    a. Who did the supervisor want to talk to?
    b. What kind of letter did they sign?

PRACTICE 4-5 Identifying People

First, your classmate will write each of the following names onto the nametag of one of the people in the picture without showing them to you.

Men: Tim, Dan, Bob, Ken
Women: Sue, Amy, Beth, Liz

Your job is find out who these people are. Ask a question about each name. Your classmate will tell you who each person is, using an adjective clause. Using the information that your classmate gives you, write the names on each person's nametag. When you finish, compare your nametags to your classmate's.

Student A: Which person is Sue?

Student B: Sue is the person who . . .

FOCUS 5   Type IV Adjective Clauses: Connecting Word Indicates a Place

What is a hardware store?

A hardware store is a place **where you can buy tools.**

What is the adjective clause?
What is the noun being described?
What is the connecting word?

A.   Type IV adjective clauses: Connecting word

This type of adjective clause uses the connecting word **WHERE.**

B.   Role of the modified noun

The noun being described in this type of clause is a word that refers to a place, such as a *city, country,* or *general location.* Do not use the preposition *IN, ON, AT,* or *TO* in an adjective clause with *WHERE.*

A hardware store is *a place.* You can buy tools at a hardware store.

A hardware store is *a place* **where you can buy tools.**

PRACTICE 5-1   Type IV Adjective Clauses

A.   *Match each location on the left with a description or definition on the right.*

1.	delicatessen	a.	You can practice hitting golf balls there.
2.	health spa	b.	You can withdraw money from a machine there.
3.	mall		
4.	drive-in	c.	Many kinds of sandwiches are sold there.
5.	driving range	d.	People go there to get in shape.
6.	automatic bank teller	e.	You can walk from store to store there without going outside.
		f.	People watch a movie from their cars there.

B.   *Now use the information from Part A to complete these sentences.*

1.   A delicatessen is a restaurant where _____.

2.   A health spa is a place where _____.

3.   A mall is a shopping center where _____.

4.   A drive-in is a movie theater where _____.

5.   A driving range is a place where _____.

6.   An automatic bank teller is a place where _____.

PRACTICE 5-2   Using Type IV Adjective Clauses

Use the information in the situations to respond to the questions. Your responses should contain adjective clauses with the connecting word **WHERE.**

EXAMPLE   You can buy tools in a hardware store.

What kind of store is a hardware store?

It's a store **where you can buy tools.**

1. The president of the United States lives in the White House.
   What is the White House?

2. The first settlers to the United States from Europe landed at Plymouth Rock, Massachusetts.
   What is special about Plymouth Rock?

3. American money is printed at the U.S. Mint.
   What is the U.S. Mint?

4. The faces of four American presidents are carved in rock at Mount Rushmore.
   Why is Mount Rushmore a famous tourist site?

5. Many immigrants entered the United States at Ellis Island.
   What is Ellis Island?

FOCUS 6   Type V Adjective Clauses: Connecting Word Refers to a Time

What is Memorial Day?

Memorial Day is the day **when Americans remember and honor the dead.**

What is the adjective clause?

What is the noun that is described?

What is the connecting word?

A.   Type V adjective clauses: Connecting word

This type of adjective clause uses the connecting word **WHEN.**

B.   Role of the modified noun

The noun being described in this type of adjective clause is a word that refers to a general time, such as a *day, time, year,* or *season.* Do not use the preposition **IN, ON,** or **AT** in an adjective clause with **WHEN.**

Memorial Day is a holiday. Americans honor and remember the dead on Memorial Day.

Memorial Day is *the holiday* **when Americans honor and remember the dead.**

PRACTICE 6-1   Type V Adjective Clauses

A.   Complete the following adjective clauses.

1. Mother's Day is the day when . . .
2. Spring is a season when . . .
3. The year 2000 is the year when . . .

*B.   Respond to the following questions. Use adjective clauses with **WHEN** if appropriate.*

1. What is the name of a special holiday in your country? Why is it special?

2. Is there a day that is special to you personally? Why?

3. Is there a year that you will always remember? Why?

A WIDER ANGLE

Definitions

Your teacher will give you a word, an expression, or the name of a person, place, or thing to define or explain. Begin your definition with the word or phrase that you are given. Try to use what you know about adjective clauses in your answer.

EXAMPLE   Teacher: Who was Christopher Columbus?
Student: Christopher Columbus was the man who discovered America.

Writing Practice: Sentence Combining

This exercise describes an unusual event in American medical history. Combine the information given in each group of sentences into one sentence. The symbol (*) indicates that you should not make any changes in that sentence. Write the sentences in paragraph form. Follow the example.

EXAMPLE   *The leading cause of death in the United States is heart disease.
a. There are many factors.
b. These factors can increase the risk of heart disease.

a. Stress is one factor.
b. It can affect the heart.
*Another factor is diet.

The leading cause of death in the United States is heart disease. There are many factors **that can increase the risk of heart disease.** Stress is one factor **that can affect the heart.** Another factor is diet.

FIRST PARAGRAPH

In 1987, for the first time in America, a living man, Clinton House, donated his good heart to another man, John Couch. House then had a combination heart and lung transplant from another donor. How did this strange "domino donor" situation come about?

SECOND PARAGRAPH

a. Clint House is a man.
b. He suffers from cystic fibrosis.

a. Cystic fibrosis is a disease.
b. It affects the lungs.

*House had a healthy heart but needed new lungs.

a. The doctors were performing the operation.
b. The doctors decided that it was safer to transplant a heart and lungs together.

*A donor heart and lungs were found.

a. House immediately went to the hospital.
b. The surgery was going to take place there.

a. The person had died in a car accident.

b. House received this person's heart and lungs.

THIRD PARAGRAPH

a. John Couch is a man.

b. He was suffering from severe heart disease.

a. Couch is the person.

b. House donated his heart to him.

*Both Couch and House were grateful to have a second chance at life.

a. After the operation, Couch was looking forward to the time.

b. He could thank House personally at this time.

a. This was the first time.

b. A heart recipient could personally thank the person.

c. The person had given him some extra years of life.

Sources: David Copen and Mark Rubinstein, *Heartplan* (New York: McGraw Hill, 1987).

Meyer Friedman and Diane Ulmer, *Treating Type A Behavior and Your Heart* (New York: Alfred A. Knopf, 1984).

Claudia Wallis, "The Hearts of the Matter," *Time*, May 25, 1987.

DEVELOPING YOUR SKILLS AND KNOWLEDGE

Chapter Exercises

EXERCISE 1

Understanding Adjective Clauses

Put the adjective clause indicated into the sentence. Do not add or change any words.

EXAMPLE
The airlines lost one of my suitcases.

The suitcase contains all of my shoes. (that they lost)

The suitcase **that they lost** contains all of my shoes.

1. I need to have the suitcase. (that is lost)
2. The airline representative was very apologetic. (I talked to)
3. He looked for my suitcase in the baggage area. (where they keep unclaimed luggage)
4. I told him to look for a green suitcase. (that had a big scratch on one side)
5. He couldn't find any suitcases. (that matched my description)
6. The man made some phone calls to other airports. (who was helping me)

EXERCISE 2

Adjective Clauses: Type I

Use the information from each situation to complete the response to the question. Include an appropriate adjective clause.

Meyer Friedman is a doctor. He identified the Type A personality.

Who is Meyer Friedman?
He is the doctor **who identified the Type A personality.**

1. Somebody lost these gloves. That person is probably upset.

   Who is upset? _____ is probably upset.

2. Somebody is looking for these gloves. That person should check the Lost and Found.
   Who should check the Lost and Found?

   _____ should check there.

3. I have lost some gloves. The gloves are made of leather.

   What gloves did you lose? I lost _____.

4. A glove is an article of clothing. It gets lost easily.
   What's the problem with a glove? A glove is

   _____.

EXERCISE 3   Adjective Clauses: Type II

Use the information in the situations to complete each sentence with an adjective clause. Use an appropriate connecting word, or omit the connecting word if it is not necessary.

EXAMPLE   I bought this book. It's very interesting.
               The book **(that) I bought** is very interesting.

1. Martha collects stamps. Some of the stamps are quite valuable.

   Some of the stamps _____ are quite valuable.

2. I enjoy doing many things. One of them is playing racquetball.

   One of the things _____ is playing racquetball.

3. We watched a movie on TV last night. Had you ever seen it?

   Had you ever seen the movie _____?

4. Jim has a map in his room. He should have brought it with him.

   The map _____ is in his room.

5. You were making a quilt the last time I saw you. Have you finished it?

   Have you finished the quilt _____?

EXERCISE 4   Prepositions with Adjective Clauses

Fill in each blank with one word.

1. The doctor from _____ I got this prescription is an old friend of mine.

2. The man I introduced you _____ earlier is a famous photographer.

3. I would like to see the new movie _____ everybody is talking _____ these days.

4. That is an idea with _____ I can never agree.

5. You are a person with _____ I always seem to disagree.

6. Your encouragement is something _____ I depend _____.

7. The space program is a subject in _____ John has a great deal of interest.

8. The space program is a subject _____ John is interested _____.

9. The space program is something _____ which I know very little.

10. Sarah is a person with _____ I have a great deal in common.

EXERCISE 5   Type I and II Adjective Clauses

Read each situation and answer the questions that follow. Include an appropriate adjective clause in each answer. Explain your answers.

1. There are two new students at this party, and George would like to meet both of them. At the moment, his roommate is talking to one of the new students. The other one is sitting alone.
   Which student do you think George will talk to first?
   Which student is probably having a better time at this party?

2. You and your friends are planning to go to a movie tonight. There are two movies on campus. Your teacher recommended one. Your friend recommended the other.
   Which movie will you and your friends probably go to?

3. There are different kinds of neighbors in apartment buildings. Some neighbors make a lot of noise. Some people never hear their neighbors. Some neighbors come over all the time. Others are friendly, but they never come over. Some people feel comfortable asking their neighbors for help.
   What kind of neighbors would you rather have?
   What kind of neighbors would you rather not have?
   What kind of neighbors do you have right now?

4. Imagine that you are looking for a roommate to share your house or apartment.
   What kind of roommate are you going to look for?

EXERCISE 6 **Type III Adjective Clauses**

Complete each sentence with adjective clauses, using the information given.

EXAMPLE   His father is a professor at this college.
                I talked to someone **whose father is a professor at this college.**

1. At the party last night, I talked to someone whose

   _____.

   a. I couldn't pronounce his name.
   b. His parents own a jet.
   c. His roommate is in my chemistry class.

2. The people whose _____ are over there.

   a. Their car is blocking the driveway.
   b. We visited their house earlier this month.
   c. David would like to borrow their lawn mower.

EXERCISE 7 **Mixed Adjective Clauses**

Use the information given to complete the sentences with adjective clauses. Supply connecting words if necessary.

EXAMPLE   She lives with an American family.
                I met a woman **who lives with an American family.**

1. That woman over there _____ knows a lot about international affairs.

   a. Her hair is pulled back in a braid.
   b. Jim was talking to her when we arrived.
   c. She is laughing.

2. Mehmet is trying to find a gift _____.

   a. He can give this gift to his grandmother.
   b. The gift won't take up much space in his luggage.
   c. His grandmother will like the gift.

3. We adopted a puppy _____.

   a. Its owner didn't want to keep it.
   b. It has big brown eyes.
   c. It was being taken to the animal shelter.

EXERCISE 8 **Type IV Adjective Clauses**

Complete each sentence with an adjective clause.

EXAMPLE   A hardware store is a store where **you can buy tools.**

1. A beauty salon is a place where _____.

2. I would like to take a vacation someplace where

   _____.

3. Mike always misplaces his keys. He should keep them in a place where _____.

4. Uh-oh! I think we just drove by the exit where _____.

5. Fred can't buy spare parts for his home computer because the store where _____ has gone out of business.

EXERCISE 9   Type V Adjective Clauses

Complete each sentence with an adjective clause.

EXAMPLE   l776 was the year when **the United States declared its independence.**

1. Winter is a season when _____.

2. If you want to call someone, you should try to call at a time when _____.

3. The year 19_____ was a special year for me because that is the year when _____.

4. Valentine's Day is a day when _____.

5. Sunday is a day when _____.

15 Possibilities and Probabilities

```
┌─────────────────────────────┐
│ THE BIG PICTURE             │
├─────────────────────────────┘
│ Possibilities: MAY, MIGHT, COULD
│ Probabilities: MUST
│ Modal Expressions: Past and Present
└─────────────────────────────
```

AT A GLANCE

Why is this woman here (Fig. 15–1)? What is she doing? Maybe she . . .

FIGURE 15–1

In this chapter, you will practice using modal auxiliaries to talk about
possibilities and conclusions. You will see how to use these auxiliaries
to give your reactions about current and past situations.

FOCUS 1   Current Possibilities: **MAY, MIGHT**

The modal auxiliaries **MAY** and **MIGHT** can be used instead of **MAY BE** to offer
possible explanations about current situations.

> Max: What is the woman doing?
> Judy: Maybe she is waiting for someone.
> She **may be waiting** for someone.
> She **might be waiting** for someone.

A.   Current states and general situations

For possibilities with stative verbs or about general situations, use **MAY** or **MIGHT**
with a base form verb. For negative verbs, put **NOT** after the modal auxiliary.

Subject	+	Modal (NOT) "possibility"	+	Base Form Verb	+	Rest of Sentence
She		may		be		on her lunch break.
She		might		enjoy		spending her lunch hour outside.
She		may not		have		anything else to do.

B. Activities in progress

For possible explanations about activities currently in progress, use **MAY** or **MIGHT** with **BE** and an **-ING** verb.

Subject	+	Modal (NOT) "possibility"	+	BE + -ING verb "in progress"	+	Rest of Sentence
She		may		be taking		her lunch break.
She		might		be thinking		about a problem.
She		might not		be doing		anything in particular.

C. Ability and necessity

It is *not* possible to have two modal auxiliaries in one verb. Therefore, do not use the auxiliaries **CAN** or **MUST** in the same verb with **MAY** or **MIGHT**. Instead, use the modal expressions **BE ABLE TO** and **HAVE TO**.

1. Possible ability

   a. She **might not be able to walk** any more because she is very tired.

   b. She **may be able to see** some dolphins from where she is sitting.

2. Possible necessity

   a. She **may not have to go** to work today.

   b. She **might have to wait** for someone there.

PRACTICE 1-1   Forming Possibilities

Remove the adverb MAYBE from each of the following sentences. Then make a new sentence with the same meaning using MAY or MIGHT.

EXAMPLE   Why isn't Jim here at this meeting? *Maybe* he's sick.

   He **might be** sick.

Why isn't Jim here at this meeting?

1. Maybe he is late.
2. Maybe he isn't feeling well today.
3. Maybe he doesn't know about the meeting.
4. Maybe he has other plans.
5. Maybe he is talking to his professor.
6. Maybe he has to work late today.
7. Maybe he can't come.

PRACTICE 1-2   Offering Possible Explanations

Use MAY or MIGHT with the cues to respond to each question with two possibilities. Fill in empty brackets with your own cues.

Why isn't Jim at the meeting?

(have other plans // not know about it)

I don't really know. He **might have** other plans, or he **might not know** about it.

1. Why are Ralph and Katie sitting on the steps of the library?

   (take a study break // not have anything else to do at the moment)

2. Miriam is sitting with her friends in the cafeteria. Everybody is eating except her. Why isn't Miriam eating?

   (not hungry // [   ])

3. Why doesn't Sam ever go to parties?

   ([   ] // [   ])

FOCUS 2   Conclusions with **MUST**

John is in bed. His nose is red. His eyes are watering. He is holding a tissue.

What can you conclude about John's condition?

Use the auxiliary **MUST** to form conclusions about a *current situation*. A conclusion with **MUST** is based on current evidence, logic, and past experiences.

Current information:	Conclusions:
His nose is red.	He must have a cold.
His eyes are watering.	He must not be feeling very well.
He's holding a tissue.	He must be sick.
He's in bed.	

A.   Using MUST for conclusions

There are two main uses for conclusions with **MUST**.

1. To show sympathy for or understanding of a situation

   Tom: I was up all night coughing and sneezing.
   Sue: You poor thing! You **must be** tired!
   Tom: I am.

2. To give a probable logical explanation for a situation

   Hank: What's wrong with my car? It won't start!
   Jim: Look! You left your headlights on. The battery **must be** dead.

B.   States and general situations

Use **MUST** with a base form verb to form conclusions about states or general situations. For a negative conclusion, add **NOT** after **MUST**.

Subject	+	MUST (NOT) "probability"	+	Base Form Verb	+	Rest of Sentence
He		must		have		a cold.
He		must not		feel		very well.

C.   Activities in progress

Use **MUST** with **BE** *and an* **-ING** *verb* to form conclusions about current activities.

Subject	+	MUST (NOT) "probability"	+	BE + -ING verb "in progress"	+	Rest of Sentence
His head		must		be aching.		
His nose		must		be running.		
This guy		must not		be feeling		very well.

D. Ability and necessity

To make a conclusion about ability and necessity, use **MUST (NOT)** with the modal expressions **BE ABLE TO** and **HAVE TO**.

1. Conclusions about ability

   a. He **must not be able to go** to work today.

   b. He **must not be able to get** out of bed.

2. Conclusions about necessity

   a. He **must have to stay** in bed today.

   b. He **must have to get** extra rest.

PRACTICE 2–1   Forming Conclusions

*A.   Use **MUST (NOT)** to form a logical conclusion based on the information in each situation.*

EXAMPLE   Mary's bedroom is painted purple. Her bed is purple. Her curtains are purple. Her carpet is purple.
Conclusion: She **must like** the color purple.

1. Mrs. Ricardo has just come home. Her husband isn't in the house, but his car is in the garage. The lawn mower is not in the garage. Mrs. Ricardo can hear the sound of the lawn mower in the backyard.

   Conclusion: Her husband _____.

2. JILL: Let's go to a Mexican restaurant for dinner.

   SAMI: Oh no, not a Mexican restaurant! Any kind of restaurant but Mexican!

   CONCLUSION: Sami _____.

3. Joey has pictures of the singer Michael Jackson all over his walls.

   Conclusion: Joey _____.

*B.   Show that you understand each situation by reacting with **MUST** and the cue. Your classmate will respond with a short answer to confirm your conclusion.*

EXAMPLE   Student A: I was up all night coughing and sneezing.
Student B: (tired) You **must be** tired.
Student A: You're right. **I am.**

4. STUDENT A: It's four o'clock, and I haven't had a thing to eat all day!

   STUDENT B: (hungry) _____.

   STUDENT A: _____.

5. STUDENT A: I go to school full-time.

   STUDENT B: (busy) _____.

   STUDENT A: _____. And on top of that, I have a part-time job!

   STUDENT B: (not have much free time) _____.

   STUDENT A: _____.

6. STUDENT A: Vang hasn't seen his family for six years.

   STUDENT B: (miss them) _____.

   STUDENT A: _____.

GETTING READY TO FOCUS *Mysteries of the Universe*

UFOs

Have you ever heard of UFOs (**U**nidentified **F**lying **O**bjects)? Have you ever seen a UFO?

Arthur C. Clarke is a famous scientist and science-fiction writer. In the following passage, he talks about seeing a strange light in the sky:*

> It was late afternoon and I was standing in the shadow of my Colombo house, pointing out the planet Venus to one of my friends.
>
> I pointed to the tiny, dazzling star high in the western sky, about forty degrees above the hidden sun. "There she is!" I said.
>
> My friend pointed almost a right angle round to the north and said: "No—there!" The argument lasted for some time: finally, to my utter astonishment, I realized that Venus had an identical twin. At about the same elevation in the northwest was a brilliant, motionless star.
>
> Then I ran for my telescope, and the mystery was solved.

Can you think of explanations for the "mysterious star" that Clarke saw? What are some possibilities?

Maybe he saw . . .   Maybe it was . . .

(After you have finished guessing, turn the page upside down to find out what it was.)

The solution to the mystery:

It was the local meteorological balloon, released every afternoon to measure conditions in the upper atmosphere. Hanging becalmed perhaps 10 kilometers above the earth, it was catching the last rays of the setting sun. There was no way in which the naked eye could have distinguished it from Venus.

---

*Source: Simon Welfare and John Fairley, *Arthur C. Clarke's Mysterious World* (New York: A & W Publishers, 1980).

FOCUS 3 Possible Explanations for Past Situations

MAY and MIGHT can make predictions about the future. They can refer to *future possibilities*.

> Scientists **might discover** more about UFOs someday.

MAY and MIGHT can refer to *current possibilities*.

> Life **may exist** on other planets.
> Beings from other planets **might be trying** to communicate with us at this moment.

MAY and MIGHT can also be used to give possible explanations for *past situations*.

> Clarke **might have seen** an undiscovered star.
> He **may have been looking** at a UFO.

A. Past events

Use MAY or MIGHT with HAVE and a past participle to talk about past possibilities. To make the verb negative, add NOT after the modal auxiliary.

Subject	+	Modal (NOT) "possibility"	+	HAVE "past"	+	Past Participle	+	Rest of Sentence
The light		may		have		come		from a UFO.
The light		might		have		been		an undiscovered star.
Clarke		might not		have		looked		at it carefully.

B. Past activities

Use MAY or MIGHT with HAVE BEEN and an -ING verb to talk about possible past activities in progress.

Subject	+	Modal (NOT) "possibility"	+	HAVE "past"	+	BEEN + -ING verb "in progress"	+	Rest of Sentence
An airplane		may		have		been flying		overhead.
A balloon		might		have		been reflecting		the sun.
Clarke		might not		have		been thinking		about other possibilities.

C. Ability and necessity

To offer possibilities about past ability and necessity, use the appropriate form of the modal expressions BE ABLE TO and HAVE TO.

1. Possibilities for past ability

> Question: Why didn't Jenny go to the party?
> Answer: Well, she **might not have been able to get** a ride.

2. Possibilities for past necessity

> Question: Why is Melissa late?
> Answer: Who knows? The parking lots are very full today. She **might have had to park** very far away.

Possibilities with **MAY** or **MIGHT**

Have you ever heard of the Bermuda Triangle (Fig. 15–2) off the southeast coast of the United States? The Bermuda Triangle is an area where an unusual number of planes and ships have disappeared over the years.

> On December 5, 1945, five United States bomber planes disappeared in the Bermuda Triangle. According to the story, the leader of the group radioed back, "Everything is wrong, strange. We can't be sure of any direction. Even the ocean doesn't look as it should."

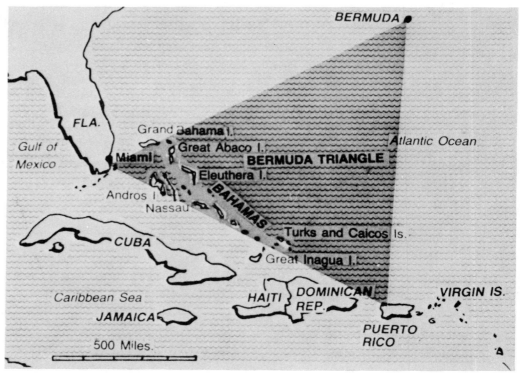

FIGURE 15–2

What happened to the five bombers?
Here are some possible explanations that have been offered for their disappearance.
*Replace the adverb **MAYBE** in each sentence with the auxiliary **MAY** or **MIGHT** to make a sentence with the same meaning.*

EXAMPLE   Maybe they got lost.
           They **might have** gotten lost.

1. Maybe they ran out of fuel.
2. Maybe they crashed in the ocean.
3. Maybe their equipment wasn't working right.
4. Maybe they weren't familiar with the area.
5. Maybe they were not experienced pilots.
6. Maybe they couldn't control the planes.
7. Maybe they had to make an emergency landing in the ocean.

Possible Explanations

*Look at the picture (Fig. 15–3). Then use the cues with **MAY** or **MIGHT** to give possible answers to the questions. Think about the time focus of the action. Fill in empty brackets with your own cues.*

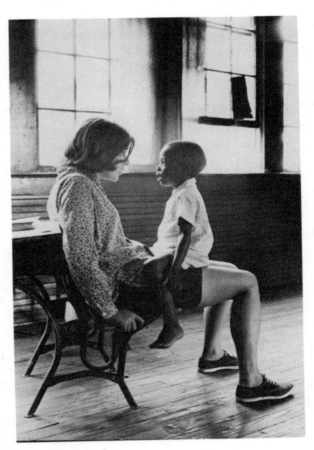

FIGURE 15-3

EXAMPLE   Where are these people?

a. school

b. house

c. camp

They **might be** in a school.
They **may be** in a house.
They **may be** at camp.

1.   Who is this woman?

a. teacher

b. babysitter

c. [   ]

2. What are they doing? Why?

    a. ask question

    b. do something wrong

    c. tell a story

    d. hurt himself

    e. [   ]

FOCUS 4   Missed Opportunities and Unfulfilled Possibilities

*What do the expressions with **COULD HAVE** mean in the following situations?*

Jim: How did you get home from the library last night?

Paul: I rode my bike.

Jim: You what? You're crazy!

Paul: Why?

Jim: You don't have a light on your bike. A car **could have hit** you! A car **could have killed** you!

Paul: You're right. I guess I was pretty lucky.

Did a car hit Paul? Do you think he was lucky? Why?

Mary: Why weren't you at the party last night?

Dave: I didn't feel like going out last night.

Mary: You should have come. You **could have met** a lot of people there.

Dave: Maybe next time.

Did Dave have the opportunity to meet a lot of people last night? Did he take advantage of this opportunity?

There are two special uses of **COULD* HAVE** with a past participle that refer to events that did *not* happen.

1. Use **COULD HAVE** with a past participle to talk about opportunities that were missed. This is a type of suggestion given too late.

    You *should have come* to the party. You **could have met** a lot of nice people.

    [It is too late. You missed this opportunity.]

2. Use **COULD HAVE** with a past participle to talk about things that did not happen but were possible in the past.

    A car **could have hit** Paul.

    [He was lucky; this did not happen. However, it was possible.]

PRACTICE 4-1   Possibilities that Did Not Happen

A.   Your classmate will tell you about a past situation. React to each situation using **SHOULDN'T HAVE . . . , COULD HAVE . . . ,** *or* **SHOULD HAVE.** *Follow the sample conversation. Fill in empty brackets with your own cues.*

---

*It is also possible to use **MIGHT HAVE** + **past participle** to talk about possibilities that did not occur.
   A car **might have hit** Paul.

Student A: Jack rode his bike in the dark last night.

Student B: [**shouldn't have**] He **shouldn't have ridden** his bike in the dark.

Student A: Why not?

Student B: [**could have**]   (car / hit) A car **could have hit** him.

[**should have** (instead)] He **should have called** a taxi instead.

Student A: You're right. He was foolish (lucky, crazy).

1.   STUDENT A: I bought a new coat for $500 in Johnson's Department Store last week.

STUDENT B: [**shouldn't have**]

STUDENT A: Why not?

STUDENT B: [**could have**]   (you / get a cheaper one at Wilson's Coat Discounts)

(**should have** [instead])

STUDENT A: [   ]

2.   STUDENT A: I went swimming alone last night.

STUDENT B: [**shouldn't have**]

STUDENT A: Why not?

STUDENT B: [**could have**]   (you / drown)

[**should have** (instead)]

STUDENT A: [   ]

3.   STUDENT A: A man opened his umbrella in the elevator a few minutes ago.

STUDENT B: [**shouldn't have**]

STUDENT A: Why not?

STUDENT B: [**could have**] [   ]

[**should have** (instead)]

STUDENT A: [   ]

B.   Read the following situations. Then offer suggestions about what these people **COULD HAVE DONE** *differently.*

EXAMPLE   David's car wouldn't start this morning. Because he couldn't drive, he wasn't able to come to class.

He **could have taken** a bus.

(He **could have called** a taxi.)

1.   Alicia doesn't know how to type, so she handed in a handwritten term paper that was 30 pages long. Her professor refused to read it.

2.   Tan missed all of the deadlines for university applications. His excuse was that he didn't know how to apply. He also said that he didn't have any information or addresses for universities offering degrees in his field.

3.   Last weekend was beautiful, but Ted and Lynn couldn't think of anything to do, so they stayed inside and watched TV all weekend.

How do you think Arthur C. Clarke probably felt when he saw the strange light that he had never seen before?

How did he probably feel when he realized that it was only a weather balloon?

He **must have felt** confused when he first saw the strange light.

He **must have felt** silly when he saw that it was a weather balloon.

The auxiliary **MUST** can make logical conclusions or indicate an understanding about past situations.

A.   Past events

Use the auxiliary **MUST** with **HAVE** and a past participle to indicate a past time focus. To form a negative conclusion, add **NOT** after **MUST**.

Subject	+	MUST (NOT) "probability"	+	HAVE "past"	+	Past Participle	+	Rest of Sentence
Clarke		must		have		felt		silly when he saw the balloon.
His friend		must not		have		known		it was a weather balloon either.

B.   Past activities

To make a conclusion about a past activity, use **MUST (NOT)** with **HAVE BEEN** and an **-ING** verb.

Subject	+	MUST (NOT) "probability"	+	HAVE "past"	+	BEEN + -ING verb "in progress"	+	Rest of Sentence(s)
The balloon		must		have		been reflecting		light from the sun.
The air		**must not**		**have**		**been moving.**		**The light was motionless.**

C.   Ability and necessity

To make conclusions about past ability and necessity, use the appropriate form of the modal expressions **BE ABLE TO** and **HAVE TO**.

  1.   Conclusions about past ability

> Bob: Why didn't Jenny come to the party last week?
>
> Jim: I haven't talked to her, but I know she was worried about getting a ride. She **must not have been able to get** one.

  2.   Conclusions about past necessity

> Kim: I heard that people stood in line all night to buy tickets to the rock concert. I also heard that the concert had sold out by 9:30 A.M. of the day the tickets went on sale.
>
> Jessica: Well, Gina got tickets.
>
> Kim: She did? Wow! She **must have had to wait** in line all night!

PRACTICE 5–1   Probable Explanations

*A.   Use **MUST** with the cues to give a probable explanation for each situation. Fill in empty brackets with your own cues.*

EXAMPLE   There's frost on the glass. (cold last night)
           It **must have been** cold last night.

1. When Mr. Wang came back to his apartment, he noticed that a light was on. (forget / turn off / this morning)
2. I did my homework, but it isn't in my bookbag. (leave / home)
3. Sarah feels fine today, but yesterday she felt terrible. She was weak and dizzy. Sometimes she felt very hot, and sometimes she felt very cold. (have / fever)
4. There was a lot of noise coming from the apartment below Jim's. He could hear music and laughter and lots of different voices until 3:00 A.M. [   ]

PRACTICE 5-2   Using **MUST** to Show Understanding

*Use **MUST** with the cues to show that you understand each situation. Think about the time focus.*

EXAMPLE   Alice just got back from a three-week trip to Hawaii.

           (have a good time) She **must have had** a good time there.
           (have a great tan) She **must have** a great tan now.

1. Eduardo usually eats breakfast, but he didn't today. It's noon now, and he hasn't had lunch yet.

   a. in a hurry this morning
   b. not have time to eat
   c. hungry now
   d. his stomach / growl

2. Jackie almost never sings, but I can hear her singing in the shower now!

   a. something great / happen
   b. get a good night's sleep
   c. in a good mood today
   d. not realize // someone else / here

CLOSE-UP   **Passive Past Modal Expressions**

Many people claim to have seen the humps of a monster's back in the waters of Loch Ness, a very deep lake in Scotland. The following passive sentences offer explanations about what caused these humps.

To form a past passive sentence about probabilities and possibilities, use a modal auxiliary with **HAVE BEEN** and a *past participle*.

Possible Explanations	Subject +	Modal (NOT) "possibility/ probability"	HAVE "past" +	BEEN + past participle "passive"	+ Rest of Sentence
Maybe waves caused the "humps."	They	might	have	been caused	by waves.
Maybe waves did not cause the "humps."	They	may not	have	been caused	by waves.
A large animal probably made them.	They	must	have	been made	by a large animal.

Close-Up

PRACTICE **ACTIVE AND PASSIVE**

Read the following letter to Ann Landers. Then complete the sentences.

ANN LANDERS
Don't leave children alone in automobile

DEAR ANN: I just read an article in the newspaper that upset me terribly. A mother left her three children, ages 4, 2, and 2 months, alone in the car on the side of the highway after she ran out of gas. The woman walked to a gas station almost a mile down the road. When she returned, she became hysterical when she discovered that her children were gone.

This story had a happy ending because, luckily, a friend happened to recognize the car. She stopped and took the children home with her.

I shudder when I think of what might have happened to those kids. Someone could have abducted them. The car could have been struck by a passing truck. The children could have wandered out onto the highway and been killed.

I hope all parents will heed this.—Little Rock

Dear Rock: I am horrified to think that a woman would leave three small children in a car alone—and the baby only 2 months old! The sensible procedure would have been to raise the hood of the car, signaling car trouble, and try to flag down some help. Never, but never should children be left alone in the car, either on the highway or on a city street.

According to Ann Landers and the person writing the letter . . .

1. The children shouldn't have _____.

2. Their mother should have _____.

Permission granted by Ann Landers and Creators Syndicate.

3. They were very lucky. Something terrible could have

   _____.

4. The car could have _____, and the children could

   have _____.

5. When the mother came back to her car and saw that her children

   were gone, she must have _____.

Modal Review

Use the information from the situation to complete the sentences that follow. All the auxiliaries are given. Just add an appropriate verb, and then complete the sentence.

Dave's trouble began when he borrowed his father's car without permission last week. As he was backing out of the garage, he accidentally hit a tree and caused $300 worth of damage to the car. There was also considerable damage to the tree.

1. Dave shouldn't have _____.

2. If he needed to go somewhere, he could have _____.

3. When he was backing out, he must not have _____.

4. He should have _____.

5. When his father saw the car, he must have _____.

A WIDER ANGLE

Group Discussion

Divide into small groups. Choose one of the following topics to discuss with your group.

TOPIC 1: Do you believe that there might be life on other planets? Why or why not? What kind of life do you think there might be out there? Do you think there is a connection between the UFOs reported around the world and life on other planets? Many ordinary people claim to have seen UFOs. What are some possible explanations for these sightings? What do you think about UFOs?

TOPIC 2: ESP (extrasensory perception) is the ability to know about something it seems impossible to know about. For example, a person with ESP might be able to describe a picture that he or she has never seen. Sometimes the police use help from psychics (people with this "sixth sense") to help solve cases. Have you ever had a personal experience with ESP, or do you know someone who has? Tell your classmates about the experience. What are some possible explanations for this event?

Writing Practice

What is happening in the following photograph (Fig. 15-4)? Write a short composition that discusses the possibilities and probabilities of the situation. Use modal auxiliaries where appropriate.

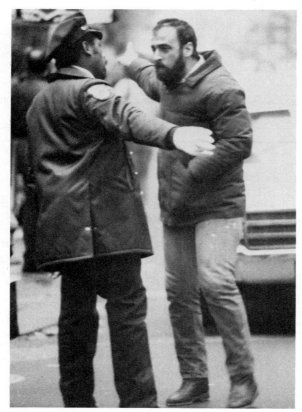

FIGURE 15-4

DEVELOPING YOUR SKILLS AND KNOWLEDGE *Chapter Exercises*

EXERCISE 1 **Forming Possibilities**

Remove the adverb MAYBE from each sentence. Then add the modal auxiliary MAY or MIGHT to make a new sentence with the same meaning.

EXAMPLE   Why doesn't Martha ever come to our meetings?
                Maybe she doesn't like meetings.

                She **might not like** meetings.

Why is Bruce walking along the highway?

1.   Maybe his car is out of gas.
2.   Maybe he is taking a walk.
3.   Maybe his car isn't working.
4.   Maybe he doesn't have a car.
5.   Maybe he's looking for something.
6.   Maybe he can't get a ride.
7.   Maybe he has to get somewhere important.

EXERCISE 2 Offering Possible Explanations

FIGURE 15–5

Look at the picture of a man sitting on a chair (Fig. 15–5). Use MAY or MIGHT with the cues to answer the following questions. Fill in empty brackets with your own cues.

EXAMPLE   Where is this man? (gymnasium)

He **might be** in a gymnasium.

1. What is the man doing?

   a. wait for someone
   b. rest
   c. cry
   d. not have anywhere else to go
   e. [   ]

2. How does the man feel?

   a. lonely
   b. happy
   c. guilty
   d. [   ]

EXERCISE 3 Logical Conclusions

Complete the conversations using MUST (NOT) with the appropriate forms of the verbs indicated.

1. JOE: Where's Mike?

   PACO: I think I hear his stereo. He _____
   (listen)
   to music in his room.

2. STUDENT: Excuse me. Is the secretary here?

   TEACHER: I don't see her. It's twelve-thirty. She _____

   _____ lunch.
   (eat)

3. WALTER: We're moving to a new apartment this afternoon.

   CAROL: You _____ a hand. What can I do to help?
   (need)

4. JULIA: Why isn't Linda's name on the sign-up list for the trip?

   FRANK: She _____ to go.
   (plan)

EXERCISE 4   **Possible Explanations**

FIGURE 15–6

*Look at the photograph of the boy (Fig. 15–6). Why is he hanging on the clothesline? How did he get into this situation? Write five sentences using **MAY** or **MIGHT** to offer possible explanations for this boy's situation. Think about the time of the action in your sentences.*

EXERCISE 5 **More Conclusions**

*Use the verb cues to form conclusions with **MUST**. Think about the time focus of each action.*

1. MARTY: A giant dog chased me while I was jogging yesterday.

   CINDY: You _____ afraid.
   (be)

   MARTY: You bet I was!

2. HENRY: Look at all the branches in the yard. The storm last night

   _____ them down.
   (blow)

3. ARTHUR: Sherry looked very discouraged when she left the library

   yesterday.

   BETTY: She _____ the information she
   (not / find [= *ability*])
   needed.

4. TONI: I can hear music and talking coming from the next

   classroom.

   MILLIE: They _____ a movie.
   (watch)

5. JACKIE: Last night I heard you talking in your sleep. You were

   saying something about your homework.

   TERRI: I _____ about my work for
   (dream)
   marketing class. We have a big assignment due today.

EXERCISE 6 **Active or Passive**

Fill in each blank with an appropriate form of the verb indicated. Add any necessary auxiliaries. Think about the time focus.

1. HECTOR: These directions are in German. This watch must

   _____ in Germany.
   (make)

   PAOLO: Not necessarily. It could _____
   (manufacture)
   in Switzerland.

2. JENNY: Jim drove without a license last night.

   CARRIE: He shouldn't _____ that! He
   (do)
   could _____.
   (arrest)

   JENNY: I guess he was just lucky.

3. LAURA: I accidentally left my purse in the classroom yesterday. When I went back, it was gone. Somebody must

_____ it.
(steal)

BEVERLY: It might _____ at the Lost and
(turn in)

Found.

LAURA: I didn't think of that. I hope you're right!

4. SHELLY: Children should never _____ to
(allow)

play with matches. They might accidentally

_____ a fire.
(start)

16 *Wishes and Other Unrealities*

THE BIG PICTURE

Unreal Conditions: Past and Present

Wishes: Past, Present, Future

AT A GLANCE

Wishful Thinking

Time in a Bottle (a song by Jim Croce)

If I could save time in a bottle,
The first thing that I'd like to do
Is to save every day 'til eternity* passes away
Just to spend them with you.

If I could make days last forever,
If words could make wishes come true,
I'd save every day like a treasure and then,
Again, I would spend them with you.

(Chorus)
But there never seems to be enough time
To do the things you want to do once you find them.
I've looked around enough to know
That you're the one I want to go through time with.

If I had a box just for wishes
And dreams that had never come true,
The box would be empty except for the memory of
How they were answered by you.

(Chorus)
But there never seems to be enough time
To do the things you want to do once you find them.
I've looked around enough to know
That you're the one I want to go through time with.

1. What person is the singer singing to?
2. The singer would like to do something that is impossible. What?
3. Have you ever wished that you could make time stop? Why?
4. In this song, the singer talks about things that are real and about things that are in his imagination. Look at each of the following sentences. Does the sentence describe a *real* or an *unreal* situation?
   a. The singer can put time in a bottle.
   b. The singer wants to spend all his life with the other person.
   c. The singer is happy with the other person.
   d. The singer has an empty box.
   e. The singer is planning to save days in a bottle or a box.

People often talk about things that are not real: their ideas come from imagination, dreams, and wishes. In this chapter, you will practice talking about imaginary or hypothetical situations.

---

*eternity: all time; time without end

Introduction to Unreal Conditions

A.   Review of real conditions

Read the following sentence. Then answer the questions that follow.

The singer will be happy if the woman agrees to marry him.

1. Is it possible that the woman will agree to marry the singer?
2. Is it possible that the singer will be very happy?

Use future and present verb forms with an **IF clause** to talk about conditions that might actually happen. These are *real* conditions.

B.   Understanding unreal conditions

It is also possible to talk about conditions that do not or cannot really exist. Notice the verb forms in the following examples.

ACTUAL SITUATION

> I **can't save** time in a bottle, so I **won't save** every day like a treasure.

IMAGINED SITUATION

> If I **could save** time in a bottle, I **would save** every day like a treasure.

ACTUAL SITUATION

> I **don't have** any powers, so I **won't make** time stop.

IMAGINED SITUATION

> I **would make** time stop if I **had** the power to do so.

In order to communicate that a general or future situation is imaginary, there are two "unreal signals" that must be included in the sentence.

1. The main clause must contain the auxiliary **WOULD** or **COULD**.
2. The **IF clause** must have a *simple past* or *past progressive* verb.

Andras is homesick, but he isn't planning to go home during the summer. He's planning to stay in this country because it's too expensive to go home for vacation. Besides, he needs to go to summer school.

Real Situation	Main Clause: "Imaginary Result"	IF Clause: "Imaginary Condition"
Present/Present Progressive	**WOULD/COULD**	+ **IF + Simple Past/Past Progressive**
He doesn't have enough money.	Andras **would fly** home this summer	**if he had** enough money.
He isn't planning to go home.	He **would be** happy	**if he were planning to go** home.
He can't go home.	He **wouldn't be** depressed	**if he could go** home.
He has summer school classes.	He **could go** home	**if he didn't have** summer school classes.

PRACTICE 1–1   Understanding Conditions

Use the information from each situation to decide if the statements are true *or* false.

1. Sam **will give** us a ride to the party tomorrow if he **can borrow** his parents' car.
   TRUE or FALSE:

   a. Sam might be able to get the car.
   b. Sam might not be able to get the car.
   c. We might get a ride with Sam.

d. We might not be able to get a ride with Sam.

e. We won't be able to get a ride with Sam because he can't borrow his parents' car.

2. Sam **would give** us a ride to the party tomorrow if he **could borrow** his parents' car.

TRUE or FALSE:

a. The party is over.

b. Sam is planning to give us a ride.

c. Sam might be able to get the car.

d. Sam doesn't want to give us a ride.

e. Sam can't give us a ride.

FOCUS 2 Forming Unreal Conditions: Present/Future

A. Forming the IF clause

1. The **IF clause** must have a simple past or past progressive verb.

2. Do not use **WOULD** in the **IF** clause.

3. There is only one form of the verb **BE** in an **IF clause**: use **WERE** for all subjects.

Here are some examples of unreal **IF clauses** with a present or future time focus.

Miguel has no money right now for a number of different reasons.

Real Situation	Unreal Situation: "Present Time"	
Present / Present Progressive	**IF + Simple Past / Past Progressive +**	**Main Clause**
He doesn't have a job.	If he **had** a job,	he **could buy** a car.
He eats out a lot.	If he **didn't eat out** so often,	he **could afford** new clothes.
He isn't careful with money.	If he **were** more careful with money,	he **wouldn't spend** as much.
He is a student.	If he **weren't** a student,	he **wouldn't be** broke.
He can't find a job.	If he **could find** a job,	he **would have** more money.
He isn't working.	If he **were working,**	he **would be** happier.
He is living alone.	If he **weren't living** alone,	he **wouldn't have to pay** so much rent.

B. Forming the main clause

Use **WOULD** or **COULD** in the main clause; these two auxiliaries signal that the situation is not real.

Here are some examples of unreal main clauses with a present / future time focus.

Miguel is here on a student visa, so he cannot work legally.

Real Situation	Unreal Situation		
Present / Present Progressive	**Main Clause WOULD / COULD +**		**IF Clause**
He doesn't have a job.	He **would have** a job		
He has to study full-time.	He **wouldn't have to study** full-time		
He isn't working.	He **would be working**		
He isn't allowed to work.	He **would be allowed** to work		**if** he weren't here on a student visa.
He can't work legally.	He **would be able to work** legally		
	He **could work** legally		
He has financial problems.	He **wouldn't have** financial problems		

Unreal **IF** Clauses

Phil is a very unhappy person. Here are some things that make him unhappy. Imagine what conditions would make him happy instead of unhappy. Complete each sentence with an IF clause.

1. Phil is unemployed.

   Phil would be happier if _____.

2. He can't find a good job.

   He would feel better if _____.

3. He doesn't get enough exercise.

   He wouldn't be so unhappy if _____.

4. He isn't living with anyone.

   He wouldn't be so lonely if _____.

Unreal Main Clauses

Sally lives in a big house. Living in a big house has disadvantages as well as advantages.

How would Sally's life be different if she didn't live in such a big house? Complete each sentence with a main clause.

1. Sally can have big parties.

   If she didn't live in a big house, _____.

2. She can have a lot of house guests.

   If she lived in a smaller house, _____.

3. She has to spend a lot of time taking care of her house.

   If her house weren't so big, _____.

4. She is paying high property taxes.

   If she didn't have such a big house, _____.

Imagined Conditions

Here is some information about a student and his life here. How would his life be different if these conditions were different? Make sentences using IF.

EXAMPLE   Chan doesn't have a car, so he has to use public transportation.
    If he had a car, he **wouldn't have to use** public transportation.

1. Chan doesn't speak English, so he is taking English courses.
2. Because Chan is a little shy, it is difficult for him to make friends.
3. He is living with his cousin's family because he can't afford to live by himself.
4. He doesn't get lonely because he is living with relatives.
5. He doesn't practice his English at home because he isn't living with English speakers.

Choose some of these characteristics to make true statements about yourself. Your true statement can be negative or affirmative. Then imagine how your life would be different if you did not have these characteristics.

tall	single	get regular exercise
short	the leader of my country	speak perfect English
patient	a movie star	know how to cook
married	a millionaire	have a lot of free time

EXAMPLES   **I'm not tall. But if** I were tall, I would be able to erase the blackboard.

I know how to cook. But if I didn't know how to cook, I would eat frozen dinners every evening.

FOCUS 3   Wishes about the Present

In the song at the beginning of this chapter, "Time in a Bottle," what is the singer hoping for? Is it possible that this will happen? What does he wish he could do? Will he ever be able to do this? Why or why not?

A.   Comparing wishes and hopes

1. In English, the verb **HOPE** expresses a desire for something that is possible. It refers to a possible real situation.

The singer **hopes** that the woman in the song will marry him. [*Maybe she will.*]

He **is hoping** to spend the rest of his life with her. [*Maybe he will.*]

2. The verb **WISH,** however, expresses a desire for something that is not possible. In the present tense, **WISH** expresses a desire to change a real situation to an unreal situation. Use **WISH** for **unreal situations.**

The singer **wishes** he could make time stop. [*Of course, he can't.*]

B.   Forming wishes about current and general situations

To express a present **wish,** use the same "unreal" verb forms that are used in **unreal IF clauses:** simple past or past progressive. Once again, there is only one form of the verb **BE:** use **WERE** for all subjects.

Current Real Situation	Wish (Present Time Focus / Past Verb)
The singer can't put time in a bottle.	He **wishes** he **could put** time in a bottle.
Fred has bad vision.	He **wishes** he **didn't have** bad vision.
	He **wishes** he **had** good eyes.
Luis lives alone.	He **wishes** he **didn't live** alone.
	He **wishes** he **lived** with someone.
My family isn't here.	I **wish** my family **were** here.
It is raining.	I **wish** it **weren't raining.**
	I **wish** the sun **were shining.**
I am very short.	I **wish** I **were** taller.
	I **wish** I **weren't** so short.

PRACTICE 3-1 Wishes and Hopes

*Read the following situations. Then complete each sentence with a form of **WISH** or **HOPE**.*

1. It's raining right now and I have to walk to class.
   a. I _____ it weren't raining.
   b. I _____ I didn't have to walk to class in this rain!
   c. I _____ the rain stops before my class finishes.
   d. I _____ I don't have to walk home in this rain after class!

2. I don't have a car now. Maybe I'll buy one in a few years.
   a. I _____ I had a car now.
   b. I _____ I can buy one in a few years.
   c. I _____ cars weren't so expensive.
   d. I _____ it were easier to get around without a car.
   e. I _____ I have enough money to buy a car after I graduate.

PRACTICE 3-2 Wishes

A. *Look at the following real situations. Complete the sentences to explain what these people wish.*

EXAMPLE   The little girl can't reach the candy jar.
She wishes she **could reach it.**

REAL SITUATIONS

1. George is living in a dorm.
   He wishes _____.

2. Jim has to fill out his income tax form today.
   He wishes _____.

3. I drive an unreliable car.
   I wish _____.

4. I have a test tomorrow.
   I wish _____.

5. The teacher gives a lot of homework.
   The students wish _____.

6. Jim's roommate is so shy!
   Jim wishes _____.

B. *Think about your current life and lifestyle. What do you wish could be different?*

A.   Wishes about future plans

Use **WERE GOING TO** with a base form verb to make a wish about plans for the future.

ACTUAL PLANS

The government **is going to raise** taxes.

WISH

Everybody wishes that the government **weren't going to raise** taxes.

B.   Future wishes as requests

Use a wish with **WOULD** and a base form verb to communicate a type of request. Speakers use a wish with **WOULD** to indicate that they want something to happen or change. This type of "request" may express irritation or the feeling that the other person may not be willing to carry out the request.

I want you to stop smoking.
I wish you **would quit** smoking.

I want it to stop raining.
I wish it **would stop** raining.

I would like you to be quiet.
I wish you would be quiet.

Why do you always interrupt me?
I wish you wouldn't interrupt me!

My friends never write to me.
I wish they would write to me!

PRACTICE 4–1   Wishes about the Future

A.   Use the information from the real future plans to make sentences with **WISH.**

EXAMPLE   We are going to have a test next Monday.

I **wish** we **weren't going to have** a test next Monday.
I **wish** we **were going to have** the test on Tuesday instead.

ACTUAL PLANS

1.   Jim is taking the bus to Washington, D.C., next month. He'd rather fly, but it's too expensive.
2.   Gail is going to spend Christmas at her in-laws' home. She'd rather spend Christmas with her parents.
3.   Some of the students are going to spend their holidays in the dormitories.

B.   Use the first cue in each of the following groups to form a question. Your classmate will use the second cue to make a wish with **WOULD** *to answer the question. Follow the example. Fill in empty brackets with your own cues.*

EXAMPLE   my stereo / bother?

Student A: Is my stereo bothering you?
(yes) wish / turn down

Student B: **To tell you the truth, it is.**
I wish you would turn it down.

1. STUDENT A: my cigarette / bother?
   STUDENT B: (yes) wish / put out
2. STUDENT A: you / angry / me?
   STUDENT B: (yes) wish / call more often
3. STUDENT A: you / upset / Roger?
   STUDENT B: (yes) wish / not make jokes / my country
4. STUDENT A: you / like / this music?
   STUDENT B: (no) wish / [   ]

GETTING READY TO FOCUS

Real-Life Dilemmas

A **dilemma** is a situation where you must make a difficult choice between two imperfect or undesirable courses of action. Perhaps you have found yourself *in a dilemma* at some point in your life.

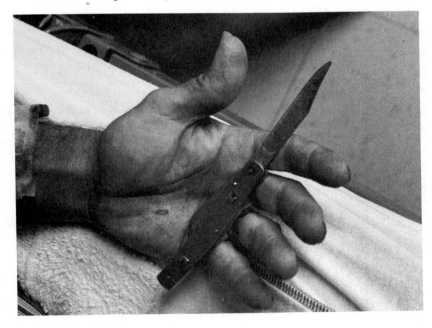

Dan Wyman's Dilemma

On July 20, 1993, Dan Wyman of Pennsylvania found himself in an unusual and difficult situation: He had to choose between dying and cutting off his own leg with a small, dull pocketknife. How did he end up in such a dilemma?

On that day, Dan Wyman was alone in the woods chopping down trees when a large oak tree fell on him and pinned the lower part of his leg to the ground. He tried shouting for help, but no one was within earshot. He couldn't reach the tree, so he used his chain saw to try to dig his leg out from under the tree trunk. When he hit a large rock, he realized that he would not be able to dig himself out of this mess. He also knew that nobody was expecting him home until later, so no one would start worrying about him and come looking for him for a long time. He was afraid that if he waited for help, he might bleed to death.

It soon became clear to Wyman that he was going to have to cut off his leg. He had only a small, dull, three-inch pocketknife, which he sharpened as best he could on a nearby rock. Then he took the cord from his chain saw and tied it around his leg to help stop the bleeding. Finally, he worked up his courage and began to cut off his left leg.

Cutting off his own leg was not the end of his problems. Once he was free, he had to crawl 135 feet uphill to his bulldozer. He climbed into the bulldozer and drove it 1,500 feet to his truck, which had manual transmission. Using a tool to push in the clutch when he shifted, he drove a mile and a half to the nearest house. He was then taken to a nearby emergency room.*

What gives people the ability to do amazingly courageous things like this?

Although it is not possible to change the past, it is possible to *imagine* how things could have happened differently. In this section, you will practice talking about past events and situations and about the different circumstances that could have produced different results.

FOCUS 5   Understanding Past Unreal Conditions

Certain actual past conditions resulted in certain outcomes. Use unreal conditions to imagine different conditions with different results.

Actual Events	Imagined Past Events
Dan Wyman had a knife, so he was able to cut off his leg.	**If he hadn't had a knife, he wouldn't have been able to cut it off.**
He didn't die, because he cut his leg off.	**He probably would have died if he hadn't cut it off.**

PRACTICE 5-1   Understanding Unreal Past Conditions

The following sentences describe imaginary situations. What actually happened?

EXAMPLE   Dan Wyman would have died if he had waited for someone to find him.

Dan Wyman didn't wait for someone to find him, and he didn't die.

1. John would have been killed if he hadn't been wearing his seatbelt when his car hit the pole.

2. If you hadn't helped me yesterday, I'd never have been able to move all that furniture.

3. If I had had Maria's address with me, I would have visited her when I went to her country.

4. We could have given you a ride if we'd known that you didn't have one.

5. Dan Wyman would never have found the strength to cut off his own leg if he hadn't had so much to live for.

*Source: Based on an article from *People Weekly*, August 9, 1993, pp. 42–43.

FOCUS 6 Forming Unreal Past Conditions

There are two "signals" that indicate that a past situation did not really happen:
1. The **IF clause** has a past perfect or past perfect progressive verb.
2. The main clause has a modal verb (**WOULD, COULD, MIGHT**) + **HAVE** + past participle.

A. Forming the IF clause

Use a past perfect or past perfect progressive verb in the **IF clause** to indicate an imaginary condition in the past.

Actual Event	Imaginary Past Condition (IF Clause)	
Dan was very brave.	If he **hadn't been** so brave,	
He didn't panic.	If he **had panicked**,	
He was able to cut his leg off.	If he **hadn't been able to cut** it off,	he probably would have died.
He was thinking clearly.	If he **hadn't been thinking** so clearly,	

B. Forming the main clause

Use a modal auxiliary (**WOULD, COULD, MIGHT**) with **HAVE** and a past participle in the main clause to indicate an imaginary result in the past. **COULD HAVE . . .** means "would have been able to . . ." or "might have . . ."; **MIGHT HAVE . . .** means "maybe would have . . . ."

Actual Event	Imaginary Past Result (Main Clause)	
Dan didn't bleed to death.	He **might have bled** to death	
He was able to cut his leg off.	He **wouldn't have been able to cut** it off	
He wasn't lying there all night.	He **would have been lying** there all night	if he hadn't kept his wits about him.
He survived his ordeal.	He **might not have survived** his ordeal	
He didn't pass out.	He **could have passed out**	

PRACTICE 6-1 Unreal Past Conditions

*A.   Use the information from the first sentence in each group to complete the **IF** clause in the second sentence.*

1. Wyman tied a cord around his leg in order to stop the bleeding.
   He probably would have bled to death if

   _____ .

2. No one else was with him, so nobody could move or cut the tree off his leg.

   If _____ , they might have been able to get the tree off his leg.

3. He cut his leg off because there was no other way to get out from under the tree.
   He certainly wouldn't have cut off his leg if

   _____ .

4. He had the inner strength to survive because he had a family who needed him.

If _____, he might not have found the strength to survive.

B. *Continue the exercise. This time, complete the main clause.*

1. He had a knife, so he was able to cut off his leg.

If he hadn't had a knife, _____.

2. It was difficult to use the knife because it was pretty dull.

_____ if it hadn't been so dull.

3. They weren't able to reattach his leg because there was too much tissue damage.

If there hadn't been so much tissue damage,

_____.

4. He was ready to lose his leg in order to live.

If he hadn't been willing to lose his leg,

_____.

C. *Complete the following sentence.*

If I had been in Dan Wyman's situation, I

_____.

PRACTICE 6-2 More Practice with Unreal Conditions

*Read the real situation. Then write a conditional sentence explaining how the situation could have been different. Begin your sentence with **BUT IF**. . . .*

EXAMPLE   Dan Wyman survived because he never gave up.
But if he had given up, he probably wouldn't have survived.

1. We didn't know that you needed a ride to the party, so we didn't offer to take you.
2. You weren't told about the meeting because we didn't know that you were in town.
3. I wasn't waiting for you at the airport because you didn't tell me your arrival time.
4. John didn't study for the test, so he didn't get a high score on the test.
5. I wasn't paying attention in class, so I didn't hear the assignment.
6. Martin got fired yesterday for missing too many days of work.
7. Alicia wasn't allowed to take the test because she arrived late.
8. I didn't know that it was going to be cold today, so I didn't wear my gloves.
9. Salima wasn't in class yesterday because she was sick.
10. The students weren't given much time to do the test, so they didn't get high scores.

Conclusions and Conditions

Use each cue to form a conclusion based on the situation. Your classmate will then ask you to explain your conclusion. Give an explanation using an IF clause.

EXAMPLE   Student A: Lisa walked by me this morning without saying hello.

            Student B: (not see you) She **must not have seen** you.

            Student A: What makes you say that? (Why do you say that? How do you know?)

            Student B: **If she'd seen you, I'm sure she would have said something.**

1. STUDENT A: Richard wouldn't help me with my math homework last night.

   STUDENT B: (busy)

2. STUDENT A: Ruth missed three days of school last week.

   STUDENT B: (sick)

3. STUDENT A: Carlos wouldn't tell me his TOEFL score earlier this week.

   STUDENT B: (not pass)

4. STUDENT A: Joseph couldn't answer a very easy question in class this morning.

   STUDENT B: (not listen)

5. STUDENT A: Karen got mad when I called her at around midnight last night.

   STUDENT B: (sleep)

Questions about Unreal Past Conditions

Read the real situation. Then use the cues to ask questions about how that situation could have been different. Answer each question with a complete sentence.

EXAMPLE   Bill studied very hard for the test and, as a result, he did very well.

        What / happen // if / not / study?

        Student A: What **would have happened if** he **hadn't studied?**

        Student B: He probably **wouldn't have done** so well.
            (He **would probably have failed** the test.)

1. There was a fire in Jennifer's apartment last night. Fortunately, her smoke alarm was working. She heard the alarm, woke up, and got out of the building safely.

   a. what / happen // if / not / have / smoke alarm?

   b. what / happen // if / it / not / work?

   c. what / happen // if / not / hear / alarm?

2. At first, David wasn't planning to buy medical insurance, but his friends convinced him that he should. David was glad that he'd listened to his friends, because three weeks later, he slipped and broke his leg. The insurance paid his medical expenses.

   a. who / pay [= *necessity*] / David's medical bills // if / not / buy / insurance?

b. what / happen // if / David's friends / not / talk to him about insurance?

c. how / David / feel // when / break / leg // if / not / buy / insurance?

FOCUS 7 Regrets about the Past: Wishes for the Past

Dan Wyman is very grateful to be alive. Do you think he might also regret the way things worked out? Can he change what has already happened? What do you think he regrets doing? What do you think he regrets not doing?

The verb **WISH** can be used to show **regret** about the way a past situation happened. This is another type of *unreal* situation because, of course, nothing can be done to change the past.

To indicate regret about the past, use **WISH** with a clause in the *past perfect* or *past perfect progressive* tense. Do not use **WOULD** in a wish about the past.

> Dan Wyman probably wishes that he **had been** more careful cutting down that tree.
>
> He also probably wishes that he **hadn't been working** out there all alone.

PRACTICE 7-1 Regrets

A.   In each sentence, change the verb regret to wish. *Make any other necessary changes.*

EXAMPLE   Fernando regrets not studying English in his country.
        Fernando **wishes that he had studied** English in his country.

1. Lucia regrets not bringing some cassettes of Italian music with her to the United States.
2. Pierre regrets staying up so late last night.
3. Melina regrets that she wasn't able to bring her guitar with her.

B.   *What are some things that you regret doing or not doing? Make sentences using* **WISH**.

PRACTICE 7-2 Wishes and Hopes

Write a sentence using the verb **WISH** *or* **HOPE** *to describe how the person in each of the following situations feels. Then explain your idea with an* **IF** *clause.*

EXAMPLES   David is waiting for some money from home so he can pay his rent.
        David **hopes** that the check **will arrive** soon.
        If it doesn't get here soon, he won't have enough money to pay the rent.

        Maria wants to be a singer, but she has a terrible voice.
        Maria **wishes** she **had** a nice voice.
        If she had a nice voice, she would (could) be a singer.

        I packed in a hurry to come here, and I forgot to bring pictures of my family.

I **wish** I **hadn't packed** so quickly.

If I **hadn't packed** quickly, I **wouldn't have forgotten** to bring pictures.

1. Mac ate too much pizza last night, and, as a result, he has a terrible stomachache today.
2. I wasn't wearing a raincoat yesterday, so I got all wet.
3. Melissa needs to get a good grade on her final exam in order to pass the biology course.
4. The woman Jim voted for was not elected as mayor.
5. Sonia can't begin her university studies this semester because she has to study English first.
6. I'd love to have one million dollars . . . tax-free!

A WIDER ANGLE

Class Discussion: Baby Jessica

The following passage is about a real-life dilemma.*

On February 8, 1991, a single mother, Cara Clausen, gave birth to a baby girl. She had decided to give the baby up for adoption because she didn't feel that she could raise a child by herself. In order for an adoption to be legal, both the mother and the father have to sign papers agreeing to the adoption. Cara contacted the man who she claimed was the baby's father, and he agreed to sign the papers too. Lawyers then arranged for the baby girl to be adopted by the DeBoers. The DeBoers had been trying to adopt a child for several years and were delighted to finally have a baby, whom they named Jessica, to take home.

Shortly after the DeBoers took Jessica home, the biological mother changed her mind about giving up the baby, but her parental rights had already been lost. However, she had lied about the identity of the biological father; the man who had signed the legal documents was *not* Baby Jessica's father. The *real* biological father had not agreed to give the baby up for adoption, and he also wanted the baby back. A long court battle followed between the biological parents (who ended up getting married) and the adoptive parents.

During the first two and a half years of her life, when all of the legal proceedings were going on, Jessica knew only her adoptive parents, the DeBoers. Then the final ruling came in 1993: the judge ruled that Jessica was to go live with her biological parents. In August, the biological parents took Jessica home with them to another state, where her name became Anna.

Discuss with your classmates what you would have done and how you would have felt . . .

1. if you had been the biological mother or father.
2. if you had been the adoptive mother or father.
3. if you had been the judge in this case.

Writing Practice

Write a short composition on one of the following topics.

---

*Based on articles from *People Weekly*, July 19, 1993, pp. 48–54, and *People Weekly*, December 27, 1993, pp. 69–70.

TOPIC 1: A Real-Life Dilemma

Perhaps you have read or heard or know about other dilemmas that people have faced. In the first part of your composition, write about one such dilemma and about what actually happened. In the second part of your composition, write about how the situation could have happened differently.

TOPIC 2: How I Would Do It

Write a composition telling what you would do if you were the person in charge of something. You can choose one of the following topics, or you can use your own topic.

the leader of this country

the leader of your country

the director of this English program

an ESL teacher

[   ]

TOPIC 3: A Turning Point in My Life

Write a composition about a point in your life when you had to make an important decision. First write about the decision that you made. Then write about what would have happened if you had made a different decision.

DEVELOPING YOUR SKILLS AND KNOWLEDGE *Chapter Exercises*

EXERCISE 1 **Present Unreal Conditions**

A. *Fill in each blank with the appropriate form of the verb indicated.*

1. I'm broke. But if I _____ some money, I
       (have)

    _____ some new clothes.
       (buy)

2. Parking is such a problem for students. If I _____ the
                                                    (be)

    president of the university, I _____ more parking
                                        (provide)

    facilities.

3. Oh no! It's raining, and I have to walk to class now. I

    _____ walking if I _____ my umbrella
       (not / mind)   (have)

    with me. If it _____, I _____ my
                       (not / rain)   (not / need)

    umbrella.

4. Andras _____ on the next plane home if he
                 (be)

    _____ the price of a plane ticket.
       (afford [= *ability*])

B.   *Read each actual situation. Then write a conditional sentence describing an unreal situation.*

EXAMPLE   Chan is broke because he doesn't have a job.
                     He **wouldn't be** broke **if** he **had** a job.

1. Scott can't get a job as an actor, so he is waiting tables at a restaurant.
2. Barbara won't be going to the meeting because she has to go to class.
3. My roommate is sleeping, so we can't ask him for a ride to the park.
4. Fred is having a party because his parents are visiting him.
5. I don't have a calculator, so I'm not able to balance my checkbook quickly.

EXERCISE 2   Wishes

Read the real situation. Then write a sentence telling what each person wishes.

EXAMPLE   It's raining. I wish <u>it weren't raining.</u>

1. I have a terrible cold. I wish _____.

2. Hamid feels lonely because he doesn't have a roommate. He wishes

   _____.

3. I love these shoes, but they are expensive. I wish

   _____.

4. The students don't have time to watch TV. They wish

   _____.

5. Boris is living far away from school. He wishes _____.

EXERCISE 3   Future Wishes

Read each situation, and write a wish using **WOULD** *to express the desire for a change in the future.*

EXAMPLE   George always smokes when he comes to my house, and I don't like it.
                     I wish he **wouldn't smoke in my house.**

1. It bothers me when you joke around all the time.

   I wish _____.

2. You are rarely serious.

   I wish _____.

3. You don't pay attention to my feelings.

   I wish _____.

4. You don't like it when I am so serious.

   You probably wish _____.

5. You don't think I laugh very much.

   You probably wish _____.

EXERCISE 4 Unreal Past Conditions

Read the following article.

Baby On Board

The first person to witness Allison Hoary's wild ride was Peg Ransom, who was driving through Wauconda, Ill., on her way home to Libertyville, a Chicago suburb. It was 4:50 p.m on March 28. The white panel truck ahead of her on Route 176 was doing about 55 m.p.h.—and a little blonde girl was perched on the 10-inch-wide back bumper, clinging to the door latch.

Ransom, a 57-year-old public relations consultant, gave chase, honking her horn and trying to get the driver's attention. At the wheel of the van, unaware of the teetering tot behind him, Mike Hoary, 36, a vending machine routeman, was driving from his Wauconda home to his office in Chicago. Ten minutes before, he had said goodbye to his wife, Pam, and his children, Ross, 5, and Allyson, 2 1/2. Shortly after he pulled out of the driveway, Pam realized Allyson was missing. She conducted a frantic five-minute search, then called police and reported her daughter gone.

On the road, Ransom swerved periodically to catch Hoary's attention. Thinking she had been drinking or was falling asleep, he speeded up. At this point, Dick McGill, 47, an off-duty fire captain, was driving into town. "I just happened to turn around to see this little kid on the back of the truck," says McGill. He did a quick U-turn and fell into line behind Hoary and Ransom. As the three cars approached an intersection, McGill pulled up next to Hoary and rolled down his window to yell, "There's a little girl on the bumper of your truck!"

Thunderstruck, Hoary jumped out and saw Allyson. "It was like, oh, my God, this couldn't be happening," he says. "It was like I was underwater." Composed all during her 5.9-mile ride, Allyson finally began crying. After five minutes together on the shoulder of the road, father and daughter drove home.

Allyson has since been warned about the dangers of playing on Daddy's van—and Hoary is planning to buy a fish-eye mirror to detect any future rear-bumper passengers.

A. Each of the following sentences describes what actually happened. Write a second sentence to show how the situation could have been different. Each sentence should contain an IF clause.

EXAMPLE   Mike Hoary didn't see his daughter on the van when he started it.
If he had seen her, he wouldn't have started the van.

1. Mike Hoary didn't know Allyson was playing on the van, and he drove the van out of the driveway.
2. Mike Hoary didn't have a special mirror to see the back of the van, so he couldn't see Allyson.
3. Hoary found out that Allyson was on the van because Dick McGill was able to get his attention at an intersection.
4. Allyson was in a dangerous situation because she had been playing around the van.

5. Allyson was okay because she didn't fall off the back of the van.

6. Allyson was able to hold on to the doorlatch, so she didn't fall off.

B. *Answer the following questions.*

1. What could have happened if Hoary had continued driving?

2. What would you have done if you had seen 2½-year-old Allyson hanging onto the back of a van or truck?

3. How would you have felt if you had been Mike Hoary? Write about three different emotions that you would have felt in that situation.

4. How could this situation have been avoided?

EXERCISE 5 **Wishes and Regrets**

Read the situations. What does each person wish?

EXAMPLE   I failed the driving test.

I wish **I hadn't failed it.** (I wish **I had passed the test.**)

1. Antony wasn't paying attention in class yesterday, so he didn't understand the homework assignment.

   He wishes _____.

2. I wasn't able to watch the documentary on Japan last night.

   I wish _____.

3. The children got books for Christmas. They had been hoping to get toys.

   The children wish _____.

4. Tom and Melissa got divorced last year. Now they are miserable because they miss each other a lot.

   They wish _____.

EXERCISE 6 **Questions and Answers**

Answer each question with a complete sentence.

1. If you could give new students one piece of advice about being a successful student here, what would you tell them?

2. If you could go back in time to witness one historical event, which event would you choose?

3. If you hadn't come here to study, where would you have gone, or what would you have done instead?

4. If you have some free time tonight, what will you do?

5. If you had had more free time last night, what would you have done?

Appendix A: Spelling and Pronunciation of Verb and Plural Noun Endings

I. Spelling and Pronunciation of -S or -ES Endings

A. Spelling

There are five rules for spelling the **-S** form of simple present tense verbs.

1. If the base form ends with *s, z, sh, ch, x,* or *o,* add **-ES**.

   miss—miss**es**   teach—teach**es**
   fizz—fizz**es**   fix—fix**es**
   wash—wash**es**   echo—echo**es**

2. If the base form ends with a **consonant + Y,** change **Y** to **I** and add **-ES.** (Consonants are *b, c, d, f, g, h, j, k, l, m, n, p, q, r, s, t, v, w, x, y,* and *z.*)

   study—stud**ies**   try—tr**ies**   empty—empt**ies**

3. If the base form ends with a **vowel + Y,** just add **-S.** (Vowels are *a, e, i, o, u.*)

   play—play**s**   enjoy—enjoy**s**

4. The verb **HAVE** is irregular.

   have—**has**

5. For all other verbs, just add **-S** to the base form.

   get—get**s**   see—see**s**   live—live**s**

B. Pronunciation

There are three different ways to pronounce the **-S** or **-ES** ending of a simple present tense verb. The pronunciation of the **-S/-ES** ending depends on the last sound, not the last letter, of the base form:

1. If the base form ends with the sounds *"p," "f," "t,"* or *"k,"* pronounce the **-S/-ES** ending *"s"* (as in Sam).

   sleeps—*"slee**p**s"*   sits—*"si**ts**"*
   laughs—*"la**fs**"*   works—*"wor**ks**"*

2. If the base form ends with the sounds "s," "ks," "z," "sh," "ch," or "j," pronounce the -S/-ES ending "iz" (as a new syllable).

misses—"mis*siz*"	loses—"lu*ziz*"	watches—"wat*chiz*"
fixes—"fi*ksiz*"	washes—"wa*shiz*"	changes—"chan*jiz*"

3. If the base form ends with any other sound, pronounce the -S/-ES ending "z" (as in zoo).

studies—"stu*diez*"   decides—"deci*dz*"   goes—"go*z*"

NOTE: The -S form of the verb **DO** has an irregular pronunciation: do—does (pronounced *"duzz"*).

II. Spelling and Pronunciation of Regular Plural Nouns

Regular nouns take the plural ending **-S** or **-ES**. The spelling and pronunciation rules for plural nouns are the same as the rules for the third-person singular present tense verb (the **-S** form). (See Section I.)

EXCEPTION: Nouns that end with a *consonant* + **O** have special spelling rules.

1. Some singular nouns that end with a **consonant + O** have a plural form with **-ES.**

tomato—tomato**es**	potato—potato**es**
echo—echo**es**	torpedo—torpedo**es**

2. Some singular nouns that end with a **consonant + O** have a plural form with **-S.**

piano—piano**s**   photo—photo**s**   disco—disco**s**

3. Some singular nouns that end with a **consonant + O** can take either **-S** or **-ES.**

tornado—tornado**es**	volcano—volcano**es**
tornado**s**	volcano**s**

4. If the singular noun ends with a **vowel + O,** just add **-S.**

radio—radio**s**   zoo—zoo**s**   video—video**s**

III. Spelling and Pronunciation of -D or -ED Endings

A. Spelling

There are four basic rules for spelling the **-D/-ED** ending of regular simple past verbs and past participles. A fifth rule, the rule for doubling the final consonant, is listed separately at the end of this Appendix in Section V.

1. If the base form ends with a **consonant + Y,** change **Y** to **I** and add **-ED.**

study—stud**ied**   try—tr**ied**

2. If the base form ends with a **vowel + Y,** just add **-ED.** Do not change the **Y.**

enjoy—enjo**yed**   stay—sta**yed**

3. If the base form ends with **E,** just add **-D.**

arrive—arriv**ed**   announce—announc**ed**

4. For all other regular verbs, add **-ED**.

   finish—finish**ed**   echo—echo**ed**
   look—look**ed**   ski—ski**ed**

B. Pronunciation

There are three different ways to pronounce the **-D/-ED** ending. The pronunciation of the ending depends on the last sound of the base form.

   1. The **-ED** ending is pronounced "*t*" (as in *T*om) if the base form ends with these consonant sounds:

"*p*"	jump—jum**ped**	("*jumpt*")
"*k*"	work—wor**ked**	("*workt*")
"*s*"	miss—mis**sed**	("*misst*")
"*ks*"	fix—fi**xed**	("*fixt*")
"*sh*"	wash—was**hed**	("*washt*")
"*ch*"	watch—wat**ched**	("*watcht*")
"*f*"	laugh—laug**hed**	("*laft*")

   2. The **-ED** ending is pronounced "*id*" (an extra syllable) if the base form ends with these consonant sounds:

"*t*"	wait—wai**ted**	("*waitid*")
"*d*"	need—nee**ded**	("*needid*")

   3. The **-ED** ending is pronounced "*d*" (as in *D*avid) for all other regular verbs.

"*l*"	call—cal**led**	("*calld*")
"*b*"	disturb—distur**bed**	("*disturbd*")
"*j*"	judge—jud**ged**	("*jujd*")

IV. Spelling Rules for -ING Verbs

There are three rules for spelling the **-ING** form of the verb. The fourth rule, the rule for doubling the final consonant, is given in Section V.

   1. If the base form ends with a **consonant + E**, take out the **E** and add **-ING**.

   write—wri**ting**   announce—announ**cing**

   2. If the base form ends with **IE**, change **IE** to **Y**, and add **-ING**.

   d*ie*—d**ying**   l*ie*—l**ying**

   3. For all other verbs, just add **-ING**. (See the rule for doubling final consonants in the following section.)

ski—ski**ing**	call—call**ing**	study—study**ing**
agree—agree**ing**	talk—talk**ing**	enjoy—enjoy**ing**

V. Rules for Doubling the Final Consonant

Regular verbs with the **-ED** or **-ING** ending follow a special spelling rule.

   1. *Double* the final consonant of the base form before adding the ending **-ED** or **-ING** in the following situation:

If the base form ends with **consonant + vowel + consonant,** *and* the final vowel of the base form is stressed, double the final consonant and add **-ED** or **-ING.**

stóp—stópped / stópping   admít—admítted / admítting

2. Do *not* double the final consonant in the following situations:

a. Do *not* double the final consonants **H, X, W,** or **Y.**

fix—fixed / fixing   sew—sewed / sewing

b. Do *not* double the final consonant if the final syllable does not have the stress.

vísit—vísited / vísiting   devélop—devéloped / devéloping

Appendix B: Irregular Verb Forms

Base Form	Simple Past	Past Participle
be	was / were	been
beat	beat	beaten (or beat)
become	became	become
begin	began	begun
bend	bent	bent
bet	bet	bet
bite	bit	bitten (or bit)
bleed	bled	bled
blow	blew	blown
break	broke	broken
bring	brought	brought
build	built	built
burst	burst	burst
buy	bought	bought
catch	caught	caught
choose	chose	chosen
come	came	come
cost	cost	cost
creep	crept	crept
cut	cut	cut
dig	dug	dug
do	did	done
drink	drank	drunk
draw	drew	drawn
drive	drove	driven
eat	ate	eaten
fall	fell	fallen
feed	fed	fed
feel	felt	felt
fight	fought	felt
find	found	found
flee	fled	fled
fling	flung	flung
fly	flew	flown
forbid	forbad(e)	forbidden

Base Form	Simple Past	Past Participle
forget	forgot	forgotten
freeze	froze	frozen
get	got	gotten*
give	gave	given
go	went	gone
grind	ground	ground
grow	grew	grown
hang	hung / hanged**	hung / hanged**
have	had	had
hear	heard	heard
hide	hid	hidden (or hid)
hit	hit	hit
hold	held	held
hurt	hurt	hurt
keep	kept	kept
kneel	knelt (or kneeled)	knelt (or kneeled)
knit	knit (or knitted)	knit (or knitted)
know	knew	known
lay	laid	laid
lead	led	led
leave	left	left
lend	lent	lent
let	let	let
lie	lay	lain
light	lit (or lighted)	lit (or lighted)
lose	lost	lost
make	made	made
mean	meant	meant
meet	met	met
mistake	mistook	mistaken
overcome	overcame	overcome
pay	paid	paid
put	put	put
quit	quit	quit
read	read†	read†
ride	rode	ridden
ring	rang	rung
rise	rose	risen
run	ran	run

*__gotten__ is the past participle in American English; __got__ can be used for the past participle in British English.

**__hang-hung-hung:__ to suspend. "I _hung_ some pictures on the wall."

   __hang-hanged-hanged:__ to kill by hanging. "They _hanged_ the criminal."

†__read-read-read__—pronounced "reed"-"red"-"red"

Base Form	Simple Past	Past Participle
say	said*	said
see	saw	seen
seek	sought	sought
sell	sold	sold
send	sent	sent
set	set	set
shake	shook	shaken
shine	shone / shined**	shone / shined**
shoot	shot	shot
shrink	shrank	shrunk
shut	shut	shut
sing	sang	sung
sink	sank	sunk
sit	sat	sat
sleep	slept	slept
slide	slid	slid
speak	spoke	spoken
speed	sped	sped
spend	spent	spent
spin	spun	spun
spit	spit (or spat)	spit
split	split	split
spread	spread	spread
spring	sprang	sprung
stand	stood	stood
steal	stole	stolen
stick	stuck	stuck
sting	stung	stung
stink	stank	stunk
strike	struck	struck
swear	swore	sworn
sweep	swept	swept
swim	swam	swum
swing	swung	swung
take	took	taken
teach	taught	taught
tear	tore	torn
tell	told	told
think	thought	thought
throw	threw	thrown
undergo	underwent	undergone

---

*said—pronounced "sed"

**shine-shone-shone: to radiate (intransitive). "The sun *shone* brightly."

shine-shined-shined: to polish (transitive). "I *shined* my shoes."

Base Form	Simple Past	Past Participle
understand	understood	understood
wake	woke	woken
wear	wore	worn
weave	wove	woven
weep	wept	wept
win	won	won
wind	wound	wound
withdraw	withdrew	withdrawn
withhold	withheld	withheld
withstand	withstood	withstood
write	wrote	written

Appendix C: Inseparable Multiple-Word Verbs: Verb and Adjective Combinations with Prepositions

Many verbs and adjectives occur with prepositions. Here is a list of some common verbs and adjectives with prepositions that usually occur with them. Look in the dictionary to find the meaning of any expressions you are not familiar with.

be **acquainted with** (something / someone)
be **afraid of** (someone / something)
agree with (someone) **about** (something)
be **angry with / at** (someone) **about** (something)
apply for (a job, admission, membership)
apply to (an institution or organization)
argue with (someone) **about** (something)
arrive at (a building, activity, general location)
arrive in (a city, state, country)
believe in (something / someone)
benefit from (something)
be **bored with** (something / someone)
borrow (something) **from** (someone)
break down
break up (with someone)
bump into (something / someone)
burn down
burn up
call on (someone)
calm down
care about (someone / something)
care for (someone / something)
catch up on (something)
catch up with (someone / something)
come up with (something)
be **comfortable with** (someone / something)
complain to (someone) **about** (something)
be **composed of** (something)
concentrate on (something)
consist of (something)
count on (someone / something) **for** (something)
be **crazy about** (someone / something)

deal with (someone / something)
decide on (something)
be **dedicated to** (something / someone)
depend on (someone / something)
be **dependent on** (someone / something)
die down
die out
disagree with (someone) **about** (something)
be **disappointed about** (something)
be **disappointed with / in** (someone / something)
be **divorced from** (someone)
do without (something)
be **done with** (something)
dream about / of (someone / something)
drop in (on someone)
drop out (of school, an organization)
eat out
end up
be / get **engaged to** (someone)
escape from (something / someplace)
be **excited about** (something)
fall behind
fall down
fall off
fall through
be **familiar with** (something)
feel sorry for (someone)
fight for (something)
fight with (someone) **about** (something)
figure on (something)
find out about (someone / something)
be **finished with** (something)

focus on (something)
be **friendly with / to** (someone)
be **frightened of** (someone / something)

get along with (someone)
get away with (something)
get by
get in (a car, taxi, truck)
get off (a plane, bus, train, bicycle, horse)
get off (work)
get on (a plane, bus, train, bicycle, horse)
get out of (a car, taxi, truck)
get over (something)
get rid of (something)
get up
give up
go on with (something)
go out (to eat)
go out with (someone)
go over (something)
grow up

be **happy about** (something)
be **happy with** (someone / something)
hear about (something / someone)
hear from (someone)
hear of (someone / something)
hide from (someone)
hide (something) **from** (someone)
hold on
hold on to (something)

be **in charge of** (something)
insist on (something)
be **interested in** (someone / something)
be **involved in** (something)
be **involved with** (somebody)

be **jealous of** (someone)

keep on (doing something)
keep up (with someone / something)

laugh about (something)
laugh at (someone / something)
lie down
look after (someone / something)
look at (someone / something)
look for (someone / something)
look forward to (something)
look into (something)
look through (something)

be **mad about** (something)
be **mad at** (someone)
be / get **married to** (someone)
move from (someplace)
move over
move to (someplace)

be **nervous about** (something)

participate in (something)

be **patient with** (someone)
be **pleased with** (someone / something)
point at (someone / something)
prepare for (something)
be **prepared for** (something)
profit from (something)
be **proud of** (someone / something)
put up with (someone / something)

quiet down

be **ready for** (something)
be **related to** (someone / something)
rely on (someone / something) **for** (something)
respond to (someone / something)
be **responsible for** (someone / something)
run across (something)
run into (someone / something)
run out of (something)
rush off

be **safe from** (someone / something)
be **scared of** (someone / something)
see about (something)
settle down
shout at (someone)
show up (**for** an event or activity)
sit down
sit up
slow down
be **sorry for** (someone)
speak to / with (someone) **about** (someone / something)
speak up
stand for (something)
stare at (someone / something)
start out
stay up
suffer from (something)
be **sure of** (something)
be **surprised at / about** (something)

take advantage of (someone / something)
take care of (someone / something)
take off
take place
talk on (the telephone)
talk to / with (someone) **about** (something / someone)
tell (someone) **about** (something / someone)
think about / of (someone / something)
be **tired of** (something)

be **upset about** (something)
be **upset with** (someone / something)

wait for (someone / something)
wait on (someone)
work for (someone / someplace)
work for / toward (something)
work on (something)
worry about (someone / something)
be **worried about** (someone / something)

Appendix D: Separable Multiple-Word Verbs

Here is a list of some common multiple word verbs. These verbs usually occur with a direct object. The direct object can go after the verb or in the middle of the verb. Many of these verbs have additional meanings and uses.

ask (someone) **out**	invite someone to go out
ask (someone) **over**	invite someone to come over
beat (someone) **up**	give a severe beating to someone
blow (something) **up**	(1) cause something to explode; (2) fill with air
bring (someone) **up**	raise (as *children*)
bring (something) **up**	introduce or call attention to something (such as *a topic*)
call (someone) **back**	return a phone call to someone
call (something) **off**	cancel something
call (someone) **up**	telephone someone
check (something) **out (of)**	borrow something according to an official procedure (such as *a library book*)
clean (something) **up**	clean something completely
cover (something) **up**	to hide something; to cover something completely
cross (something) **out**	draw a line through something to indicate that it should be omitted
cut (something) **up**	cut something into pieces
do (something) **over**	do something again
drop (someone / something) **off**	leave someone or something somewhere
figure (someone / something) **out**	solve a problem or puzzle
fill (something) **in**	write in the blanks or spaces
fill (something) **out**	complete a form
fill (something) **up**	fill completely
give (something) **away**	make a gift of something
give (something) **back**	return something
hand (something) **in**	submit something (such as *homework, an assignment, a test*)
hand (something) **out**	distribute something
hang (something) **up**	put something on a hook or clothes hanger
have (something) **on**	wear something
help (someone) **out**	help someone
keep (something) **up**	continue something
kick (someone) **out**	expel someone; force someone to leave
leave (something) **out**	omit something
let (someone) **down**	disappoint someone
look (something) **over**	examine something

look (something) **up**	try to find information in a reference (such as *a dictionary, phone book*)
make (something) **up**	(1) create something from the imagination; (2) do work that was missed
pass (something) **out**	distribute something
pick (something) **out**	choose something
pick (someone) **up**	stop to get someone; stop to give someone a ride
pick (something) **up**	(1) lift something with your hands; (2) stop to get something; (3) learn something
point (something) **out**	focus attention on something
put (something) **away**	put something in its place
put (something) **back**	return something to its place
put (something) **off**	postpone or delay something
put (someone) **on**	play a trick on someone; deceive someone
put (something) **on**	get dressed in something
put (something) **out**	extinguish something (such as *a cigarette, a fire*)
put (something) **together**	assemble something; join the pieces of something
see (someone) **off**	watch someone leave (such as at *the airport, the bus station*)
shut (something) **off**	stop the operation of something (such as *a machine*)
straighten (something) **out**	settle a problem
straighten (something) **up**	make something neat; organize something
take (something) **off**	remove something (such as *an article of clothing*)
take (someone) **out**	invite and go out with someone
take (something) **out**	(1) remove something; (2) take something outside
take (something) **over**	take control of something
take (something) **up**	begin a new activity as a hobby
tear (something) **down**	destroy completely
tear (something) **up**	tear into pieces
think (something) **over**	consider something
throw (something) **away / out**	get rid of something
try (something) **on**	put on an article of clothing to see how it looks
try (something) **out**	experiment with something; use something to see how it works
turn (someone) **down**	refuse an offer, invitation, or request from someone
turn (something) **down**	(1) refuse something (such as *an invitation, an offer, a suggestion*); (2) decrease the volume of something
turn (something) **in**	submit something to the teacher (such as *homework*)
turn (something) **off**	stop the power to something
turn (something) **on**	start the power to something
turn (lights) **out**	extinguish the lights
turn (something) **up**	increase the volume of something
wake (someone) **up**	cause someone to wake up
work (something) **out**	find a solution to something
wrap (something) **up**	(1) cover something with paper; (2) bring something to a conclusion

Index